BEYOND
THE LEGEND

Speakman's VC. (*National War Museum of Scotland*)

Speakman after receiving the VC ribbon from Major General Cassels in Korea on 30 December 1951. (© *IWM KOR/U6*)

BEYOND THE LEGEND

BILL SPEAKMAN VC

DEREK HUNT
& JOHN MULHOLLAND

First published 2013

by Spellmount, and imprint of
The History Press
The Mill, Brimscombe Port
Stroud, Gloucestershire, GL5 2QG
www.thehistorypress.co.uk

British Library Cataloguing in Publication Data.
A catalogue record for this book is available from the British Library.

ISBN 978 0 7524 9430 2

Typesetting and origination by The History Press
Printed in Great Britain

CONTENTS

ILLUSTRATIONS

MAPS

PHOTOGRAPHS

ACKNOWLEDGEMENTS

We are indebted to the staffs of the following institutions, which have been of great assistance, many of them allowing us to reproduce material from their archives: The National Army Museum for access to the Canon Lummis VC files, The Victoria Cross and George Cross Association, especially Mrs Didy Grahame OBE MVO, the Secretary of the Association, The King's Own Scottish Borderers, especially Lieutenant Colonel G. Wood MBE, the regimental secretary, and Lieutenant Colonel G.C.O. Hogg OBE DL, former regimental secretary, William Foster, curator and Ian Martin, archivist, The National Archives at Kew, National Museums of Scotland/National War Museum in Edinburgh, Australian War Memorial, Printed Books Department and the Sound Archive of the Imperial War Museum, British Korean Veterans Association, Altrincham History Society, Jane Carmichael, Director of Collections, National Museum of Scotland and Kate Swann, Department of Archives, Photographs, Film & Sound at the National Army Museum.

We should also like to thank the many newspapers and publishers that have generously given us permission to use short extracts from their publications in this book, including: *Sunday Express*, *The Times*, Newsquest Media Group for quotes from the *Altrincham, Hale and Bowdon Guardian*, and the *Canberra Times*.

Many individuals have helped us and we should particularly like to thank: Rupert Allison, Reg Clements, John Cowell, Peter Fisher, John Hayward, Medal Consultant at Spink, Peter Hennerley, Colonel Michael Hickey, Christopher Hunt, Tom Johnson BEM, Rose Jones, the late James Murdoch MBE DCM, Sir William Purves CBE DSO, Geoff Scott, Steve Scott-Spence, Peter Arnold, Alan Speakman and the Victoria Cross Database Users Group, comprising Doug and Richard Arman, Vic Tambling, Paul Oldfield and Alan Jordan, with apologies if we have inadvertently omitted to thank anyone.

ACKNOWLEDGEMENTS

Our thanks are also due to Gail Balfour and Barbara Hunt for typing/producing drafts of the manuscript.

For the photographs reproduced we would like to thank: Bill Speakman VC, Australian War Memorial, The Victoria Cross and George Cross Association, Imperial War Museum, National War Museum of Scotland, British Pathé, www.militaryimages.net, the late James Murdoch, James Bancroft, Erling Breinholm and John Mulholland. We are particularly grateful for the co-operation and assistance of William Foster, curator and Ian Martin, archivist at the KOSB Museum. Details of the Museum can be found in Appendix IV. Whilst every effort has been made to trace the copyright holders or the photographers of illustrations used this has not always proved possible.

Our special thanks to David Balfour for producing the maps and Mark Adkin for permitting us to use information from one of his maps.

Finally, we are greatly indebted to Bill Speakman VC, without whose assistance this book could never have been written. He generously gave us much of his time, taking part in numerous interview sessions and answering questions, in addition to allowing us access to his Army records and private papers and photographs.

PREFACE

Anyone growing up in the 1950s and 1960s, as we did, would have been familiar with the story of 'Big Bill' Speakman VC. He was, literally, a larger than life hero and his exploits in holding off a Chinese attack on a hilltop in Korea for over four hours had become a legend. But while the details of how he won his Victoria Cross were well known, almost nothing was known about the man behind the legend.

Bill Speakman, despite his physical size, is a shy and modest man and does not seek attention and rarely talks about himself. Although he has been mentioned in several books about the VC and the Korean War, he has never contributed to a biography or written his memoirs.

We had a chance to meet Bill and get to know him better a few years ago and later he kindly agreed to write the foreword to one of our previous books. Following on from those first meetings, when we became friends, he requested us to write his biography. We have always respected and admired Bill Speakman and were delighted to be offered this unique opportunity to write about him.

He has spared us the time to be interviewed, covering every aspect of his fascinating life, and has allowed us access to his personal records as well as providing answers to the many queries which arose during the course of writing. In this book, the first biography of Bill Speakman VC, we have disproved all the myths surrounding his life and how he won his VC as well as giving an account of the VC action in his own words. We have also covered his childhood in Altrincham and his later life in South Africa – a period about which little has been known previously – and have looked beyond the legend.

Derek Hunt and John Mulholland, 2013

ABBREVIATIONS

A&SH	Argyll and Sutherland Highlanders
AWOL	Absent Without Leave
BAOR	British Army of the Rhine
BCOF	British Commonwealth Occupation Force
BEM	British Empire Medal
BKVA	British Korean Veterans Association
CB	Companion of the Order of the Bath
CBE	Commander of the Order of the British Empire
CCS	Casualty Clearing Station
CDC	Civil Defence Corps
CMF	Central Mediterranean Forces
CO	Commanding Officer
CSM	Campaign Service Medal/Company Sergeant Major
CT	Communist Terrorist
DCM	Distinguished Conduct Medal
DF	Defensive Fire
DL	Deputy Lieutenant
DP	Displaced Person
DSO	Distinguished Service Order
ERE	Extra-Regimentally Employed
FARELF	Far East Land Forces
GC	George Cross
GCB	Knight Grand Cross, Order of the Bath
GDP	Gross Domestic Product
GHQ	General Headquarters
GOC	General Officer Commanding
GSM	General Service Medal

ABBREVIATIONS

HM	His/Her Majesty
HMSO	His/Her Majesty's Stationery Office
HQ	Headquarters
HRH	His/Her Royal Highness
KBE	Knight Commander, Order of the British Empire
KD	Khaki Drill
KOSB	King's Own Scottish Borderers
KSLI	King's Shropshire Light Infantry
LRDG	Long Range Desert Group
MBE	Member of the Order of the British Empire
MC	Military Cross
MCP	Malayan Communist Party
MM	Military Medal
MMG	Medium Machine Gun
MP	Member of Parliament
MVO	Member of the Royal Victorian Order
NAAFI	Navy, Army and Air Force Institutes
NCO	Non-Commissioned Officer
NHS	National Health Service
NLF	National Liberation Front
OBE	Officer of the Order of the British Empire
POW	Prisoner of War
RAF	Royal Air Force
RAR	Royal Australian Regiment
RMS	Royal Mail Steamer
RNF	Royal Northumberland Fusiliers
RSF	Royal Scots Fusiliers
RSM	Regimental Sergeant Major
TB	Tuberculosis
SAS	Special Air Service
TD	Territorial Decoration
UK	United Kingdom
UN	United Nations
US	United States
VC	Victoria Cross
VE DAY	Victory in Europe Day
VJ DAY	Victory over Japan Day

PROLOGUE

When news was received that two members of an SAS patrol had been killed in a terrorist ambush in the jungle, plans were made for the immediate recovery of their bodies. A helicopter was requested to fly them back to base for a proper burial, but first the dead soldiers had to be brought out of the jungle.

It was November 1953 and Britain faced a new type of enemy in the jungles of Malaya – communist terrorists (CTs). The CTs had grown from the resistance groups which Britain had supported and armed in the fight against the Japanese occupiers during the Second World War. After the end of the war, however, the communists planned to seize power for themselves. A campaign of killing rubber planters and tin miners later developed into a lengthy guerrilla war against colonial rule, which became known as 'The Emergency'. British and Gurkha troops were sent to restore order, with the SAS being in action for much of the conflict. The 22nd Special Air Service worked deep in the jungle, sending in small patrols, often no more than four men, to seek the enemy and kill them.

An SAS patrol, under the command of Corporal K.B. 'Digger' Bancroft, ran into a CT ambush and Bancroft and Trooper F.W. Wilkins were killed. The rest of the patrol engaged the enemy, who retreated into the jungle. News of the deaths was sent by runner and received by C Squadron commander, Captain Johnny Cooper – one of the original founders of the SAS during the Second World War.

Cooper had been given the task of penetrating the thick jungle in the mountains of Pahang to establish a fort from which to control the local area and send out patrols. The clearing of the site and construction of a helicopter landing area were progressing to plan when the patrol was ambushed and the two SAS men killed on 26 November 1953. This tragedy marked the only

British deaths during the squadron's 122 days in the jungle. Captain Cooper informed headquarters and a helicopter was put on standby to collect the bodies; it was considered a priority to bring back fatal casualties for burial.

Trooper Bill Speakman VC, a Korean War veteran who had joined the elite regiment less than six months earlier, was one of the men who volunteered to go into the jungle to recover the bodies. He had known both men and wanted to do whatever he could to help. At 6ft 6in tall and well built, he was ideal for such a dangerous mission. The rescue party set off on foot towards Bancroft's base, while another party continued to search for the enemy. The next day, around noon, Speakman returned to camp carrying Corporal Bancroft strapped to a bamboo pole across his shoulders. Three other SAS troopers supported the back end of the pole.

The body was placed near the waiting Royal Navy helicopter and a second recovery party organised to bring back Trooper Wilkins. Bill Speakman volunteered once more, saying that he should go as he was stronger than the others, and went back into the jungle. When the volunteers returned, Speakman was again in the lead taking the weight of the second body on a bamboo pole across his broad shoulders. Both dead SAS men were then flown out and were buried in Cheras Road Christian Cemetery (Military Annex), Kuala Lumpur. Corporal Bancroft's parent unit was the East Surrey Regiment and Trooper Wilkins' parent unit was the Army Catering Corps. Johnny Cooper later wrote about the ambush and the jungle rescues in his memoirs (1). Trooper Speakman was typically modest about his part in the two rescue missions:

> I was laid up beforehand because I had cut my feet to ribbons. Unfortunately they could never find jungle boots to fit me. I was told to stand down for a while because a soldier has to have two feet working. So I stayed behind for a couple of days to get my feet treated; because of the weather they were giving me problems with septic healing up. While I was laid up I did some administration duties in the fort and I was there when Digger Bancroft, who I knew personally, and a trooper got ambushed.
>
> Johnny Cooper said: 'Look, we have to get those guys out.' Everyone else was out on patrol and couldn't be called in. Once an SAS patrol was in the jungle no one knew where they are and that is the whole point of a secret patrol. So I said; 'I'll go, sir'. We went in and got one body out but couldn't get the other one. We brought the first one, which was Digger, out on a bamboo pole. Johnny Cooper said: 'We have got one more body to retrieve.'

So we went back and found Trooper Wilkins and brought him back. I think we carried him out on a pole as well.

These rescue missions were dangerous for all involved, because of the risk of further terrorist ambushes, but more so for Speakman as he had no adequate footwear. Because of his size it was impossible to obtain boots that fitted him. Size fourteen jungle boots were just not available and so he had to wear a smaller size with the toes cut out. This made walking through the jungle hazardous and, not surprisingly, his feet were severely cut and injured when he returned to camp. He had cut his feet to ribbons before they had healed properly following a previous venture into the jungle.

Displaying the same courage and determination he had shown in the Korean War two years earlier, Speakman accomplished his mission. He received no award for the jungle rescues and, although he was mentioned in a report by Captain Cooper, he did not receive an official Mention in Despatches. For the earlier act of heroism when besieged on a hilltop in Korea he had been awarded the nation's highest award for valour: the Victoria Cross.

NOTES

(1) *One of the Originals: The Story of a Founder Member of the SAS* by Lieutenant Colonel John Murdoch Cooper MBE DCM. (Pan Books, London, 1991)

EARLY YEARS
1927–1945

'Big Bill' Speakman VC has not always enjoyed an easy relationship with the media. In fact, for much of his life, this relationship has been characterised by resentment and suspicion. It all started off so well, with the media displaying genuine affection for the young VC winner, so where did it go wrong?

Speakman returned home to a hero's welcome in January 1952 after being awarded the Victoria Cross for his gallant stand against a Chinese attack on United Hill in Korea. He had organised a defence against thousands of enemy soldiers who were as determined to capture this position as he was to defend it. Back in England his heroism had made him a legend and he was greeted at RAF Lyneham by huge numbers of newspaper reporters, photographers, television and newsreel cameramen and well-wishers. All of this was unexpected and he was completely overwhelmed by the media attention he received. As he would later remark, his life changed the moment he stepped off the plane. Over the following weeks the media were at every event he attended – every official reception, football match and dinner dance. He was followed around by newspaper reporters looking for stories with which to satisfy the nation's craving for a new hero in austerity Britain. They would say that they were just doing their jobs, but it was not always viewed that way by Speakman.

He did not consider himself a hero and pointed out that others, who had not received the VC, had performed the same actions in Korea. He felt uncomfortable being singled out for this special attention and hated being in the spotlight. Despite his size, he was a shy person and soon found the expectations of others difficult to live with. 'They won't let you be normal,' he said at the time. 'All the time they are watching you to see if you are getting above yourself.' Public speaking was something he found very difficult and he shunned interviews and social occasions wherever he could. This, inevitably, led to accusations of aloofness and feelings of resentment.

Eventually, in March 1952, he decided to return to active service in Korea to escape the media attention. As a result of his reluctance to talk to the press, or even to correct inaccurate stories, errors have been perpetuated and myths have grown about how he won his VC. When he returned to Korea he would not have considered co-operating with the writing of a biography, but he has mellowed over the years and now, at 85, thinks it is time to put the record straight.

Bill Speakman is the best remembered of the four VCs awarded for Korea, but often for the wrong reasons. Many people have heard the story that he was drunk when he repelled wave after wave of Chinese soldiers with grenades and beer bottles. This is a myth; he was not drunk when he fought the enemy who were attacking his battalion's position. It is something he has always denied and there is no evidence to support this scurrilous accusation. Speakman was a born fighter; he did not need alcohol to spur him into action and when in a fight he was unbeatable.

Since 1952 he has been known as 'The beer bottle VC' and it will surprise many people to learn that the story behind this is also a myth. When he ran out of grenades he is said to have thrown anything he could lay his hands on at the advancing Chinese, including rocks and beer bottles. He threw rocks but there were no beer bottles. This myth is partly based on a misquote and despite his protestations the legend persists. 'Where would you get bottles of beer from?' asks Speakman. 'Whoever started the story, it seems to have caught on.' One of the most bizarre claims made about Speakman is that when the Chinese attacked he got hold of beer bottles and hit the attackers over the head with the bottles.

Although he served in several Scottish regiments, including The Black Watch (Royal Highland Regiment), The King's Own Scottish Borderers and The Royal Scots Fusiliers, William Speakman (always known as Bill) is not Scottish. His first choice of regiment was influenced by his stepfather, who had served in The Black Watch during the First World War.

He was born in Altrincham, a market town in north Cheshire 8 miles to the south-west of Manchester. Altrincham has a long history; it was originally an Anglo-Saxon settlement, meaning 'the homestead of Aldhere's people', and became a chartered borough in 1290. It is interesting to note that the name of the town was spelt Altringham (which is how it is pronounced) up to about 1800 at which time the 'c' spelling was adopted (1). Altrincham has a population of approximately 41,000 and is now part of the Metropolitan Borough of Trafford.

Bill Speakman was born on Wednesday, 21 September 1927 into a working-class one-parent family at 17 Moss Lane, Altrincham. The area has since been redeveloped and the terraced house has been demolished. It is now the site of the Ice Ring and is on the same road as the ground of Altrincham Football Club.

THE YEAR 1927

The year 1927 was an eventful year during a decade of social and political change when both Britain and the rest of the world were still coming to terms with the aftermath of the First World War. On the day that Speakman was born, 21 September 1927, *The Times* reported that the Irish general election had ended inconclusively with the Government Party having a very small majority over their opponents. The political fallout from President Paul von Hindenburg's Tannenberg Memorial speech, in which he repudiated Germany's responsibility for the First World War, was covered in some detail. The Soviet Fleet's Black Sea manoeuvres around Odessa were reported, as was the Air Race across the United States, which had so far claimed two lives.

He was illegitimate and is one of many men who overcame their less fortunate start in life to win the Victoria Cross. His mother, Hannah Speakman, was a 'general servant (domestic)' but nothing is known of his father, whose name does not appear on Speakman's birth certificate. In an era when there was still a stigma attached to illegitimacy and little help available to single mothers, Hannah Speakman decided to keep her child. Social habits change over the years, however, and at the time of writing 47 per cent of UK births occur outside marriage. Hannah Speakman registered her son's birth on 18 October 1927. He was named William after his maternal grandfather.

Bill Speakman never knew his father. Whoever he was, he must have been a man of means as he made regular maintenance payments to Hannah's father to support her and her child. Speakman did not discover this until many years later. His mother never revealed the name of his father, although she had the opportunity, and to speculate on his identity would be futile. Speakman accepts the reality of the situation. 'I am not ashamed of it because it was not my fault', he says.

CHAPEL STREET, ALTRINCHAM

Bill Speakman was not the first war hero to come from Altrincham; during the First World War, Chapel Street, Altrincham was said to be the most patriotic street in the country. It was a short walk from Moss Lane where Speakman was born. In a street of just 60 houses, 161 men fought for King and country and 29 of them never returned. Chapel Street was in a working-class area of the town and many of the inhabitants were of Irish descent who had come to Altrincham looking for work.

In April 1919 Lord Stamford unveiled a memorial, or Roll of Honour, outside All Saints Church, Chapel Street dedicated to the local men who had helped to win the war. The names of all 161 men were recorded on the memorial and King George V sent a telegram expressing his appreciation of the sacrifices made. Chapel Street was demolished in the 1960s as part of a slum clearance programme. All Saints Church was also demolished and the glass-fronted memorial was taken into storage at Altrincham Town Hall.

In September 2009 Trafford Council erected a blue plaque honouring the 161 men who volunteered. The plaque was fixed to the wall of a restaurant in Regent Road which stands on part of the rebuilt street. Bill Speakman VC attended the plaque unveiling as a guest of the organiser, Peter Hennerley, who is a descendant of one of the Chapel Street volunteers.

Hannah Speakman had been a resident of Altrincham all her life, and was born at 4 Back Moss Lane, Altrincham on 28 December 1902. Her father, William Speakman, was born about 1867 and was the second of ten children of William and Elizabeth Speakman. He was a general labourer when Hannah was born. Her mother, Elizabeth Speakman, formerly Fowles, registered the birth on 6 February 1903. In the 1911 census, Hannah was the youngest of four children: her sisters were named Mary and Emily and her brother was Joseph. Two further sisters followed: Jessie was born in 1914 and Grace in 1916. The two older girls, Mary and Emily, had left home by the time Bill Speakman was born and he does not remember them.

At the time of her son's birth, Hannah was in service as a general servant to the owners of one of the many large houses in the area. She was in service for one particular Bowdon family for many years; the staff were expected to work long hours for low wages. When the First World War gave women the opportunity to undertake new areas of work previously performed by men, many of them never returned to work in service. Hannah Speakman was 15 years old when the war ended so would not have had the chance to try other work and was a domestic cleaner all her life.

Max Arthur OBE noted in *Symbol of Courage* (2) that 'over 75 per cent of VC awards have been made to a man who has grown up as the responsible child of an early widowed mother or the eldest child in a large family'. For almost eight years of his life, until his mother married Bert Houghton in 1935, Bill Speakman was an only child to an unmarried mother and must have learnt responsibility at an early age.

John Percival in *For Valour: The Victoria Cross, Courage in Action* (3) also commented on the qualities of men who were awarded the VC. He said that they all showed a strong sense of responsibility for others which they developed early in their lives.

On 15 June 1935 Hannah Speakman, aged 33, married Herbert Houghton, a 46-year-old widower, at the local register office. Herbert had previously

The Speakman family's home, 27 Moss Lane, is the house with the Union Flag above the door to commemorate Speakman's homecoming in 1952. Speakman was born nearby at 17 Moss Lane. (*British Pathé*)

married Lily Venables in 1919 but she died in 1928, aged 37. Herbert and Lily had two daughters: Lillian and Margaret, known as Peggy, who was born in 1926, just two years before her mother died.

Herbert was recorded as a potato salesman living at 15 Shaw's Road at the time of Peggy's birth in 1926 but had become an engineers' storekeeper by the time of his marriage to Hannah in 1935. Shaw's Road is close to Moss Lane, so Herbert and Hannah were in the same neighbourhood and it is likely that this is how they met.

Bill Speakman was 7 years old at the time of the marriage but cannot recall the event. Houghton's eldest daughter, Lillian, had left home by the time of her father's remarriage. So the new family in Moss Lane was Herbert, Hannah, Peggy and Bill. Peggy was a year older than Bill and was fond of him. She later married Norman Broadbent and named her first son after Bill. Peggy died in Sheffield in 1995. Herbert and Hannah Houghton had two children: Ann Houghton, born in 1937, and Herbert Houghton, born in 1939.

Herbert Houghton senior was born in Wigan on 1 November 1888, the eldest son of William and Mary Houghton. Herbert was the eldest of three children; his siblings were William and Annie. Prior to his service during the First World War, he was employed as a railway clerk, in the engineers' department, and lived at Linwood Terrace, 13 Stockport Road, Altrincham. He enlisted, as a volunteer, in The Black Watch (Royal Highland Regiment) on 17 November 1915 and was posted to the 2nd Battalion, then serving in Mesopotamia (now Iraq) (4). He joined the battalion, via India, in June 1916.

Houghton's health soon suffered as a result of the climate and conditions in Mesopotamia, and he contracted malaria and dysentery. He was evacuated to India, where he spent several months in hospital. Although he returned to Mesopotamia in June 1917, he suffered further ill health and was again invalided to India to recover. He spent a total of one year and 227 days in India and just 127 days in Mesopotamia.

Houghton was invalided to England in February 1918 and, after attachments in England and Ireland with other Black Watch battalions, arrived in France just before the end of the war. However, his health had not improved and he developed pleurisy in November 1918 and was admitted to hospital in France. He was discharged from the Army in March 1919, and his poor health later contributed to his death at the relatively early age of 60. Houghton was said to have been gassed during the First World War, but there is nothing in his extensive medical records to confirm this.

THE BLACK WATCH

The regiment began its history in 1725 as a number of independent companies to patrol, or 'watch', the Highlands for smugglers. Through amalgamation of these companies, the 43rd (Highland) Regiment of Foot was formed in 1739. The new regiment was renumbered the 42nd Regiment twelve years later, and in the 1881 reorganisation became known as The Black Watch (Royal Highlanders). In 1920 the name was changed again, to The Black Watch (Royal Highland Regiment). After amalgamations of Scottish infantry regiments in 2006, the regiment became The Black Watch, 3rd Battalion Royal Regiment of Scotland.

The regiment has served all over the world and fourteen men serving in The Black Watch or its predecessors have been awarded the Victoria Cross (eight of them for the Indian Mutiny).

Speakman got on well with his stepfather, who he remembers as 'a short, stocky man', and when he was old enough he joined Bert's old regiment:

I wanted to join the Army from an early age because my stepfather was in The Black Watch and was gassed in the trenches in the First World War. So he brought his gear with him, including his kilt. They used to have an apron when they went in the trenches to keep it clean and his shoes, apron and tackle were stored in the bottom cupboard. I used to sit on that cupboard and go through his collection of badges. In those days if you had a Black Watch badge you could take it to pieces and put it back together again.

Bert was a good stepfather. Bit tough at times, but then again that was the way it was. He was very grumpy at times because he was gassed in the First World War. Later on he often used to sleep downstairs. He couldn't always make the stairs because of his coughing. He always used to smoke a pipe which didn't help.

He had a son and a daughter with my mother and he must have thought and wondered, 'Who the hell is Bill's father?' He didn't really treat me differently from my half-brother and half-sister, although he had a preference for young Bert. My stepfather was a smallish guy – but a tough little guy. He would go down the pub for his pint and come back and spend the time of day with me.

Bert Houghton would often tell his young stepson about his experiences in The Black Watch during the First World War. He told about the battalion standing in water in the trenches, how his kilt floated on the water and the time he was gassed by the enemy. There was an element of exaggeration in some of these stories, but they gave Bill Speakman his desire to join the Army. He later said that another reason for joining the Army was to get away from home and his mother.

Although he admits that his mother worked hard to provide for him, Speakman grew to dislike her. As he was growing up he spent long periods in childcare and with his grandparents while she worked in service. He felt he was being 'farmed out' and became a loner, although he liked his own company. Speakman particularly resented the fact that his mother would never reveal the name of his real father, even when he was an adult. He felt he should have been told and this is something which still haunts him to this day. It was this detached relationship with his mother which made him leave home to join the Army as soon as he was old enough.

Speakman recalls that his mother, Hannah, was 'lithe and tall and with a skinny build'. He also remembers her as a very hard-working woman:

She worked all her life but was around for me when she could be. She worked in service at Bowdon and Hale, where all the cloth barons lived. There are some plush areas in Hale. The staff were expected to work long hours every day; sometimes they were in early and sometimes they stayed overnight. As a consequence I saw not a great deal of my mother really. But then as a child I was always outside, I loved it. You couldn't keep me indoors: I had a wonderful life in the fields. But, of course, that's the way Cheshire was in those days, mainly fields. You only had to go out and within ten minutes you were in the country.

I had a very happy childhood. I was mainly brought up by my grandfather, William, and my grandmother, Elizabeth, while my mother went to work. My grandfather taught me about the birds and the bees and the like. When he retired he was always in the country. Both my grandparents were superb. When my mother married Bert Houghton and became a Houghton and had their children, I said, 'Shall I change my name?' They said, 'No, you are still Bill Speakman'. My grandfather had something to do with that.

The family was living in rented accommodation at 17 Moss Lane when Bill Speakman was born and later moved up the road to 25 Moss Lane. The next move was to 27 Moss Lane after Hannah married Bert in 1935. Bill Speakman spent his entire childhood living in various houses in Moss Lane and remembers being brought up at 25 Moss Lane by his grandparents. He knew the area well:

> We lived in a row of houses leading down to the railway yard. They belonged to the brewery, which also owned the Bridge Inn next door. I believe I spent some time at 17 Moss Lane but I can't remember. I do remember living at 25 Moss Lane and then when my mother married Bert, my stepfather, we moved into 27 Moss Lane. Bert applied for this house, to have a house of our own. It wasn't a bigger house, just a convenient house because we all lived together. There was me, Bert and Ann, my mother and my stepfather. They weren't big houses – upstairs and downstairs.

Bill Speakman was educated at Oakfield Road Infants' School in Altrincham from the age of 5 and then Wellington Road Boys' School in Timperley. He recalls his school days with great affection:

> I went to Oakfield Road School from the age of 5 to the age of 10. Oakfield Road School was marvellous because there were women teachers: Miss Royal, Miss White and Miss Wilkinson. That's where I learned to write and add up. They told you things of interest. There was no hard arithmetic and no hard geography. They prepared you for the adult world, ready for senior school. They were so kind it was a pleasure to go to school. It was absolutely wonderful.
>
> I was in charge of dishing out the milk, because it was free milk in those days. And then you had your little favourites, two bottles here you are and chain straws all coming out of the same jar. Funny little things like that. You had lunch to take to school with you, usually a jam butty. We would swap things over. 'What have you got today?' we would say. We had no worries whatsoever.
>
> But then when we got older we had to go to Wellington Senior; that was all men teachers. They were toughies, but then it was a very new school. There was Wellington for girls and Wellington for boys, but not mixed. It was a tough school. They drummed it into you. In a way it was good schooling; it toughened you up. It was excellent teaching as far as I was concerned. They really applied themselves to us.
>
> I always remember maths used to be at the end of the day. Sometimes you would get an air raid warning and everyone would go to the shelter and there were times when the maths started and I said, 'I hope the bombers come over today!' Then we would all go to the air raid shelter. Those were the days of being naughty and being spoken to rather harshly. We lost a couple of good

teachers who got called up during the war – Mr Gerathy, a biology teacher, lovely man, was one of them.

Maths was not one of Speakman's favourite subjects. He admits that he never applied himself to maths as he thought it a waste of time. 'Every other subject I used to wallow in it,' he says:

> My favourite subjects were geography, geology and history. I was very fond of history because we used to go and look at a map for all the ruined things around there. That was lovely. I was also a sports person. I played football and rugby, but I was excellent at swimming. All the Speakmans were good at swimming, every one of them. I used to go swimming in the canals with my friends and also regularly attended Altrincham Baths.

The Second World War began on 3 September 1939, less than three weeks before Bill Speakman's twelfth birthday. The effects of the war were felt everywhere, including rural Cheshire.

The local area helped the war effort by providing men for the armed services, converting factory production to armaments, raising money for ships and aircraft and accommodating evacuees whose homes in Manchester had been bombed.

The factories in the Broadheath area of Altrincham became military targets as well as nearby Manchester. Ships on the Manchester Ship Canal, just 5 miles to the north-west of the town, were also targeted by the Luftwaffe. Sometimes bombs fell short on Altrincham and at other times they were jettisoned by the bombers. On one occasion a bomb fell on Speakman's favourite shop – Mrs Pearson's sweet shop – and on another occasion a house on the corner of Oakfield Street and Moss Lane, Altrincham received a direct hit, killing twelve people. The first air raid on Altrincham took place at the end of August 1940 and the last on the evening of 25 October 1941. Between these dates, there were 130 local casualties, 26 of them fatal and over 1,000 houses were damaged (5). Bill Speakman remembers the air raids:

> Our house at 27 Moss Lane had a lovely cellar which during the war we turned into an air raid shelter. It was really nice – that's where we lived half the time … There was an air raid shelter at school for the boys and one for the girls. It was a separate school for the girls. There was a field between us but during an air raid we used to meet. I used to get this girl named Miriam to carry my books. After the air raids passed over there was not much time left

so we all mixed and talked of our experiences. Sometimes there was time for a kiss or a cuddle with some of the girls. I remember one girl charged a toffee, and toffees were rationed at the time!

Rationing was not a problem. I didn't take any notice of rationing; I got sufficient food. In Cheshire we seemed to live on what we got because a jam butty would suffice us: porridge in the morning then a jam butty. We never saw the black market.

During the war my stepfather worked at Old Trafford, Manchester. He worked on the rooftops and watched where the bombs fell in air raids and where heavy fires broke out. He would monitor these things with his buddies and tried to put out the fires from incendiaries. There were a lot of big factories near the docks at Old Trafford and he worked in that environment, like a warden. He couldn't do much because of his wounds but he was very alert and he made sure that if anything started, something was done about it.

Since the Scout Movement was founded in 1907, approximately forty-five former Scouts have been awarded the Victoria Cross (6). Scouting principles, with their emphasis on duty to country and other people, no doubt prepared many Scouts for the challenges they overcame to win the VC. Bill Speakman VC is proud to belong to that gallant group:

I was a Cub first of all and then I became a Scout in the Altrincham Scout Group. We had a Cub mistress and then a Scout leader. In those days Scouts did all sorts of things to help out. We did things like running messages when the lines were down and I used to be a messenger for the Scouts during air raids. We were very streetwise and knew all the short cuts when we were carrying messages. Altrincham was a close-knit place and we knew everyone and everything. But we would help out – sometimes during the day, sometimes at night. We got involved in the civil defence side as well by helping the air raid warden and making cups of tea for people when they were pulled out of rubble. It was all part of being a Scout.

Although many Scouts undertook valuable civil defence work during the war, their efforts did not qualify them for the Defence Medal. Scouts over the age of 14, however, were awarded the Scout War Service Badge for sustained work. During the Second World War a total of 60,000 badges were awarded. This red rectangular badge, featuring a crown and the initials 'NS' (National Service), was designed to be worn on the arm of a Scout uniform.

Speakman left school, aged 14, in 1941 with no academic qualifications and no desire for further education. Britain was still at war at the time and his ambition was to join the Army. A plaque at his school records his 'great gallantry and utter contempt for his own personal safety' when he earned his VC ten years later.

He had shown he was capable of great gallantry, in the school playground one day in 1940, when a group of older boys started bullying his friend, Harold Cook. Despite the odds of three to one against them, and Speakman and his friend being small for their age, they took on the bullies and beat them. Unfortunately, the fight was witnessed by a teacher and Speakman was caned by the headmaster for fighting in the playground. The headmaster said that Bill Speakman had no respect for rules and discipline and it was apparent from his behaviour that he would never make a good soldier.

There was probably an element of truth in what the headmaster said, which would become apparent years later. He was at times ill-disciplined and lacked sufficient respect for authority, and his disciplinary record while in the Army confirms this. There was no doubting, however, that Bill Speakman was an exceptionally brave person and a good man to have on your side in a difficult situation. He remembers the headmaster making the comments, 'and yet he was a good headmaster,' says Speakman. 'He knew I wanted to join the Army from an early age.'

To anyone who has met Bill Speakman it is hard to imagine that he was small for his age, even at 13. He remembers that he was 'like a bean pole'; tall and quite skinny and so was Harold:

> We always hated bullies. In Wellington, because there were bigger boys, they picked on Harold, and Harold was a friend of mine along with Peter Kelly. But Harold was a very popular boy with the girls and with everyone. As I watched him being slapped around I thought 'stuff them' and I waded into this great big guy and, do you know, I put him down. He was the biggest of the lot. 'Just don't mess about with my mates like that,' I said. I just went to Harold's aid like anyone else would do.

Having been told that he would never make a good soldier, Bill Speakman was determined to prove his headmaster wrong. Aged 14, he enlisted as a drummer boy in A Company (Hale) 1st Cadet Battalion (Altrincham and Hale), The Cheshire Regiment. His school friend, Harold Cook, enlisted with him. *The Cadet Journal*, in February 1952, recalled that Speakman was 'a very keen cadet and always hankered after service in the regular Army'. He remained with the cadets until August 1945 and enjoyed the experience it gave him:

> We had a good time in the cadets. Major Halliwell was in charge. We used to do exercises with the local Home Guard – they had weapons and fired live ammunition.

After leaving school Speakman worked for two years as an apprentice turner at Edward Holme & Co Ltd, a firm of electrical engineers. Though he had left school and got a job, he retained his links with the Scouts. 'Even when I started work, I still kept in contact with the Scouts,' he says. Edward Holme & Co made switch gear for cranes at the docks and, as Speakman got older, his employers took him to Manchester Docks to install the equipment. He recalls that he had to climb up the cranes and watch them operate. He then worked for Churchill Machine Tools until August 1945, when, at nearly 18, he was old enough to join the Army. But by then the Second World War was almost over.

NOTES

(1) Information supplied by the Altrincham History Society.

(2) *Symbol of Courage: A Complete History of the Victoria Cross* by Max Arthur OBE. (Sidgwick & Jackson, 2004)

(3) *For Valour: The Victoria Cross, Courage in Action* by John Percival. (Thames Methuen, London, 1985)

(4) British and Indian troops invaded Mesopotamia (now Iraq) in November 1914 in response to Turkey's entry into the war on the side of the Central Powers. The strategic port of Basra was captured on 23 November. Allied casualties of the fighting increased with diseases such as dysentery and malaria, the extreme heat and the Turkish ill-treatment of prisoners of war, particularly after the British surrender at Kut. The war in Mesopotamia continued until November 1918.

(5) Information from Altrincham History Society and *The Story of Altrincham* by Patricia Southern. (Amberley Publishing, 2008)

(6) Among the Boy Scouts who were later awarded the Victoria Cross are Boy 1st Class Jack Cornwell, who received a posthumous VC in the First World War, and Wing Commander Guy Gibson, who led the Dambusters raid in the Second World War.

ARMY
1945–1951

The war in Europe ended on VE Day, 8 May 1945, but the fighting in the Far East continued for another three months. Japan finally surrendered after the USA dropped atomic bombs on Hiroshima and Nagasaki. VJ (Victory over Japan) Day was celebrated on 15 August – although the Second World War did not officially end until 2 September 1945 when the formal Japanese surrender was signed aboard the US battleship *Missouri* in Tokyo Bay.

Bill Speakman signed to join the Army in Manchester on Friday, 10 August 1945, aged 17 years and 11 months. His attestation papers recorded that he was on 'deferred embodiment – due to join 20 September 1945' (the day before his eighteenth birthday). He had to obtain a copy of his birth certificate from Sale to join the Army and remembers being surprised to see a blank under 'Father's name'. Being underage did not prevent him from joining:

> I told nobody I was joining up. I think it was July or August 1945 that I sloped off and went to Dover Street in Manchester. I looked at the Royal Navy recruiting office and thought 'No. It's got to be the Army'. They said 'Come inside', and I signed on. I was underage but they didn't seem to mind. Within weeks I was on the railway up to Perth to the Depot of The Black Watch. I did my training at Kingshorn Castle. Then I went to an Infantry Training Centre at Winchester. They taught me at Perth but then sent me down to Winchester for weaponry.

The attestation form noted that 14471590 Private William Speakman had a fresh complexion, brown eyes and brown hair. He was 6ft 4in tall at the time and weighed 157½ pounds. His medical category was A1. To save any embarrassment or awkward questions, he listed his stepfather as his next of kin, under the name Herbert Speakman. He was assigned to the General Service

Corps until he was legally old enough to join and sent to No 15 Primary Training Centre for his military training.

After completing his basic training, he was transferred to the 1st Battalion The Black Watch (Royal Highland Regiment), his first choice of regiment, on 1 November 1945. On the same day he was posted to No 8 Infantry Training Centre. He had enlisted for an initial period of seven years, with a further five years in the reserves. He had long wanted to join the British Army and his choice of regiment was influenced by the fact that his stepfather, Bert Houghton, had served in The Black Watch during the First World War. He was transferred to the 10th Battalion The Black Watch on 26 January 1946.

At the time he attested, the Second World War had not yet ended but by the time he officially joined the Army on 20 September the war had ended 18 days earlier. Speakman, therefore, was not eligible for the War Medal 1939–45 or any campaign medals as he had not served the minimum period necessary for these awards (1). In late 1945 when he joined the Army, many servicemen were eager to leave – they had joined up, or were called up, for the duration of the war and now wanted to return home to their families.

On 9 August 1945, an atomic bomb had been dropped on the Japanese city of Nagasaki and the Russian Red Army launched an offensive against Japanese forces in Manchuria. The newspapers of 10 August, the day Speakman attested to join the Army, reported these developments which showed that the war was still being fiercely fought in the Far East.

Demobilisation was a huge logistical undertaking, at a time when most of Europe was still in chaos, and was regarded as one of the greatest challenges facing the post-war government. In the UK, the farming and fishing industries desperately needed newly demobilised forces personnel to fill vacancies to meet the country's food requirements. However, the filling of vacancies in the food and other industries was dependent on the speed of demobilisation from the armed forces and the munitions industries.

On VE Day there were over five million British men and women in uniform, and full demobilisation was not completed until the end of 1946. At the time Bill Speakman was transferred to The Black Watch in January 1946, only 20 per cent of British servicemen had been demobilised and returned home.

Speakman's Army career did not get off to a good start and his rebellious nature soon landed him in trouble. In February 1946 he was disciplined for 'stating a falsehood to an NCO' and for being absent from Church Parade and, as a result, was confined to barracks for ten days and placed under open arrest. On 13 June 1947 he was confined to barracks for fourteen days for failing to be alert whilst on duty and he was deprived of five days' pay for a further offence a week later. Whenever Speakman appeared before his commanding officer on a charge and he was asked if he was guilty he would always say 'Yes'. He never made excuses and he believes the CO respected him for that.

On 20 March 1946, six months after his official date of joining the Army, Private Speakman was upgraded to class I rates of pay. He served in the UK until 20 June 1946 and then with the British Army of the Rhine (BAOR) in Germany from 21 June to 9 August 1946. Speakman was transferred to No 8 Holding Battalion on 2 July 1946, before being posted to Central Mediterranean Forces (CMF) on 10 August 1946. He was attached to Brigade Headquarters in Trieste, in north-east Italy, and served in a transit camp. At the time, neighbouring Austria was still occupied by Allied troops and Trieste was an important transit port for central Europe.

Speakman was compulsorily transferred from The Black Watch to The Gordon Highlanders and posted to the 1st Battalion London Scottish on 13 August 1946. He remained with CMF, though not with the same battalion, until 31 July 1947:

When I joined the Army, I never joined The Black Watch, even after battalion training. I was posted to Italy to reinforce the London Scottish in Italy. I remained with The Black Watch all the time but I was transferred temporarily.

THE LONDON SCOTTISH

The London Scottish Regiment was raised as The London Scottish Rifle Volunteers by a group of London-based Scots in 1859. When the Volunteer Force became the Territorial Force in 1908, the regiment became the 14th (County of London) Battalion, The London Regiment (London Scottish). In 1936, individual battalions were linked to other regiments and the London Scottish became a territorial battalion of The Gordon Highlanders. The London Scottish fought in both World Wars and three Victoria Crosses have been awarded to men serving in the regiment.

Bill Speakman recalls that 'the London Scottish was affiliated to The Gordon Highlanders. They were territorials – the Inns of Court – a posh regiment'. They are now 'A' (London Scottish) Company, The London Regiment (Guards Division).

On 9 December 1946 Speakman was posted to the newly formed No 1 Special Guards Battalion:

> I finished up in Trieste with the London Scottish and then we moved down to Rimini on the Adriatic coast and formed the 1st Special Guards. We were guarding 10,000 German POWs at Rimini airfield. They were due for vetting before going back to Germany, 1946–47.

He had joined the Army on his own, leaving his friends behind in Altrincham, but Speakman soon made new friends:

> When I was with the London Scottish I learned a very good lesson that these old soldiers taught me. 'Do your best. Pick a mucker and stick with him.' It was Paddy Hayley with me for a long, long time. Paddy and I went everywhere together and no matter where we were, especially in the Far East, he would always pick up a stray dog. What a marvellous person he was.

THE GORDON HIGHLANDERS

The regiment can trace its roots back to the 75th Highland Regiment, raised in 1787, and the 100th (Highland) Regiment, raised by the 4th Duke of Gordon in 1794. (In 1798 the 100th Regiment became the 92nd Regiment of the Foot.) These two regiments amalgamated in 1881 to form the 1st and 2nd Battalions of The Gordon Highlanders.

They have fought with distinction throughout the world, and will be particularly remembered for the forced march under the command of General Sir Frederick Roberts VC from Kabul to Kandahar in Afghanistan in 1880 and the rearguard action, as part of the 51st (Highland) Division, at Dunkirk in 1940. Eighteen Victoria Crosses have been awarded to men serving in the regiment or its predecessors. After amalgamations with other regiments, The Gordon Highlanders became The Highlanders (Seaforth, Gordons and Camerons) in 1994 and after further amalgamations were renamed The Highlanders, 4th Battalion Royal Regiment of Scotland in 2006.

After the war there were huge population transfers across Europe as prisoners of war were released from captivity, and slave labourers, the majority of them taken from Russia to work in factories and farms, tried to make their way home. In addition, millions of Germans were expelled from Poland and Czechoslovakia. These displaced persons (DPs) created huge welfare and administrative problems for the Allies. The German POWs at Rimini, and elsewhere, had to be vetted before sending them home to ensure there were no Nazi war criminals hiding amongst them.

Private Speakman rejoined his original regiment on 14 February 1947, the same day he was promoted to lance corporal. At his own request, he reverted to the rank of private three weeks later on 6 March, while at Riccione, northern Italy. Although his Army record does not state the reason for his decision, he signed a memo stating that the reversion to the permanent rank of private was 'at my own request and not to avoid trial by FGCM [Field General Court Martial]'. He entrained for a period of private leave in the UK on 9 March 1947, returning on 11 April.

An undated note on his Army record, between June and August 1947, states that he was awarded a Second World War medal. The rubber stamp entry 'Awarded War Medal 1939–45' was no doubt a clerical error as Speakman had not served the twenty-eight days qualifying period. This may, however, explain why he later wore the ribbon or medal even though he was not officially entitled to do so; if he had been informed by the Army that he had been awarded the medal he would have assumed that this was correct. Second World War medals had to be claimed from the War Office but Speakman would not have been able to claim the War Medal 1939–45.

He served again in BAOR, from 1 August 1947 to 2 April 1951, and was posted to No 3 Leave Centre on 8 September 1947 and then HQ BAOR Leave Unit on 13 June 1948. Also in June 1948, he attended an education course at Formation School in Dahlerbruck in the Ruhr. Bill Speakman remembers the early part of his Army career:

From Italy I went up to Austria and even then I did not rejoin my regiment because I was ERE'd (2) to another transit camp, a place called Biederfeld in Germany. When we got to Biederfeld, we were told that the regiment did not want us. So we asked why. I said, 'Since joining The Black Watch, I've been put through the London Scottish and The Gordon Highlanders.' They said, 'Yes, but you're a young soldier, you have not fought a four-year war.' They had filled their strength and we were not needed.

After that I was posted back to The Black Watch but for some reason I couldn't get back to my old battalion immediately. You had 2nd Battalion from India and men were being posted to 1st Battalion. They were coming back to finish their time, so they didn't want us. But when they got rid of these guys and then asked, 'Where were you?' We rejoined our regiments – The Black Watch 1st Battalion at Duisburg just outside Dusseldorf and from there to Berlin before the wall went up.

We went into Berlin on a convoy because we escorted the NAAFI by road through the Russian sector. We were the escort and saw Berlin in ruins, long before they built the wall.

Just after the war there was still a bit of fighting, but we didn't mind. We were seeing what we joined up to see. When I got back from the escort duty my mate, Ginger Hartwell, and I were posted. I was posted to No 3 Leave Centre at Möhne See, near where the dams raid took place and Guy Gibson VC got his decoration.

Speakman home on leave. (*Bill Speakman VC*)

Wing Commander Guy Gibson received the VC for leading Operation *Chastise*, the Dambusters raid, on the Möhne and Eder Dams on 16–17 May 1943. The attack on the Möhne was successful and the wall of the dam was breached. The resulting loss of water flooded huge areas and disrupted German industry in the Ruhr, although not to the extent which had been anticipated. It did not take the Germans long to repair the dam, as Speakman noted:

I was put in charge of the Officers' Leave Hotel, right next to the dam which Gibson bombed. It's amazing how it goes a full cycle. I used to walk on that dam. They repaired it after the raid and then tried to drain it to recover the bodies of the aircrew and the wreckage of the planes that had gone in. It was a hopeless task.

'You are here to help out on the general staff,' they told me and so I helped to run the boat section. From there I got transferred to No 6 Leave Centre – a skiing and winter leave place. I was in charge of the ski stores at Winterbergen, in Germany. In those days if you got a 72-hour pass you couldn't get back to the UK because you were on Mediterranean lines of communication – it took at least two weeks to get home so the Army initiated leave centres where you could spend a weekend.

After the Second World War, Germany was divided into zones of occupation by the victorious Allies. The west of Germany was occupied by Britain, the USA and France and the east by the Soviet Union. Berlin, which had been captured by the Russians and was in the Soviet sector, was also divided into zones, with a road and rail link to the west. The British Zone was occupied by the British Army of the Rhine (BAOR). Speakman served with BAOR from 21 June 1946 to 9 August 1946 and from 1 August 1947 to 2 April 1951. While with BAOR, he returned to Berlin:

We were responsible for guarding Spandau Prison and for RAF Gatow – the airfield right on the border along with the Russians. There was no wall then. I was the battalion butcher (3) – I applied because it was a nice cushy job but while I was there I got a little bit fed up and said, 'This is not for me.' After being in Italy and all that I missed it and the Mediterranean.

I've been on leave and got really drunk, but one thing I've never been is vicious with a drink. In those days there were no spirits to buy; it was pure beer, beer, beer – even in the NCOs' and officers' mess. I remember getting back to base late and trying to climb over a barbed wire fence while wearing a kilt – hilarious! You get one leg over the barbed wire and watch you don't get anything caught on the wire while you and your mate hold it. He's half cut so he lets go – a hell of a twang. These kilts are made of so many pleats and that gets caught, made of wonderful stuff and that gets caught as you are trying to get over but you manage to do it.

When we were stationed in RAF Gatow, next to the Russian sector, we were responsible for guarding the border. We would say 'Hello' to the sentries in their boxes on the other side. They would say 'Hello' and point their cameras at us. I used to chat to them: 'Hi, Ivan.' They were conscripts and they had a job to do.

The guys in the machine gun towers used to swing their weapons round. They were East Germans. They were deadly; they cared for nobody. They would follow people trying to escape to the West: a woman or a child climbing the barbed wire. The guards would watch them climb halfway up and then turn the machine gun on them and drop them. For that they got a day's leave as a reward. They were there to discourage people.

At one time in Berlin, in the early days, you could go anywhere. Married families could go to East Berlin to get crockery and glassware, which was beautiful. Then the Berlin Airlift started in 1948.

In June 1948 the Russians escalated the Cold War by denying the Western Allies road and rail access to their sectors in Berlin. The only way into landlocked Berlin was by air across Soviet-occupied territory, and tons of equipment and food were flown into Berlin's Tempelhof Airport. The blockade ended in May 1949 but the airlift continued until September. In the same year the West and East sectors of Germany became separate Democratic Republics.

The recovery of Europe from years of war and Nazi control took time, and Speakman saw the destruction and chaos everywhere. Most towns and cities had been reduced to rubble and the road and rail infrastructure was destroyed. Many Germans were forced to clear rubble in order to make enough money to live. Living conditions in post-war Germany, in common with other countries,

Speakman home on leave.
(*Bill Speakman VC*)

were extremely harsh; food was scarce and few people could afford to buy goods on the black market. Speakman witnessed the suffering of the survivors:

> There was a lot going on. Europe was trying to get itself together after the war. There were displaced persons everywhere and the railways were out of order. The war had finished in 1945 but in all those years there was chaos. If you were going home on leave from Italy you were on the train for a week or two weeks at a time, so you were issued with haversack rations and all that food had to last you. We had cigarettes and chocolate as well. All that chocolate went to the kids on the trains. A tin of fifty cigarettes would have been worth £1,000 on the black market.
>
> We saw it all, it was bad. In displaced persons camps we saw people who had been taken from their homes and sent to work in Germany as slave labourers. It was horrific what happened. They had lost their homes. Most of the kids were motherless. No one wanted them. It was quite an eye opener – people just don't realise what went on. Everyone hated Germany, Krupp especially. But then you had to get Europe together. Money was coming in for reorganisation, so it gradually got better.

Britain also experienced a period of political, economic and social change after the war. In the 1945 general election, Winston Churchill was replaced as Prime Minister by Clement Attlee, in a landslide victory for the Labour Party. With a clear mandate for change, the new government nationalised the Bank of England, the railways, coal mines and the iron and steel industries and established the National Health Service. Britain experienced a balance of payments crisis in the late 1940s, brought about by the ending of Lend–Lease and had to be helped by the Marshall Plan for European economic recovery. These problems highlighted the weakness of the pound, which was devalued in September 1949. As the country began to recover from the war, bread rationing ended in July 1948 and clothes rationing ended the following February.

Speakman's stepfather, Bert Houghton, died on 11 June 1949, aged 60. His occupation at the time of his death was labourer at an engineering works. The cause of death was listed as cardiac failure and chronic bronchitis and emphysema, from which he had suffered for many years. Bill Speakman was home on leave at the time and was present when his stepfather died at the family house at 27 Moss Lane, Altrincham. Speakman recalls, 'One day I woke up and came down the stairs and he was dead.' He registered his stepfather's death three days later. Bill Speakman lost the father figure he had known for only fourteen years, but it was worse for his mother, Hannah Houghton, who would spend the next forty-nine years as a widow.

In January 1950 Speakman was confined to barracks for fourteen days for being absent on roll call and went Absent Without Leave (AWOL) twice in early 1951. In January he was missing for a period of 1 hour and 35 minutes and was confined to barracks for 10 days as punishment. In March 1951 he again went AWOL, this time for 1 day, 23 hours and 25 minutes. He was given 72 hours' detention, and forfeited two days' pay, and returned to duty immediately after his release from detention. It later became apparent that some of these acts of rebellion were designed to make a nuisance of himself so that he would be released by his battalion.

Speakman was still serving in Germany when the Korean War started in June 1950. A request was made later to The Black Watch, and other regiments, for volunteers to transfer to battalions which were due to go to Korea. Speakman may have been unsure where Korea was, but he knew he was bored with Army life in Germany and wanted to see some action. The idea of fighting in a real war appealed to him, so he volunteered to transfer to another battalion.

Despite the nature of the call for volunteers, it appears that some battalions were reluctant to release men for Korea if it meant depleting their own numbers:

> I was with The Black Watch when I volunteered for Korea. They would not let me go at first and then I made a bit of a nuisance of myself. They said, 'Right, then, we will get rid of this bloke.' And so I found my way to Korea … The first regiments which went over were the regiments stationed in Hong Kong. When it enlarged and the Chinese came on, they knew they had a battle on their hands and called for volunteers.

He was accepted for a transfer to Korea, initially attached to The Argyll and Sutherland Highlanders (A&SH), but by the time he arrived in Korea the battalion was ready to leave. 'When I volunteered the Argylls were in the line,' remembers Speakman, 'but by the time we got round to it the Argylls had done their stint and were on the way out.' Speakman and the other volunteers were attached to another battalion fighting in Korea – 1st Battalion The King's Own Scottish Borderers (KOSB). The *Borderers' Chronicle*, however, states that he was attached to The Argyll and Sutherland Highlanders and then posted to the KOSB when the A&SH tour was over. Once he had been attached to the KOSB he never returned to his parent regiment, The Black Watch.

Speakman returned to the UK from Germany for a short period, 3 April to 21 May 1951, before being posted to Korea. He was taken on the strength of

The Black Watch, ex-BAOR, in the UK on 3 April. Despite his many brushes with authority, the Army recognised that Speakman would make a good NCO; he had the necessary ability to lead other men and his size would enable him to keep them in order. He was a very sociable person, with a good sense of humour, who was well liked by the rest of the battalion.

On 22 May 1951 he was promoted to acting corporal and included in a draft of men being sent to Korea on the troopship *Empire Medway*. He left the 'Home Service' and was attached to the Far East Land Forces (FARELF). Unfortunately for Speakman, his problems with discipline surfaced again during the long voyage to Korea. He was deprived of his acting rank by the ship's commander for going AWOL for over five hours on 24 June 1951, and returned to the rank of private. The troopship finally reached Base Depot in South Korea on 4 July.

NOTES

(1) The qualifying period for the War Medal 1939–45 was twenty-eight days' service between 3 September 1939 and 2 September 1945.

(2) ERE: Extra-Regimentally Employed (attached to a unit other than the individual's own regiment or corps).

(3) Speakman qualified as a butcher on 23 September 1950.

KOREA

JULY–NOVEMBER 1951

The Korean Peninsula lies south of the border with the Manchuria region of China and is approximately 130 miles north-west of the Japanese mainland. After the Russo-Japanese War of 1904–05, Korea, the so-called 'Land of the Morning Calm', was occupied by Japan and remained a Japanese possession until 1945. At the end of the Second World War, America and the Soviet Union, the two occupying nations, divided Korea into two separate countries along the 38th Parallel. The communist north became the Democratic People's Republic of Korea and the pro-Western south became the Republic of Korea. In 1949, both the Soviet Union and the United States withdrew their forces from Korea. Under the pretence of a counter-attack and with the tacit approval of the Soviet Union, North Korean troops invaded South Korea on Sunday, 25 June 1950. North Korean artillery began a bombardment along the 38th Parallel at 4.00 a.m. and, as the artillery lifted, the North Korean People's Army advanced into South Korea. By 28 June the invading army had captured Seoul, the capital. A United Nations Security Council resolution demanded an immediate withdrawal of North Korean troops and called for other UN member nations to assist South Korea. (The resolution was passed unanimously as the Soviet Union had boycotted the meeting and did not vote.)

Reinforcements from a number of countries soon arrived, with US troops landing the following month. Britain could ill-afford another war and its Army was already fully stretched but, nonetheless, immediately offered military support. Britain was the second largest foreign troop contributor to UN Forces and by the spring of 1951 a total of 12,000 British troops were in Korea. During the course of the war a total of 63,000 UK troops were sent to the conflict. Seventy per cent of these were National Servicemen.

North Korean troops made rapid progress and advanced almost as far as Pusan (now Busan) in the south-east of the peninsula. A perimeter was established around Pusan, enabling the United Nations Forces, led by Supreme Commander General Douglas MacArthur, to drive back the North Koreans. A daring US-led amphibious landing behind enemy lines at Inchon on 15 September succeeded in cutting off North Korea's supply lines and Seoul, just over 20 miles east of Inchon, was liberated on 26 September.

China threatened to escalate the war by assisting its ally if UN troops crossed the border into North Korea. Despite this threat, which General MacArthur did not take seriously, the United Nations Forces crossed the border (with UN approval) on 7 October and captured Pyongyang, the North Korean capital, on 19 October. Ignoring the warnings from the Chinese, the UN Forces continued north towards the Yalu River, which marked the border with China. Chinese forces attacked on 27 November and in the face of numerically superior troops the UN Forces were forced to retreat. Chinese troops crossed the 38th Parallel into South Korea on 28 December 1950 and captured Seoul again on 4 January 1951. They were soon pushed back to the border area, aided by continuous UN aerial bombing campaigns.

The war became less mobile and the front line eventually settled around the 38th Parallel, where fighting continued for another two years. The Imjin River, scene of some of the fiercest fighting involving British troops, rises in North Korea and crosses the 38th Parallel before flowing into the Yellow Sea.

General MacArthur wanted to bomb Chinese bases in Manchuria but was overruled by President Harry Truman, who felt that this would be a dangerous escalation of the war. MacArthur publically criticised US foreign policy in Korea, and in April 1951 Truman relieved MacArthur of his command and replaced him with General Matthew Ridgway. Talks on a truce began in July 1951 at Kaesong, and later moved to a more secure location at Panmunjom, which was marked by a vertical searchlight beam to prevent accidental attack by either side. An armistice was agreed on 27 July 1953 but no peace treaty has yet been signed. Technically, North and South Korea are still at war and the USA retains troops along the Demilitarised Zone to preserve the uneasy peace.

Tension remains high in the region, especially since North Korea, under the leadership of 'Dear Leader' Kim Jong-Il, gained the capacity to manufacture and launch nuclear missiles. Whilst the leadership has built up a nuclear arsenal, the people of North Korea have suffered; one-third of the population is starving and power cuts are a daily feature in the capital Pyongyang. After the collapse of communism in 1989, North Korea found itself isolated and lost most of its economic support. In December 2011 Kim Jong-II died and was succeeded by his son, Kim Jong-Un.

Korea theatre of operations, 1950–53.

The two B Coy KOSB soldiers in the foreground are Lance Corporal John Pender, who was to win the MM in the 4 November action (light hat), and Private John Dunbar. The soldiers in background left are Private John Davine and Lance Corporal Ted Arbuthnott DCM MM, who won his DCM at Anzio and his MM in Sicily. (© *IWM K07607*)

In the 1990s a series of floods and droughts caused widespread crop failures. Observers have estimated that up to 2.5 million people have died of cold and starvation. Despite this, the regime spends large sums on keeping an army of 1.2 million soldiers and expanding its nuclear programme. It is of great concern to the West that North Korea announced it had exploded a nuclear bomb in 2006. In 2009, it tested ballistic missiles and expelled UN nuclear inspectors. In 2010, North Korea sank a submarine belonging to South Korea and the two countries exchanged artillery fire.

During the three years of the Korean War, British casualties were 1,109 dead and 2,674 wounded. In addition, more than 1,000 men were made POWs. Four Victoria Crosses were awarded – two of them posthumously. It has been estimated that more than two million Koreans died during the war. Fighting conditions were often primitive, with both sides facing each other across the type of trenches and dugouts that were common in the First World War.

KOREAN WAR VCS

Four Victoria Crosses were awarded for the Korean War:

- Major Kenneth Muir VC (1912–50) 1st Bn The Argyll and Sutherland Highlanders for action at Hill 282, on 23 September 1950. Posthumous award.
- Lieutenant Philip Curtis VC (1926–51), The Duke of Cornwall's Light Infantry, attached to 1st Bn The Gloucestershire Regiment for action at Castle Hill, near the Imjin River on 22–23 April 1951. Posthumous award.
- Lieutenant Colonel James Carne VC DSO (1906–86), the CO of 1st Bn The Gloucestershire Regiment for action near the Imjin River on 22–23 April 1951.
- Private William Speakman VC (born 1927), The Black Watch, attached to 1st Bn The King's Own Scottish Borders for action at 'United' Hilltop on 4 November 1951.

The weather in Korea is particularly unpleasant, ranging from hot and humid, with monsoon rains, in the summer to sub-zero temperatures in the winter. Frostbite was a particular problem. To combat the cold, British soldiers wore several layers of clothing including a thick pullover and parka anoraks; many battalions were not prepared for a Korean winter when they arrived, as Speakman recalls:

Those battalions which went into Korea in the beginning, like the Middlesex Regiment, went in battledress. We got the winter warfare uniform – a new type of combat dress. Korea has extreme heat in summer and extreme coldness in winter. In summertime we were in KD [khaki drill] and in winter we had to have this combat kit otherwise we would have just froze to death. If you touched metal with your bare hands it would stick to you so we wore mittens. We used special graphite grease on our weapons as graphite will never freeze.

Speakman remembers the daily tot of rum: 'The only alcohol we got was a tot of rum every day. We had a small tot at night with our tea and it was to get rid of the chills and the cold'.

When the Korean War began in 1950, 1st Battalion The King's Own Scottish Borderers (KOSB) was stationed in Hong Kong. The Borderers had been there for the previous eight months as part of an infantry division defending the colony against potential attack from mainland China. (In view of the swift Chinese advance through Korea it is debatable whether one division would have been sufficient to prevent them invading Hong Kong.) The battalion embarked for Korea on 19 April 1951, arriving at Inchon on 23 April, to relieve 1st Battalion The Argyll and Sutherland Highlanders, which had completed its tour of duty.

After a long period of training and border patrolling in the New Territories, Hong Kong, the battalion was ready for action. After arriving in Korea, 1st KOSB moved to positions just south of the 38th Parallel and was attached to the 28th British Commonwealth Brigade. By the time of Operation *Commando* in October 1951, the brigade comprised 1st KOSB, 1st Battalion King's Shropshire Light Infantry (KSLI) and 3rd Battalion Royal Australian Regiment (RAR).

In July 1951, a Commonwealth Division was established from units from Britain, Australia, Canada, India and New Zealand, and 28th British Commonwealth Brigade was incorporated into the newly formed 1st British Commonwealth Division. Before then, Commonwealth Brigades had fought under American Divisional leadership. The new Commonwealth Division, which formed part

Lieutenant Colonel J.F.M. MacDonald commanding 1st KOSB, and his escort on arrival in Korea. (*KOSB Museum*)

of the 1st US Corps, was commanded by Major General James Cassels, a career soldier who had held general rank in the Second World War. He was greatly respected by everyone in the division, and morale among the troops improved as a direct result. Major General Cassels and his father, General Sir Robert Cassels, had the distinction of both being Generals in the Second World War.

After a year of fighting across the entire peninsula, both sides faced each other across a front line which ran diagonally across the 38th Parallel. The front line remained roughly the same for the rest of the war. The King's Own Scottish Borderers were in defensive positions on the Kansas Line, south of the River Imjin, when ceasefire negotiations began in July 1951. The Kansas Line was a line of heavily defended hills and positions held by UN Forces close to the 38th Parallel.

THE KING'S OWN SCOTTISH BORDERERS

The King's Own Scottish Borderers (KOSB) can trace its origins back to 1689, when it was raised by the Earl of Leven for the defence of Edinburgh and to secure the Protestant succession to the throne in Scotland. It was known as The Edinburgh Regiment and was designated the 25th (Edinburgh) Regiment of Foot in 1751. In 1782 it was renamed the 25th (Sussex) Regiment of Foot as the colonel at the time (Lord George Lennox) had his family seat at Goodwood, in Sussex.

After service in the French Revolutionary Wars, the regiment was renamed the 25th (The King's Own Borderers) Regiment of Foot in 1805. Yet another strange renaming occurred in the army reorganisations of 1881, when the 25th Foot became the York Regiment, King's Own Borderers and the Regimental Depot was relocated to York. This proved to be a very unpopular decision and the depot was quickly moved to Berwick-upon-Tweed (Northumberland), close to the Borders. In 1887 the regiment became The King's Own Scottish Borderers. The KOSB served in South Africa and both World Wars, as well as Korea, and six VCs (four of them for the Great War) were awarded to men serving in it. The regiment is now part of the Royal Scots Borderers, 1st Battalion Royal Regiment of Scotland.

The regimental badge shows Edinburgh Castle upon a saltire surrounded by thistles, surmounted by the Royal Crest. The badge also includes the mottoes *In veritate religionis confido* (I trust in the truth of my belief) and *Nisi dominus frustra* (In vain without the Lord).

Because of Britain's expanding military burden, the Army consisted of mainly National Servicemen. Second Lieutenant William Purves, himself a National Serviceman, noted that there were more National Servicemen officers than regulars in 1st KOSB. (In October 1950, in response to the Korean War, National Service was extended from eighteen months to two years and many men were trained to become officers.)

Reinforcements from other battalions arrived in Korea following the appeal for volunteers. Private Bill Speakman was part of a new detachment of men which left England in May 1951. They disembarked at Base Depot in Korea on 4 July and Speakman, formerly of 1st Battalion The Black Watch, was taken on the strength of the Reserve List. He was attached to 1st Battalion King's Own Scottish Borderers, from the Reserve List, on 16 July.

Many veterans of the Korean War recall the monotonous existence and the endless digging of trenches in ground which was rock hard in winter and flooded in other seasons. Historian and former Borderer, Robert Woollcombe summed up the situation in *All the Blue Bonnets*:

> It was a war fought for the possession of hilltops, with ceaseless digging and wiring of positions. Digging was a feature of the campaign, not only from a fighting point of view, but also as the means of obtaining shelter. From start to finish, whenever the troops halted they dug. (1)

He joined B Company, under the command of Major Philip St Clair Harrison (2), a regular Army officer who had served in the Second World War, and was attached to Harrison's company headquarters. Operation *Commando* would be the first occasion Speakman had been in action since he joined the Army six years earlier. His duties were many and varied:

> Signaller, gofer, orderly, but never a batman, and things like that. It was in general Company HQ. In the platoons you did ordinary duties, like guard duty, but at Company HQ I was just an orderly working with Major Harrison and the company sergeant major.
>
> I was a signaller, which is also a radio operator. You worked the radio at times, when you were going forward. We didn't have Royal Signals attached to us – you were trained as a signaller. And as an orderly, I used to run messages between the lines and between platoons when the lines went down. You were, in general, a 'gofer'. Major Harrison was a gentleman, he treated me very fairly; he treated everyone fairly.

British servicemen tried to camouflage their slits and trenches, as well as make them more comfortable, with blankets. Being a Scottish regiment, 1st KOSB had tartan blankets. Taking the blankets out of the trenches to give them a shake and air them in the open almost caused an incident on more than one occasion, as Speakman recalls:

> In those days we were issued with a panel of various colours and when you displayed it the American aircraft would bomb beyond that point. We were airing our blanket around the back of our trenches and the guys on watch were around the front. The Americans had bombed the Argylls so many times [with rockets and napalm] and we realised we were inviting them to bomb our trenches. We had this bloody great tartan blanket on display like a target!

That autumn an offensive was launched by 1st Commonwealth Division, in its only attack of the war. The aims of the new offensive were to disrupt any plans the enemy might have for an advance and to improve the UN negotiating position at the peace talks by moving closer to the 38th Parallel. At the time, UN troops held positions south of the Imjin, with the enemy across the river to the north. The Chinese Army was some 6 miles away, with the area in between in no-man's-land. There had been no recent action in this area apart from occasional patrols.

The task of establishing a bridgehead over the Imjin was given to 28th Commonwealth Brigade, under the command of Brigadier George Taylor DSO★. This was achieved, without difficulty, on 8 September and the brigade moved to new positions north of the Imjin. The Chinese were taken by surprise and, apart from shelling Commonwealth positions, did not counter-attack. The next phase of the offensive was Operation *Minden*, in which British and Canadian battalions moved to within 3 miles of the Chinese defences. This phase was assigned to 25th Canadian Infantry Brigade and 29th Commonwealth Brigade – 28th Commonwealth Brigade did not take part.

The third phase of the offensive, Operation *Commando*, was planned for early October. The principal role of capturing a number of strategic hills, marking the Jamestown Line, was given to 28th British Commonwealth Brigade. The Brigade's objectives were Kowang-san (also known as Little Gibraltar or Hill 355), Maryang-san (known as Hill 317) and the adjacent Hill 217 (3). The Chinese had held these objectives for some time and were well dug in. In the southern sector, the task of capturing another line of hills was allocated to 25th Canadian Brigade. For the last part of *Commando*, 1st Battalion Royal

Two views of Hill 355. (*KOSB Museum*)

Northumberland Fusiliers (RNF) was borrowed from 29th Commonwealth Brigade and placed under the control of 28th Brigade.

On the evening of 1 October 1951 the brigade moved into the assembly area. 1st KOSB, under the command of Lieutenant Colonel John MacDonald OBE, was assigned Hill 355; MacDonald's coolness and determination during the battle for Hill 355 would earn him the DSO. After lying in wait during 2

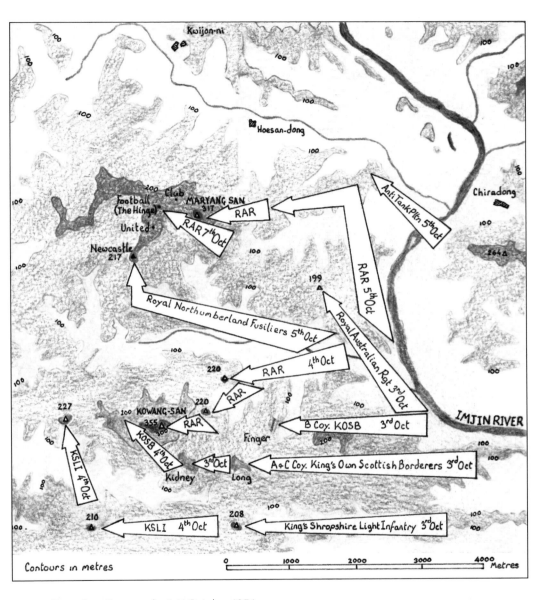

Operation *Commando*, 3–7 October 1951.

October, the battalion began the attack at dawn on 3 October. Hill 355 was protected by several other hills in between and was to prove a difficult objective. A heavy artillery bombardment of the Chinese positions, held by units of the 191st Division, preceded the infantry attack.

Using B and C Companies, the battalion advanced on two intermediate features known as Finger and Long to cover the later assault on Hill 355. The two companies began their attack at 7.00 a.m., but progress was slow due to the steep and densely wooded terrain. Speakman, and the rest of B Company Headquarters, followed B Company on the right flank towards Finger. Despite heavy enemy mortar fire, the ridge was captured with minimal resistance. Having completed its first objective, B Company began to dig in while still under fire.

It was a different story, however, for C Company, led by Major Little, on the left of the advance. They encountered stiff opposition on Long ridge and fought a long battle with the well-armed Chinese defenders. The fighting went on for over three hours, during which time the company was spread along the entire ridge mopping up snipers. Major Little was then ordered to withdraw from Long in order to regroup his company. They were reinforced by A Company, led by Major Duncan, and that afternoon a further attack was made by the two companies. They were supported by a barrage from

Hill 355 being bombarded by artillery in Operation *Commando*. (© *IWM BF 10426*)

Brigadier George Taylor and Captain Donald Lear 1st KOSB watch KOSB advance on Hill 355. (© *IWM BF 10427*)

16th Field Regiment Royal New Zealand Artillery and mortar fire, and with B Company providing covering fire from Finger. The objective, Long, was soon taken and A Company then captured the next feature, known as Kidney. All companies then consolidated their positions ready for the next day's action and removed their casualties, and during the night the Korean porters brought up further supplies.

The attack had air and artillery support and it was the aircraft dropping napalm on the enemy positions that remained in Speakman's mind:

All hell broke out. You went forward and looked up and you knew you were going to take these hills. You saw the planes going in there – the napalm going in. The Chinese were on the hills dug in and the planes never put the stuff right into the trenches. They always put it above the trenches and the stuff would roll into the trenches from above. Same with phosphorus shells – it would take all the oxygen and they would come running out of the trenches because they had no air. You could see them coming out of their dugouts with their clothes on fire. It stuck like jelly; you couldn't get it off you. It was horrific, sickening …

Taken immediately after the capture of Hill 355 on 4 October. In the background are the men of KOSB. In the foreground are two Chinese POWs, watched right by a South Korean soldier attached to KOSB.

All the immediate approaches to Hill 355 had been captured on 3 October. On the southern flank, Hill 208 had been taken by 1st KSLI. Hill 355 was attacked on 4 October after a heavy artillery bombardment which blasted the top of the hill to pieces. It was captured by a combined attack from B Company 1st KOSB advancing from the east and D Company, commanded by Major Robertson-Macleod, and the Battle Patrol from the south-west.

Australian troops from 3rd RAR attacked Kowang-san (Hill 355) from the north-west to overwhelm the Chinese defenders and prevent them from reinforcing the threatened positions. Major Jack Gerke led 3rd RAR to the summit of the hill and was awarded the DSO for this and other acts of bravery and leadership during Operation *Commando*.

There is still some dispute over which unit captured the hill. It had no clear peak; it was a large feature with several hillocks along the top. The Australians claim to have reached the summit and set up defensive positions while the Borderers were still making their way up the slopes 'accompanied by the jaunty sounds of their bagpipers playing traditional Scottish marching tunes' (4).

Other sources, including *The Borderers in Korea*, (5) give credit for the capture of Hill 355 to 1st KOSB. *The Borderers in Korea* states that: 'Early on the 4th October,

D Company, commanded by Major Robertson-Macleod, and the Battle Patrol successfully scaled and fought the enemy off the final objective of Point 355. B Company ... gave most valuable support throughout this operation.'

Although neither battalion would like to admit it, they both captured the hill in a classic pincer movement. To the left of the KOSB, 1st KSLI captured their final objective on Hill 210. The Australians soon departed Hill 355, leaving its defence to 1st KOSB, but felt aggrieved that Lieutenant Colonel MacDonald was not there personally to meet Major Gerke.

Enemy defence positions on Hill 355 were well equipped, with some of their bunkers 20ft deep and containing up to three sleeping bays. A large stores dump, which supplied the defenders, was found and destroyed. The enemy suffered many casualties, mostly from the artillery bombardment, in the taking of Hill 355.

Speakman recalls that the battalion used phosphorus grenades, the use of which is still considered controversial, during Operation *Commando*:

> Whenever we were taking ground, taking hills, we were in action. That's where the phosphorus grenades came in – nothing like it for getting people

Hill 317 bombarded with napalm and rockets during Operation *Commando*. (© *IWM BF 10430*)

View of Hill 317 from the newly captured Hill 355. (*Australian War Memorial 042315*)

out of holes in the ground. You can't get phosphorus off, it sticks to you like putting syrup on your arm. They were very handy because it was a choker and a smokescreen, very, very handy for certain things.

The KOSB Regimental History of the Korean War noted that casualties over the two days of action were seven killed and thirty-four wounded – about a third of the enemy's casualties. Phase three of Operation *Commando* involved 1st RNF and 3rd RAR capturing Hills 217 and 199, and then Hill 317 (Maryang-san). In a brilliant flanking move on 5 October, 3rd RAR took the Chinese by surprise and captured not only Hill 317, but all along to the Hinge, another ridge. Although not directly involved, 1st KOSB provided supporting fire in the opening stage. Operation *Commando* was successfully completed by 8 October and 28th Commonwealth Brigade (assisted by 1st Royal Northumberland Fusiliers) seized its main objectives of Hill 355 and Hill 317. At the end of Operation *Commando*, adjustments were made to the line of newly captured hills and on 9 October 1st KOSB took over the responsibility for the defence of Hills 217 and 317 from 3rd RAR.

On 9 October 1951, Brigadier Taylor, Commander of 28th British Commonwealth Brigade wrote a letter to all ranks congratulating them on 'their splendid achievement' in Operation *Commando*. He added: 'You have again proved your superiority over an enemy who fought with considerable determination and some skill.'

In August 1952, Company Sergeant Major 'Busty' Murdoch of B Company 1st KOSB was recommended for the DCM for outstanding service between October 1951 and May 1952. Murdoch was a regular soldier and had seen action during the Second World War in India, Burma and Norway. During Operation *Commando* he took part in the offensive and ensured the company was constantly supplied with ammunition. His DCM citation mentioned his important role:

> On Operation *Commando*, with complete disregard for his own safety, he was frequently to be seen up with the foremost troops not only ensuring that a constant supply of ammunition was immediately available but also, by his calmness under fire and personal bearing, giving confidence to the young officers and NCOs carrying out the attack. There is no doubt that the successful exploits of the company were due in great measure to the encouraging and steadying influence of CSM Murdoch and to his courageous example.

From a strategic viewpoint, Operation *Commando* was very successful – a view endorsed at ground level by Private Speakman:

> Everything went so smoothly. A bit of opposition here and there but I think it was run very smoothly. As a soldier with Company HQ, you had your platoon and in the whole battalion each company was doing its thing. Then you had special companies forming the Battle Patrols and other companies doing this and that. You weren't in action all the time. In the line, when you were in action you never met a guy from another company because that is the way it was. You were with B Company, because everything was in place and you stayed in place.

Although Brigadier George Taylor was an experienced soldier, who had won a formidable reputation in north-west Europe in 1944–45, his man management skills were less impressive. He clashed with many of his battalion commanders, including John MacDonald of 1st KOSB, Frank Hassett of 3rd RAR and John Moodie of 16th Field Regiment Royal New Zealand Artillery.

Eventually, the problems with Taylor became known at divisional HQ, and on 25 October Major General Cassels relieved Brigadier Taylor of his command of 28th Commonwealth Brigade. He was replaced by Lieutenant Colonel MacDonald, who was an experienced battalion commander and previously had commanded 1st KOSB in north-west Europe in 1944–45. Major Dennis Tadman OBE, MacDonald's second in command, took command of 1st KOSB. Their promotions were not automatic and took a little while to come through.

BRIGADIER GEORGE TAYLOR CBE DSO*

George Taylor was born into an Army family in September 1905 and was commissioned into the West Yorkshire Regiment in 1929. During the Second World War, he took part in the D-Day landings and later won a formidable reputation as a battalion commander in north-west Europe, where he received the DSO and Bar.

He was appointed commander of 28th Infantry Brigade in Hong Kong and in April 1951 took his brigade to Korea, where it became 28th Commonwealth Brigade. He led this brigade during Operation *Commando* but was relieved of his command shortly afterwards. After Korea, he commanded a brigade in Kenya to counter the Mau Mau uprising. For his part in this campaign he was appointed CBE in 1955. He retired from the Army in 1957 and died in July 1994, aged 88.

During any war, casualties are expected by every army but, as Speakman discovered, it is sometimes difficult to understand why when someone you know is killed:

> In the battalion we had a corporal, a Welshman. He was a lovely guy. He did his wartime service in Germany and was a reservist after the war. He was called up for Korea and fouteen days after arriving he lost his life. It is a terrible thing for a reservist to be called back after serving his country and then be killed. You have disrupted your life once to fight during the war and then it happens again and you are killed after fourteen days. There was no sympathy or pity.
>
> We had seen what had happened to the Glosters and the RNF, whose positions were captured by the Chinese. There were bodies strewn across the hills and the survivors trying to get them back for burial. We could understand; we only did the job we were trained to do.

With peace talks under way, the war became more static and both sides dug in ready for the winter. Many other locations, including parts of Spain, Greece and the USA, share the 38th Parallel with Korea but their climate is much more agreeable. In Korea, the Arctic winds blowing from Siberia reduce the winter temperatures to well below freezing point. The winter uniform for British soldiers included extra layers of socks and underwear, two pullovers, gloves with inner layers and a thick parka. Chinese troops, in contrast, were poorly protected by their quilted jackets. British soldiers slept fully clothed in dugouts, with their weapons by their sides in case they were attacked during the night.

Lieutenant Colonel J.F.M. MacDonald, 1st KOSB; Lieutenant Colonel Frank Hassett, 3rd RAR; Lieutenant General Bridgeford; Major General A.J.H. Cassels. (© *IWM MH 28035*)

These dugouts were usually holes in the ground with beds made of planks of wood; hygiene facilities were fairly primitive. Some units heated their dugouts and bunkers with cans of petrol, which often proved dangerous.

Both sides waited and watched each other. The periods between enemy attacks or shelling could be times of relative boredom and the Chinese would try to use psychological warfare on UN troops to make them question why they were there. Leaflets were often left on barbed wire defences and Chinese loudspeakers frequently broadcast messages, in English, to the British units facing them. Both sides sent out patrols to gather information and, where possible, carry out trench raids to capture prisoners for interrogation. Speakman recalls that British patrols went out into no-man's-land with bayonets fixed:

> The fixed bayonet is so important for close quarter work. You can swing the butt of the rifle, which is heavy wood with a brass end, and hit the enemy with that. Other times you can go straight in with the bayonet. You can use the butt to club them if you come across the enemy and want to take a prisoner. We had patrols out just to try to secure prisoners and bring them in. The butt and the bayonet were essential tools.

1st KOSB C Company reconnaissance group being briefed by company commander, Major T. Little. Left to right: Sergeant R. Mitchell, Corporal J. Roberts, Second Lieutenant E.R. Mudie, Captain R.H.S. Irvine, Second Lieutenant W. Purves, Major T. Little MC. *(Australian War Memorial HOBJ2379)*

In early November, Second Lieutenant William Purves, commanding 7 Platoon (C Company), was ordered to take a reconnaissance patrol from his position on a hill called Knoll down into the valley. He had the distinct impression that they were being watched all the time by Chinese soldiers in the surrounding hillsides. The patrol reached a deserted village and Purves decided to check inside a large two-storey house. To his great shock, he discovered a Korean girl in the hay-loft. Assuming her to be a 'comfort girl' for the Chinese senior officers, he quickly ordered his patrol back to its base. He had correctly calculated that providing they did not harm the girl or disturb the village the Chinese would not disclose their positions by firing on them. When he returned to Battalion

HQ Purves was able to report on this and described the trenches and connecting trenches dug into the foothills between the two opposing armies. The foothills were very sandy, unlike the mainly rocky hilltops occupied by KOSB, and the Chinese were able to dig their trenches very quickly.

The Chinese built defensive systems consisting of deep trenches and well-constructed bunkers and tunnels. There was usually little visible activity during the day, but at night they brought in mechanical diggers to extend their trenches forward. They were also very experienced in burrowing in holes, moving ever closer to UN lines, ready to emerge when an attack began. The Chinese felt they had been humiliated by Operation *Commando* and were determined to retake all the strategic positions they had been forced to give up. With their apparent lack of regard for human life, they were prepared to recapture the hills at any cost.

Chinese shelling of KOSB positions continued during early November, with 106 shells falling on 1 November, 133 shells the next day and 120 shells on 3 November. On 1 November a platoon-sized attack on C Company, supported by artillery and mortars, was repulsed without KOSB casualties. Later that day, a Battle Patrol reconnaissance group engaged the enemy and after a short firefight withdrew without serious casualties.

British and other Commonwealth troops made preparations for the next Chinese attack; more trenches were dug before winter set in and made the ground too hard to dig, and extensive barbed wire barriers were erected between the trees and around gun positions. Defenders had to run a gauntlet of fire to work on these obstacles. In some parts of the 1st KOSB front line the enemy were only some 300 yards away, particularly in the Hinge area.

NOTES

(1) *All the Blue Bonnets: The History of The King's Own Scottish Borders* by Robert Woollcombe. (Arms and Armour Press (now The Orion Publishing Group), London, 1980) © Robert Woollcombe, 1980.

(2) Lieutenant Colonel Philip St Clair Harrison DSO OBE was appointed Regimental Secretary of KOSB in 1957 and he was instrumental in the creation of the Regimental Museum at Berwick-upon-Tweed.

(3) Hills were named after their height, in metres, above sea level.

(4) *The Battle of Maryang San – 3rd Battalion, The Royal Australian Regiment, Korea, 2–8 October 1951.* (Headquarters Training Command, NSW, 1991)

(5) *The Borderers in Korea* by Major General John MacDonald CB DSO OBE.

VC ACTION

4 NOVEMBER 1951

By the beginning of November 1951, 1st KOSB had dug in for the winter along the battalion's front line before the sub-zero temperatures made digging impossible. An enemy counter-attack had been expected ever since the surrounding hills had been captured from the Chinese during Operation *Commando*, but no one knew when it would come. And no one could have forecast that when the attack eventually did come it would be directed at the section of the overstretched divisional line held by 1st KOSB. As Speakman later said, they were just 'waiting, waiting, waiting' for the Chinese to attack.

The new commanding officer of 1st KOSB, Major Tadman, spread his companies along his front line. This long ridge of hills and peaks, formerly part of the Chinese winter defence line, formed an arrowhead pointing both north and west into enemy-held territory. It was there that the battalion faced its fiercest fighting of the war.

To the east was the highest point, Hill 317, with steep sides to the south-west. A spur called Peak ran south from Hill 317. Both Hill 317 and Peak were held by D Company (less one platoon), commanded by Major Robertson-Macleod on 317.

About 400 yards to the west of 317 was a small hill called Knoll. The defence of this position was shared by Second Lieutenant Barney Henderson, in command of D Company (12 Platoon), and Second Lieutenant William Purves, in command of C Company (7 Platoon). Purves, aged 19, was awarded a DSO for his part in the action. About 200 yards west of Knoll was the Hinge. This was the tip of the arrow occupied by C Company, commanded by Major Little, with two platoons on its northern and western slopes.

South of Hinge was a long spur which formed the left side of the arrowhead. Approximately 400 yards from Hinge, up this ridge, was United (1), defended by 5 and 6 Platoons and Company HQ of B Company, commanded by Major Harrison.

Speakman was attached to B Company HQ as Major Harrison's runner on United, facing west. Major Harrison kept in touch with all sections of B Company by radio and telephone from his command post.

The spur continued south-west from United to a lower hillock, Point 217, defended by 4 Platoon of B Company with a section from 5 Platoon and a pair of machine guns. To the south-east of United ran another small spur for 500 yards to a position called Lock. This was occupied by the Battle Patrol, a unit of platoon strength. The spur which continued southwards was called Italy, because of its shape, and faced away from the enemy. On Italy's western slopes were the 3-inch mortars.

A Company was held in reserve, to the south of Peak, and took no part in the fighting on 4 November. Battalion HQ was situated just south of A Company. The KOSB front was 3,000 yards long, and a tricky one to defend; at one point it was a mere 300 yards from the Chinese positions. It was difficult to bring up ammunition and equipment to the forward companies, despite the best efforts of the loyal South Korean porters, without attracting the attention of the enemy and bringing down shell and mortar fire on the KOSB defences. To the battalion's left were positions held by 1st Battalion King's Shropshire Light Infantry (KSLI) and to their right, near to the Imjin River, was 3rd Battalion Royal Australian Rifles (RAR).

View of battle area 4 November 1951. (*Bill Speakman VC*)

Chinese attacks on KOSB positions, 4 November 1951.

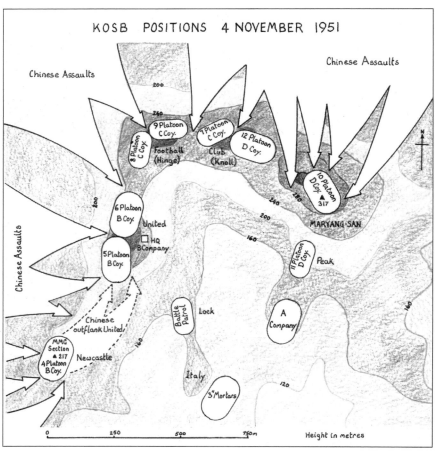

Frequent incidents had occurred since 1st KOSB occupied the hills the previous month. These usually involved platoon-sized Chinese attacks to test UN defences, sniper fire and almost daily shelling and mortar fire. During the night of Saturday, 3 November and the morning of Sunday, 4 November, there were signs that the Chinese were increasing their activity in the area and

Part of forward left B Platoon of C Company just before the battle. *(Major R.H.S. Irvine MC via KOSB Museum)*

building up their troop numbers. The enemy could be seen digging saps, using pick and shovel, towards the UN trenches. A new stretch of trench pointed towards the KOSB positions on Hinge and it was decided to call for air support. Royal Naval aircraft dropped napalm and fired rockets at the Chinese trench. From about 4.00 a.m. on 4 November, 1st KOSB positions became targets for sporadic pre-attack ranging shots from concealed enemy artillery and 180 shells had fallen by midday. This shelling soon turned into an intense bombardment and it became clear that an enemy attack was beginning. An Allied airstrike was called in, and Australian and South African aircraft repeatedly bombed the Chinese positions with napalm; the Chinese and North Koreans had no aircraft available to support their offensives. Despite the airstrikes and return fire from KOSB lines, the enemy shelling continued. The Chinese guns were hidden in tunnels, which had been bored through the hills in the weeks leading up to the attack, making it very difficult to destroy them.

The enemy shelling continued into the afternoon of 4 November and by 4.00 p.m., while the sun was setting, it had developed into a fierce bombardment. While the constant shelling continued, there was little the battalion could do

Lieutenant Colonel Tadman, commanding officer 1st KOSB, at a command post. (© *IWM MH 32343*)

except stay in their trenches. It was estimated that at one point shells were falling on the KOSB trenches at 6,000 an hour. It soon became apparent that once the bombardment lifted, an enemy infantry attack would almost certainly follow. The King's Shropshire Light Infantry were defending a point about 100 yards away but no shells fell on them. Approximately eight Chinese tanks were spotted from Hinge by C Company, adding to the shells falling on the KOSB positions. The resulting battle became known as 'Charlie Chinaman's Gunpowder Plot', even though the action took place the day before Guy Fawkes Day. The Regimental History of the war (2) noted:

> By this time, the ridge-line held by the three forward companies had become an inferno of smoke, dust, flame and explosions. All available means of defensive fire, aircraft, artillery and mortars were called on for support at this stage, as it was evident that the battalion was about to be attacked.

At about 4.15 p.m., Chinese infantry started advancing across the paddy fields in the valley facing B Company's trenches. Conventional British attacks began at dawn, with the prospect of a full day to carry the attack to the enemy's position, but the Chinese preferred night attacks. Approximately 1,500 Chinese soldiers, many of them blowing bugles, rose from their trenches and holes to attack positions along the KOSB line, particularly around Hill 217 and United. The Chinese carried all their equipment, and could cover long distances quickly. They carried satchels full of 'potato masher' style grenades, which they could throw a great distance but were less lethal than British grenades. The more senior soldiers had 'burp' guns – machine guns with a drum round which fired in a short burst and made a 'burp' sound. The

1st KOSB strengthening barbed wire defences on the forward slopes of their hill. The soldier on the left keeps a lookout with his Bren gun.
(© IWM MH 32800)

others carried rifles and bands of ammunition, although many in the first wave were unarmed and picked up the rifles dropped by dead comrades.

Private Speakman was in a group of soldiers reinforcing the wire defences when the Chinese attack began:

> We were wiring most of the day on large, tall strands of wire called Danni wire. It has two handles on it and comes apart like a concertina – it is terrible stuff. So we put the apron there. You went in and had a brew, had a meal, then went back to it – wiring, wiring, wiring. Then it started.
>
> There was a feeling that something was going to start – sporadic shelling, and then a Chinese patrol started appearing, which we had never seen before. I was out wiring and then the shelling and mortaring started. We were used to this so we never dodged for cover – it was so sporadic and we wanted to get the wiring finished. All of a sudden we knew something was going to pop. And then the shelling started. For some of the soldiers, they had never seen a shelling like it. It lasted two hours solid. The Chinese tanks were hammering us but we never had attacks from enemy aircraft – there were none. We saw the American aircraft come over us and the South African Air Force, but they were supporting another unit. Thousands of Chinese just got out of the ground and came for us. That's when it all started.

The enemy advanced under cover of their bombardment and many of them were killed by their own shelling. As these soldiers fell, they were quickly replaced by more Chinese troops, equally fanatical and many of them having a doped appearance. Many veterans reported that the Chinese soldiers appeared to be dazed as if drugged, which might explain why they didn't worry about walking into their own barrage. With disregard for their own casualties, they advanced over the frozen ground carrying pole charges and nets to lay over the KOSB barbed wire defences. B Company's forward defences and observation posts were wrecked by the accurate shelling from the Chinese self-propelling guns. With much of the barbed wire destroyed by the enemy bombardment, there was nothing to hold back the attackers once they reached the forward trenches, despite accurate KOSB mortar fire. The first wave were considered 'cannon-fodder' and threw themselves on the remaining barbed wire so that the following soldiers could walk over them. Speakman recalls the situation:

The first lot were carrying nothing – they went on the wire. Had the wire been intact they would have had a job getting to us, but it was hammered. They would go down, and then the second wave and then the third wave – nothing was stopping them. There was dead ground between us and the enemy but you could see down it. They had to get up that hill. We had the advantage. We didn't have tall barbed wire but we had aprons. You try and walk through aprons, you can't. But the shelling cleared a lot of that, so it didn't happen very much. Cut it to pieces as the ground was rock hard … They shelled us tremendously, that's how we knew something was going to happen.

Chinese soldiers on a night offensive in Korea.

An unnamed KOSB soldier reported that the Chinese had moved silently up the British-held hill with their weapons slung over their shoulders and walked across the dead Chinese soldiers on the KOSB barbed wire.

At 5.10 p.m., the War Diaries of 28th British Commonwealth Brigade (3) noted:

> 1 KOSB reported a considerable number of enemy attacking C Company 1 KOSB and also now attacking B Company 1 KOSB in considerable numbers. Arrangements made to divert air strike on them – result 2 tanks knocked out, 1 SP gun knocked out, 1 MMG destroyed and 25 KIA.

Major Little's C Company on the Hinge soon found themselves engaging the enemy in hand-to-hand fighting. Being the KOSB Company nearest the enemy, they were the first to be attacked. After a courageous two-hour stand against overwhelming odds, the company was forced to withdraw and the survivors regrouped in A Company's area on Peak. By 5.30 p.m., Hill 217, defended by slightly less than two platoons from B Company, had been overrun and a few survivors withdrew to join the Battle Patrol in reserve on Lock. Lieutenant A. McMillan-Scott and most of 4 and 5 Platoons were reported 'missing, believed killed' but it was not confirmed until after the battle that they had died in the fighting. One of the few survivors from McMillan-Scott's platoon was Private John Cowell, a 19-year-old National Serviceman.

With Hill 217 and Hinge overrun, the enemy were able to advance along the ridge and attack B Company on United from behind. Later in the day, 1st KSLI and 3rd RAR positions were also subjected to shelling and attack by the Chinese.

At the height of the battle, Private Patrick Lydon refused to fight and took no part in the desperate fighting around him. He lay in a trench, cringing with fear, and ignored orders from his officer to get up. He was eventually captured by the Chinese when C Company's position was overrun and was a prisoner of war for twenty-one months (4).

At B Company HQ on United, Company Sergeant Major 'Busty' Murdoch started to break open the grenade boxes and, with Speakman and others, individually primed each grenade. CSM Murdoch, nicknamed 'Busty' as he was broad-chested, was responsible for maintaining the ammunition reserve and ensuring that it was distributed to all companies. Murdoch was in charge of stores at Company HQ and he had realised that the grenade was the weapon of choice if there was a Chinese attack. Whenever ammunition and rations were delivered he always asked for more grenades and built up a sizeable reserve.

PRIVATE JOHN COWELL

Private John Cowell, a 19-year-old National Serviceman from Edgware, was posted to Lieutenant MacMillan-Scott's platoon in B Company 1st KOSB on 9 October 1951. This was just after Operation *Commando*, when KOSB had taken over responsibility for the whole ridge. Cowell was No 3 in one of the two machine guns on Point 217, which was a forward position and would take the brunt of any enemy attack. Cowell's responsibility was to supply ammunition to the No 2 who actually fed the gun.

Between 9 October and 3 November, Cowell and his platoon endured frequent salvos of Chinese artillery shelling on their exposed position. On 3 November, Cowell remembers being with a party detailed to go to the lower slopes of 217 to lay mines and strengthen the defences. He was one of the guard party to protect the men doing the work. Not far away he noticed farmers going about their work but it was difficult to tell if they were genuine or Chinese soldiers in civilian dress gathering intelligence on the strength of the British positions.

During the battle on 4 November, Cowell went to and from the platoon bunker getting ammunition. On one occasion he returned to find the position empty; his comrades were either dead or had disappeared. Cowell decided to return to the relative safety of the bunker to await his fate. When the first Chinese soldier shouted at the entrance, Cowell decided to remain silent but later thought he would surrender. A short while later, a second Chinese soldier arrived and Cowell surrendered. He recalled in 2008:

> I'm glad it was a Chinese soldier who accepted my surrender. If it had been a North Korean he would have thrown a grenade or shot me. When I came out of the dugout, artillery shells were raining down on the position. My Chinese guard motioned me to run down the hill, which was being strafed by Allied aircraft. After that I marched for five days before coming to a POW transit camp (5).

Cowell had been reported 'missing in action, probably killed' but his parents were later informed he was unhurt and a POW. He was held at Camp 5 near the Chinese border and released on 8 August 1953.

When the action started, he realised that the grenades stockpiled in Company HQ would need to be quickly distributed, so he organised small stockpiles which were easily accessed by those fighting the Chinese.

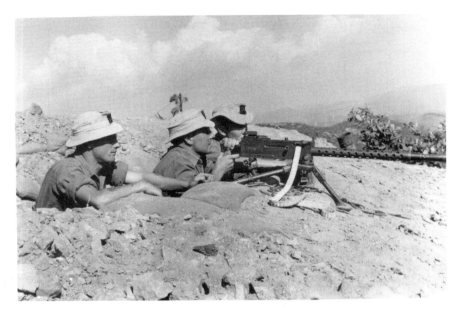

1st KOSB team, with Browning machine gun, guarding frontline positions. Left to right: Lance Corporal John Simpson, Private Tom Brown and Private Jim Elliott. (© *IWM KOR 605*)

Private Speakman, who had been at Company HQ all afternoon, heard all the messages coming in over the radio and was aware of the desperate situation in which the battalion, and in particular his own company, found itself. Major Harrison had by this time left Company HQ to take part in the fighting, leaving CSM Murdoch in charge. Speakman was determined to do something to help and filled the pockets of his combat suit with primed grenades and moved towards the entrance of the command bunker. 'Where the hell do you think you're going?' demanded CSM Murdoch. 'Going to shift some of those bloody chinks, sir,' Speakman replied. Despite his size – he stood at 6ft 6in – he was generally reckoned to be a gentle giant: slow to anger but a force to be reckoned with when roused. Often, at times of emergency, a hero emerges to save the day and on this occasion it was Private Bill Speakman.

Leaving B Company HQ, he joined the 5 Platoon trenches, which were very close to the entrance of Company HQ. At this stage the Chinese were just over the crest of the hill, having overrun the forward defences, and were no more than 20 yards away.

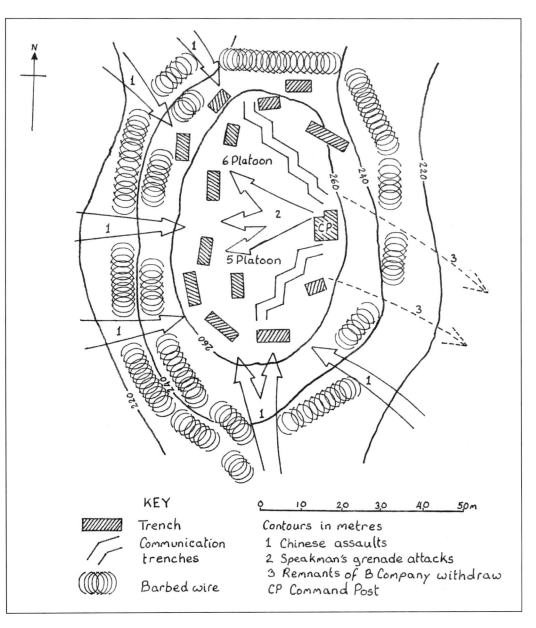

KEY

Trench

Communication trenches

Barbed wire

Contours in metres
1 Chinese assaults
2 Speakman's grenade attacks
3 Remnants of B Company withdraw
CP Command Post

KOSB B Coy positions on United, 4 November 1951.

Artist's impression of Speakman's grenade charge. (*James Bancroft*)

Taking responsibility for the left flank of the position, Speakman threw his stock of grenades at the advancing enemy. His weapon of choice was the No 36 High Explosive hand grenade, commonly known as the Mills bomb after its inventor. It was the standard issue grenade at the time and was fitted with a 4-second fuse. Speakman's great height and size made him an obvious target but also allowed him to throw his grenades twice as far as anyone else before taking cover to avoid the resulting explosion. He would not have been able to see the enemy clearly in the failing light but could hear their screams of pain and see the flashes of the exploding grenades. Although Bill Speakman could not have known it at the time, this was to be the defining moment in his life – the event for which he would later be awarded the Victoria Cross. He recalls the moment he decided to 'go out and do something':

> I was on the radio and I had all the reports of what was happening. Three companies took the brunt of 6,000 Chinese – that's 2,000 Chinese against each KOSB company. We were spread out covering hills and gullies and we started to get hammered because they were coming at us in huge numbers. I thought: 'Fuck this; I'm not sitting here waiting.' Then I climbed down and started doing what I had to do.

Others joined in the grenade throwing, inspired by 'Big Bill' Speakman's actions. Private Paddy Buchanan, Corporal Tug Wilson and Corporal Eric Wood, positioned in nearby trenches, quickly followed his example and they were later joined by Sergeant Jock Duncan and CSM Murdoch. 'I led them', says Speakman. 'I took over actually and said "Come on, let's go, let's go" and we rallied round. That was it.'

The grenade assault temporarily halted the enemy attack, but Speakman had used his stock of grenades. He hurried back to Company HQ to collect a further supply and returned to the front with his pockets and pouches full of primed grenades.

This time he charged up the slope of the hill to clear the crest. At great personal risk, he stood there and hurled grenade after grenade into the advancing Chinese infantry, adding to the ever mounting pile of enemy dead. Buchanan and the others, again, followed his example. Sergeant Duncan had been firing a bazooka over the crest of the hill before joining the others to throw grenades. CSM Murdoch said that at times the Chinese were within 20 to 30 yards and he could see them clearly. Speakman personally killed or maimed dozens of Chinese, but he soon ran out of grenades and went back for more. He says that it is another myth that he threw the grenades as if he were throwing a cricket ball:

I didn't throw them over my head. I rolled them. That's the way they train you, but with the equipment you have today you could never do that. You have to pitch them a long, long way. So you only had 7 seconds. Sometimes you get wounded in your throwing arm so you just lob them over there. You just put it where it was wanted. We used a 7-second fuse for long throws or a 5-second fuse. The ground was hard so the Chinese got the full effect rather than the ground. A good guy would have it in his hand. Then he would pull the pin, let the clip go to make sure, otherwise when you throw a grenade the pin would not strike if you didn't let the clip go. Then you know it and you have 10 seconds to get it among this lot.

Major Harrison, in his VC recommendation, stated that Speakman showed magnificent powers of leadership in keeping the hill clear of the enemy:

This he did by assembling a great pile of grenades and organising a party of six men whom he repeatedly led forward to shower a hail of grenades as each successive wave of enemy arrived on the skyline. The determination with which he led these charges caused great losses to the enemy, who fell down in heaps on the crest.

CSM Murdoch and his team continued to prime the grenades ready for Speakman to throw. Speakman rated the grenade very highly as an infantry weapon:

At the beginning of the action we had rifles, Bren guns, ammunition, grenades and supporting fire from the mortars but there were so many Chinese attacking us. They creep up and come again. There is only one thing and that's what it is all about, the grenade. You start pulling the pin and throwing those and it doesn't take care of just one of them, it takes care of half a dozen. With a grenade you can throw it into a bunch of men and blow them up. So that was an ideal little weapon. We used those grenades and we quietly settled down to a nice pattern of throwing them. In the end it was grenades where they were needed. As soon as the chinks came upon the bodies of their guys, our grenades were there.

There were six of us spread out in front of them. Until we were throwing grenades, some of the Chinese got through because they went round the side. These were the guys who nailed our machine-gunners, putting the machine guns out of action. We had a lot of grenades and we threw them. That was just on the brow of the hill. We had the advantage of seeing them coming. When we first got that hill we dug in. Good British infantry tactics to dig in.

Speakman repeated his actions several times. He made at least ten trips back for more grenades after using his stock to great effect, and probably threw over 100 grenades. Several accounts of the battle have recorded that other soldiers on the hill began shouting 'Bill Speakman' as a battle cry. The Chinese tried to find a way round the grenades by moving around the hill. Speakman also moved around and hurled grenades in every direction the enemy approached. The attacks continued and some of the enemy managed to break through the KOSB defence. 'They were getting through,' says Speakman, 'but not as many as before and our men could deal with that. When they come at you in ones and twos you could use the bayonet – that was no problem.' The Chinese had to not only scramble up the hill in freezing temperatures; they also had to climb over the bodies of their own people, of which there were hundreds. Life was held cheap by the ideologically indoctrinated Chinese foot soldiers.

During his grenade charges, Speakman was hit by mortar fragments in the left shoulder and thigh. Despite the pain he would not leave the battlefield to get his wounds treated; he was spurred on by a determination to not be moved from the hill by the Chinese. He later said that when the shrapnel hit him in the leg it felt as if a stone had hit him. Corporals Wilson and Wood were also struck by shrapnel. Major Harrison commented on Speakman's wounds in his VC recommendation:

> Private Speakman continued his task in the face of withering fire, and although after half an hour he was shot through the leg and was in great pain he refused to have it dressed and carried on without ceasing.
>
> Eventually he was made to pause to have a field dressing applied to his wound but returned immediately to lead charge after charge on the enemy as if nothing had happened.

He was treated at the company first-aid post and while he was there the medical orderly treating him was injured. Speakman recalls his visit to the first-aid post:

> Busty got hammered. Then I got hammered – I don't remember being hit but someone said to me: 'You've been wounded – in the back and in the neck'. We were in a hole in the ground and I was limping around and somebody helped me. Major Harrison said, 'What's the matter?' 'I'm wounded; I believe I have a hole in my back,' I said. When you get like that and it's freezing cold you don't mess about. He told me to get back and get the wound treated. There were two bloody great bits of shrapnel which they took out in the

hospital in Kure, Japan. His name was Roddy McDowall, funnily enough. [There was an actor with the same name.] He was the medical orderly in the company. So I got in a little trench with him. He put my leg up for a big shell dressing on it and we didn't notice the one in the shoulder because that was through a big thick pullover. While he was doing it I saw Roddy stagger, he bounced off the wall. Of course, he had been hit by something.

I said, 'What's the matter, Roddy?' He sort of shook his head and then he finished putting on the dressing. I said, 'Fuck this, I'm off,' and I went straight up again. I was angry. Very, very cross because I could do nothing for Roddy because I was in a state. I went back and just carried on with it. I was looking for more grenades.

At the time of the VC award, newspapers reported that the medical orderly was treating Speakman but was called out to bring in a wounded man and in doing so got hit by shrapnel in the neck. Speakman was reported as saying: 'I came back mad. Anyone would have felt mad at a thing like that.'

Despite the heroic efforts of Speakman and the others, the Chinese kept up their attack and were in danger of overrunning B Company. Major Harrison took the decision to request Allied artillery fire on his own position. Speakman was on the hill at the time:

Someone said, 'Let's go.' So I said, 'Where are we going?' Someone said, 'Bill, we have to withdraw. Something is happening.' There were so many Chinese on that hill that the company commander said, 'Get down, get down in the trenches. Get down in your dugouts. We are calling in a DF.' That's defensive fire to clear the hill on your own position. There was a lull, flares going all over. So we got our heads down and they called in the 16th Field Regiment of the Royal New Zealand Artillery to clear the hill of chinks. It cleared the hill. There were so many of them. Well it did clear the hill and we got up again. It helped us tremendously. They had thinned out a bit but they were still coming up the hill.

While B Company sheltered in their trenches, the guns of the New Zealand Artillery pulverised the crest of the hill. The shelling killed many of the Chinese attackers and gave what was left of B Company a temporary respite. 'And those gunners were so good,' says Speakman, 'they were dropping them just on the brow of the hill.' The enemy attack soon continued, though, with the Chinese now able to charge from every side of the hill. At this stage of the battle the

KOSB 2-inch mortar. On the left is Private Tom Lapere and on the right Private Alec Ewan. (© *IWM KOR 601*)

defenders had almost exhausted their stocks of ammunition and grenades and they engaged the enemy in hand-to-hand combat. By the end of the day the Chinese had lost over 1,000 men from a 6,000 strong division, and suffered countless injuries.

The battalion's 3-inch mortar platoon, under Second Lieutenant Peter Rooke, supported the defenders throughout the attack. The mortar pits were on the reverse slope of the hill, behind the advance trenches where Speakman and the others were holding off the Chinese. Although the mortar pits were under heavy fire from enemy artillery, they kept up a continuous fire on the enemy. It was later estimated that the mortars had fired over 5,000 rounds in four hours. The mortar tubes became so hot they had to be cooled down with water, and when water supplies ran out the platoon's beer ration was poured down the barrels. Speakman later spoke of the support given by the mortar platoon:

They were right back because the mortars sit behind you and throw the mortar bombs overhead to the enemy in front of you. They were firing everything they had got and those barrels sometimes glowed. The mortar platoon had a beer supply because they were not in the line – they were there to support. They were quite a distance behind because we had small 2-inch mortars, but they had 3-inch so they could throw them overhead and into the enemy. No point having the mortar right below you because they get bombed, so they are some distance behind to get the trajectory over there. They were right behind you all the time. We didn't want them getting hurt otherwise we would have lost a valuable means of support.

The 2-inch mortar mentioned by Speakman was used as a platoon weapon and had a range of up to 1,000 yards. The 3-inch mortar was used as a company support weapon and had a range of approximately 2,500 yards. Both types avoided hitting British troops and overcame enemy defences by firing at a steep trajectory to drop on top of the target.

With ammunition so low, B Company resorted to throwing rocks, tins and anything they could lay their hands on at the enemy. Speakman recalls the desperate situation:

When the action started there were thousands of Chinese soldiers and we were throwing grenades and then it got into twilight – not dark, not light and

1st KOSB 3-inch mortars in action. Left to right: Lance Corporal Bill Hunter, Private Jim Beveridge and Private Tony Donaldson. (© *IWM KOR 604*)

we ran out of grenades so we started to throw rocks and anything like that. If you're on the other side and you're having grenades thrown at you, you get out of the way – just like I would get out of the way. When we ran out of grenades and ammunition we threw rocks, anything we could get our hands on. If you feel something drop beside you, you automatically think it is a grenade and the ground was rock hard and the rocks didn't sink in. They were bouncing along and when they were landing, I can imagine these guys were scattering.

Although he admits to throwing anything he could get his hands on, Speakman is emphatic that he did not throw any beer bottles. The story about him hurling beer bottles at the enemy, when he ran out of grenades, has been told so many times it has passed into legend. Despite being known as 'the Beer Bottle VC' for over sixty years, Speakman insists the story is untrue. He believes it was based on a misquote, but the public back home loved the story so much it assumed a life of its own. He feels it brings the regiment into disrepute by implying they were drinking alcohol before or during the battle and trivialises the sacrifices made that day. 'The beer bottle story is very strange to me about where they got it from, how it originated,' says Speakman. 'My mates were bloody well killed; men died next to me and they say we were throwing bottles. That makes me really angry. Men died and all they want to talk about is beer bottles. Who dreamed that one up? Whoever started the story, it seems to have caught on. If I had thrown beer bottles I would have said: "Yes, I threw beer bottles".'

But according to the *Canberra Times* (31 December 1951) it was Speakman himself who mentioned beer bottles. He is quoted as saying: 'We hadn't time to use the beer ration, but it was very useful as I saw mortar crews cooling the barrels of their weapons with beer. When we ran out of grenades we threw beer bottles and stones.' However, Speakman denies ever saying this.

Some accounts reported that as many as forty-eight bottles of beer were poured down the barrels of the mortars to cool them down and this may have been the inspiration for the beer bottle throwing story. However, the mortars were some distance from where Speakman and the rest of B Company were throwing grenades at the Chinese. So it is unlikely that Speakman saw mortar crews using beer to cool their barrels as reported in the *Canberra Times*. They probably would not have known that the beer ration had been used for that purpose and if they had, would not have had time to go looking for empty bottles. The defenders on the hill threw only what was in easy reach. It is possible that other members of B Company threw a beer bottle or two, but Speakman says he did not.

Private Bill Ballinger (6), a Bren gunner in the same action, recalls that his friend Jimmy Burgess threw beer bottles at the enemy when they ran out of ammunition for the guns. Burgess was said to have opened the bottles with his teeth, drank some of the contents and then hurled the partially empty bottles at the Chinese. Both Speakman and CSM Busty Murdoch have denied that there was beer available in the trenches. The myth about Speakman throwing beer bottles has become so well established over the ensuing years it is probable that Ballinger's story is feeding the myth.

Any suggestion that Speakman drank the contents of beer bottles before throwing them and was drunk at the time is also untrue. He was far too concerned about helping to repel the Chinese attackers, and there would have been no opportunity for him to obtain any unopened bottles or time for him to drink the contents. He was at Company HQ when the battle began, and during the battle he was at the forefront of the action, in front of numerous witnesses. It was well known that Speakman liked a drink when he was off duty and would sometimes have a few too many. This reputation, no doubt, led many people to the wrong conclusion and fuelled the story which has circulated ever since. He has denied that there was any drinking on United and the story would appear to be another media distortion.

It has been repeated, nonetheless, in one book about the Korean War – *Korea: The Commonwealth at War* by Tim Carew (7). The author has alleged that most of B Company HQ staff, including Speakman, were drinking beer during the battle:

'Big Bill' was in a temper, and not only because the beer was finished: Company Sergeant Major 'Busty' Murdoch was a firm believer in the adage 'rank hath its privilege', and had seen to it that Company Headquarters was well supplied. During brief lulls in the fighting, appreciative gurgling noises from the throats of Sergeant Jock Duncan, Corporal Tug Wilson, Corporal Eric Wood, Lance Corporal Ed Buchanan and Private Bill Speakman – the loudest and most appreciative noises of all came from the two last named – told the CSM that his foresight was appreciated.

As Tim Carew died in 1980, it has not been possible to enquire about his sources. However, ex-WO1 (RSM) Murdoch MBE DCM, who was alleged to have organised the drinking session, strongly denies that it ever took place, calling it a 'scurrilous fable'. (8)

James 'Busty' Murdoch. *c.*1948.
(*John Mulholland*)

RSM JAMES DIROM 'BUSTY' MURDOCH MBE DCM

RSM James 'Busty' Murdoch MBE DCM was born in Lockerbie in March 1922 and joined the KOSB, underage, in 1938. After six months of training at Berwick-upon-Tweed he was sent to the North-West Frontier of India in 1939 to help quell a tribal rebellion.

During the Second World War he served with the 2nd Battalion in India and Burma from 1942 to 1945 and took part in the action at Imphal. Towards the end of the war, with 7th Battalion, he took part in a glider-borne landing in Norway to take the German surrender.

Murdoch served with distinction as CSM of B Company KOSB in Korea. He took part in Operation *Commando* in October 1951 and was awarded the DCM for this action and for the KOSB defence of United Hill against 6,000 Chinese troops on the night of 4 November 1951. It was under his command that Private W Speakman was awarded the VC for the action. Murdoch was wounded in the leg and sent for treatment in Japan before returning to the regiment; he departed from Korea in May 1952.

Murdoch was seconded for two years to the West Africa Volunteer Force on the Gold Coast and later served in Malaya receiving a Mention in Despatches for operations against communist insurgents. He later served in Berlin and Aden and received the MBE in the Queen's Birthday Honours in June 1963. He finally retired from the Army in December 1963 after twenty-five years' service. Murdoch died in Whitley Bay on 26 November 2010, aged 88.

Describing the hand-to-hand fighting, Speakman says:

> At the start of the fighting they were coming up in dribs and drabs. These
> were their ordinary guys. We had plenty of ammunition and grenades and
> machine guns and Bren guns. But when it started getting heavy they started
> coming in mass and the real guys started coming. As we put them down it
> was just pile after pile of bodies.
>
> We opened up from the trenches with our guns and they started coming
> through. One or two would get through to begin with, then about twenty to
> thirty-five because there were so many of them – sheer weight of numbers.
> Then when they got close they used to pop up in front of you. When they
> are on top of you, you can't just get your rifle back to stab with your bayonet.
> That's where you are taught to use the butt because you swing it around. If you
> pull back the bolt of your rifle to put the round up the spout, it takes seconds
> but they are valuable. You give him the butt and when he's down you give him
> the bayonet – there is no hesitation. They did back off a bit when they knew
> we were going to stand but it was amazing how we held onto that hill.
>
> I had to take the initiative when I did. I've often thought why didn't an
> officer or an NCO take the lead? But the Sergeant Major was in charge
> of the ammunition so he couldn't and Major Harrison was busy holding
> the line. We were losing officers and most positions had a platoon officer in
> charge. We had Lieutenant Brooks left but he was also busy holding the line.

Murdoch's decorations and medals: MBE (Military), DCM, 1939–45 Star, Burma Star,
Defence Medal, War Medal 1939–45, Queen's Korea, UN Korea, GSM (1918) *Malaya*
with Mention in Despatches, Long Service and Good Conduct Medal. *(John Mulholland)*

So it is just something you do. You take it on your initiative and think 'I'm going to help out'. I went out and did my bit. When I got there I knew the position we were in and that the Chinese were really going to overrun us. I managed to get these guys together and I said, 'Right, let's go.' Then the others caught on and they got going. We all did it.

Towards the end of the battle, the Chinese had overrun the MMG (medium machine gun) pits and entrenched themselves there. Aware of the danger of the enemy turning the Vickers machine guns on the men of B Company, Speakman and Buchanan advanced under enemy fire and destroyed the machine guns and the Chinese soldiers with hand grenades. The battalion's 3-inch mortars were moved to a safer location to prevent them falling into enemy hands.

The situation was proving hopeless, with the Chinese attacking from almost all sides, and the ground held by B Company gradually diminishing. At around 8.45 p.m., the remainder of the company was ordered to withdraw to Battle Patrol's position on Lock. Just before midnight, B Company withdrew further back to Italy. Meanwhile, Major Robertson-Macleod and the survivors of D Company were forced to withdraw from Hill 317 after a fierce battle and regrouped on Peak. A Company remained in reserve south of Peak. None of the hills lost by 1st KOSB that day were retaken and remained in Chinese hands until the end of the war. They are all in, or close to, the present Demilitarised Zone (DMZ).

During the battle, the battalion medical officer, Captain Rutledge (RAMC), and his staff worked tirelessly attending to the many casualties. The MMG drivers, under Second Lieutenant Lyal, provided excellent support by using the platoon Jeeps to evacuate wounded men from the forward positions while under enemy fire.

Nothing had been heard from the two platoons on Knoll since the beginning of the battle and it was not known whether they were still alive. Field telephone lines had been destroyed in the Chinese bombardment and the platoons could not communicate with their type 88 wireless sets as they did not work properly in the hills – the signal often could not get through unless the person receiving the message was in a line of sight. Then, about midnight, Second Lieutenant William Purves established radio contact. With the senior officer, Second Lieutenant Henderson, wounded and the Chinese attacking from three sides, he had assumed control of the C and D Company platoons. Nineteen-year-old Purves, a former bank clerk, asked Major Tadman what his orders were. His platoons were successfully fighting off enemy attacks, though very short of ammunition. He was ordered to withdraw his small force and fight his way to Peak, despite Purves' insistence that they were holding the enemy.

Purves had been wounded in the shoulder earlier in the battle, and his battledress was blood-soaked, but there had been no time to attend to his wound. He organised the men under his command and he succeeded in leading both platoons, with all their equipment, to safety while under heavy mortar fire. Purves ensured that everyone was accounted for and every wounded man was led or carried from the ridge, arriving at Battalion HQ around dawn. For his conspicuous gallantry and outstanding leadership skills that day, Second Lieutenant Purves was awarded the DSO and had the unique distinction of being the only National Service officer to receive this decoration.

During the battle, when the Chinese were attacking 1st KOSB from all directions, there were inevitable security breaches, resulting in the enemy gaining secret information from the withdrawing battalion. The War Diaries of 28th British Commonwealth Brigade noted in the early hours of 5 November:

> 1 KOSB reported that code words, etc., may have been compromised by enemy action.

At 7.05 a.m. the brigade War Diaries noted:

> 1 KOSB report point 217 and ridge to north definitely held by the enemy. C Coy [Company] reorganising at [map reference]. Copy of withdrawal operation order fallen into enemy hands.

Major Harrison organised an orderly withdrawal of B Company, with Speakman and others covering them with a final grenade charge up the crest of the hill. Speakman threw phosphorous grenades to enable his company to make a successful withdrawal. 'We used phosphorous grenades to create smoke,' he explained. 'We never had smoke grenades in those days, so we used phosphorous. When phosphorous comes into contact with air it smokes. You will never put it out.'

He had spent four hours keeping enemy infantry at bay with a number of grenade charges, and had done more than could be asked of him. He had thrown over 100 grenades and killed or seriously injured dozens of Chinese soldiers. His company was being forced to withdraw from the hill by numerically superior forces, but they had put up a good fight. It was now time to leave the battlefield but he was still concerned about those they left behind:

> It was our hill and we wanted to hang on to it. A lot of us were wounded and we just didn't want to leave any wounded behind. That was my big concern

actually because these were my friends. They were my muckers … When the order to withdraw came I immediately thought: 'What about these guys of ours who are wounded? We have got to get them out.'

You saw mates dying or dead. I saw a lance corporal getting hit with the full burst of a burp gun – a Chinese machine gun. It cut him in half and he was lying on the wire. The other half was below the wire. We just got together and then the order came through to retire. We redoubled our efforts and we managed to get all our guns off the hill.

Unfortunately, we had to leave one or two men behind – taken prisoner. But they were lucky because the Chinese had a habit when the fighting was heavy of not stopping, even for their own kind. That's the way it works, even in the British Army. There was going to be no hope for them if we left them so we did our best to get our guys away.

In the action, we saved a lot of wounded men and sent them down the line because we managed a good withdrawal. We never say retreat. Getting our wounded guys off the hill and saving the lives of the men who could fight another day is very, very important.

PRIVATE BRIAN CALVERT

Private Brian Calvert, a 19-year-old National Serviceman from Knaresborough was with B Company on United. He was wounded and wrote from hospital:

> It was hell let loose. The shelling was terrific. We could hear the Chinese as they advanced right into our positions blowing bugles and shouting to one another. At least one of our platoons was cut off completely, but they fought their way back, bringing their wounded with them.

Private Calvert went on to relate how a mortar bomb fell into his slit trench, killing one man, while another was unhurt. Private Calvert was injured by the explosion and crawled out of the trench.

> Then they told me to get on a stretcher. Another shell dropped 20 yards in front. That did it. I got up and struggled down the hill as best I could through the barbed wire and everything. I got the ambulance OK and felt safe for the first time.

Everybody was helping everybody else to get down from the hill, and somehow Speakman managed to get to safety, although he is not sure how:

> Around then I just started stumbling around and a guy said 'Come on, Bill. Come on.' I remember someone grabbing me because I went over once or twice because I couldn't walk. We had barbed wire, which we had put down ourselves, I remember tripping over that. I was very dazed by this time as I was losing blood; I was at the end of my tether. Busty had also been wounded. When the order came through to retire, Tug Wilson said: 'Sergeant Major will help you down the hill, Speakman'. I was half asleep, very dazed. So it was Busty who helped me down the hill as we were getting our wounded down. I helped Busty and Busty helped me, but I think one or two privates helped us both down the hill. I remember Tug Wilson doing something for me. By the time I got to the bottom of the hill, I didn't know I was at the bottom of the hill. I didn't even know I was on the hill. I then woke up in this first-aid station.

NOTES

(1)   United was one of several hills/points given nicknames by the Royal Northumberland Fusiliers. There were four such hills in the 217/317 area – Newcastle, United, Football (also known as the Hinge) and Club.

(2)   *The Borderers in Korea* by Major General John MacDonald CB DSO OBE.

(3)   Held in National Archives file WO 281/140.

(4)   Private Lydon of C Company KOSB was found guilty of cowardice in the face of the enemy when he appeared before a court martial at Catterick Camp in October 1953. He was sentenced to one year in prison and discharged with ignominy. He was the only British soldier to be convicted of cowardice in the Korean War and it is thought that this is the only case since the First World War. CSM 'Busty' Murdoch was instrumental in Speakman's VC award and in the conviction of Private Lydon. (See Appendix III.)

(5)   Interview with authors on 21 September 2008.

(6)   Private Ballinger lost his No 2 man and was then wounded himself. He recalls that 'most of that night is just a blur'. He was treated at an Indian Field Ambulance hospital before being sent to Kure. His memories of the Korean War can be found on: http://www.britains-smallwars.com/korea/KOSB.htm.

(7)   *Korea: The Commonwealth at War* by Tim Carew (The Orion Publishing Group). All attempts by the authors at tracing the copyright holder of this book were unsuccessful.

(8)   Interview with the authors on 13 August 2009.

AFTERMATH OF BATTLE
5–11 NOVEMBER 1951

Speaking about the evacuation from United, Speakman said, years later:

> We were lucky, we were very lucky. We lost a few men and a few were taken as POWs. They were listed as missing in action. Later we found they were OK, but they came back with tales of brutality. The Chinese didn't bother us, they took us prisoner. It was the North Koreans. The Chinese handed over POWs to the North Koreans. We saw some of the Glosters coming back – you should have seen the state they were in. Colonel Carne was a prisoner. Look at what they did to him.

For their actions that day, Speakman received the Victoria Cross, and Major Tadman, Major Harrison, Major Robertson-Macleod and Second Lieutenant Purves received the DSO. CSM Murdoch later received the DCM for his outstanding service throughout the regiment's time in Korea. (See Appendix II for a list of all awards to 1st KOSB for Korea.)

The battle continued into the early hours of 5 November and at approximately 2.00 a.m. the enemy artillery shelling of A Company and Battalion HQ lifted. The Chinese then fired tracer down the valley between Italy and Peak, but fortunately for the severely depleted battalion no further enemy attacks were made.

A counter-attack was made by 28th British Commonwealth Brigade on 5 November. The newly arrived 1st Battalion The Royal Leicestershire Regiment, borrowed from 29th Brigade, was given the objective of re-capturing Hill 217, but the attack was not successful. The Australians felt bitter about 1st KOSB not holding the ground which had been fought over and won by 3rd RAR and also that another British battalion was not able to recapture Hill 217. However, it should be remembered that the Borderers were the main objective of a Chinese divisional attack and that 1st KOSB was outnumbered by a margin of ten to one. Under such circumstances it is doubtful that 3rd RAR would have fared any better.

SIR WILLIAM PURVES CBE DSO

William Purves was born on 27 December 1931 in Kelso, Scotland and educated at Kelso High School. His chosen career in banking was interrupted by National Service in the early 1950s. He served in the 1st Battalion King's Own Scottish Borderers during the Korean War, when he became the only National Serviceman to be awarded the DSO.

Returning to banking in 1954, he moved to Hong Kong to join the Hong Kong and Shanghai Banking Corporation (HSBC) and worked in branches throughout Asia and London. Purves remained with the HSBC, becoming chief executive in 1986 and chairman in 1991. He helped with the transition from British to Chinese rule in Hong Kong's financial services sector. He was knighted in 1993 and retired from HSBC in 1998, to live in London. Sir William Purves was trustee and deputy chairman of the Imperial War Museum 1996–2004.

Casualties among 1st KOSB were 7 dead, 87 wounded and 44 missing, almost all from the three forward companies. The wounded were assessed at Casualty Clearing Stations (CCS) and taken to various hospitals for treatment. The Battalion War Diaries noted that Speakman received shrapnel wounds to his left shoulder and left thigh, and that the wounds were 'moderate'. He was admitted to Advanced Dressing Station No 60, Indian Field Ambulance on 4 November. Here he was given first aid for his wounds and a large mug of hot sweet tea to deal with the shock. He remembers arriving at the Indian station:

> The next thing I knew I woke up in this withdrawal business and I finished up in an Indian First Aid Station – a Casualty Clearing Station. The first thing I got when I got down there was a great big mug of tea. Only the Indians can make a big mug. It was sweet. I got that down me. Then I flaked out again. I must have passed out a couple of times; I was always losing blood.

Company Sergeant Major 'Busty' Murdoch also ended up at the Casualty Clearing Station. He and Speakman were among the last to leave their position on United and during the fighting Murdoch had been injured by shell splinters in his leg. This wound caused profuse bleeding, which probably looked a lot worse

Left to right: Second Lieutenant William Purves, Lance Corporal Allison, Private John Common who was decorated with the MM. (*Australian War Memorial HOBH 2378*)

than it was, but fortunately there was no long term damage. He was eventually evacuated by aircraft to Kure for treatment. While he was at the CCS, Murdoch said to the padre: 'If anyone deserves a VC it is Bill Speakman.' This is probably the first indication that Speakman was being considered for the award and the padre may have spoken to Major Harrison or Major Tadman in order to get the VC recommendation procedure under way if it had not already started.

While in a first-aid post, Speakman met an artillery officer who had news of the state of the United battlefield:

Later I remember lying in a bed somewhere, it may have been the first-aid post, and a captain in the artillery came in and he said, 'What were you?'

I said 'KOSB' and he said, 'That was something out there. Where were you?' But I didn't know where I was because I was in a daze. He said there were bodies all over the place. He was a pilot in observation duties because they were looking for tanks. He said, 'I've just been flying over there and there are bodies all over the place.' He said, 'Were you there?' I said, 'Yes, I was there but the whole battalion was there, sir. The Canadians [*sic*] and the Australians were all there.' He said, 'There were a lot of Chinese bodies there.'

On 5 November Speakman was transferred from the Indian Field Ambulance to NOR MASH, the Norwegian Mobile Advanced Surgical Hospital. India and Norway were among several countries which did not commit troops to the war but instead provided non-combatant medical units. The following day, Speakman was sent to No 26 Canadian Field Dressing Station. From there he was assessed as needing surgery to remove the pieces of shrapnel still in his wounds and transferred, on 7 November, to the British Commonwealth Occupation Force (BCOF) No 29 General Hospital in Kure, Japan. Most of Korea was still devastated by the war and did not have the hospital facilities that were available in Japan.

Speakman recalls his transfers between the Casualty Clearing Stations and hospitals and how he ended up in Kure:

They were trying to assess how badly wounded you were. Then they would get you out of there altogether or somewhere for treatment. But I passed out and lost a lot of blood. Then I finally finished up in Kure, Japan. I don't remember going there. They put me on an aircraft and I woke up in Japan, where they operated on me. I had a blood transfusion and then they opened up my shoulder and opened up my leg. There were two big pieces of shrapnel. I didn't know this because I went to theatre and they operated on me. When I woke up in this nice bed in the hospital, I was groggy – they had used some sort of anaesthetic.

I woke up and felt this great lump on my chest. 'What the hell is that?' I thought. Someone was passing and he said to me: 'Private Speakman, that's what we dug out of you. You might like to keep them as a souvenir.' They had taped two bits of shrapnel to me as a souvenir. I said, 'I don't want those.' I just took them off and threw them away because I was so glad I hadn't lost a limb like the guys around me who were blown to pieces. I regretted it later on as I would like to have kept them. He said, 'Don't you want to keep them as a souvenir?' They were wrapped in cotton wool and taped to my chest.

KURE, JAPAN

Kure is a city in the prefecture of Hiroshima, about 13 miles south-east of Hiroshima city. Historically, it was a major shipyard and naval base and during the Second World War the *Yamato*, the largest battleship at the time, was built in the Kure dock. In July 1945 Kure was extensively bombed by the American Air Force and most of the naval facilities and factories were destroyed. The present population is approximately 200,000, but in its heyday the population was as large as 400,000.

After the war, control of the area was handed over to the British Commonwealth Occupation Force (BCOF). The BCOF Headquarters was located in Kure and utilised the few remaining facilities of the naval base. The British Commonwealth General Hospital at Kure was a large military hospital, opened in 1889 as Kure Naval Hospital, with about 600 beds.

Casualties from Korea were transported by hospital ship and sometimes aircraft. They also arrived by train from Iwakuni (a port and airfield along the coast, west of Kure), and an ambulance would transport casualties from Kure Railway Station to the hospital.

Second Lieutenant Purves was wounded during his gallant attempt to hold Knoll. The Battalion War Diaries noted that he received a shrapnel wound to his right shoulder and that the wound was 'moderate'. After initial treatment at the Indian Field Ambulance, he was transferred on 8 November to BCOF No 29 General Hospital in Kure. Second Lieutenant Henderson, who had been in command of a platoon from D Company on Knoll, received more serious shrapnel wounds to his face, nose, right eye and left forearm. He was transferred to Kure on 9 November.

Private Speakman spent just over seven weeks at Kure – at first in the BCOF Hospital and then in a transit camp. Like many other British servicemen he visited nearby Hiroshima to see the devastated city for himself:

I went to see Hiroshima – everyone went to see it. There was a factory nearby which made porcelain cups and plates and beautiful china. They had beautiful boxed cups and you could pick up the cups and see a Geisha girl at the bottom. These shops they were running were managed by Australians who had been captured and taken to Japan as POWs, and when the war finished they stayed behind. I bought some stuff for my mother. Next door was Hiroshima and we went to see it. They would take you to a certain point on a hill overlooking the city as there was still some radiation about.

THE ATOMIC BOMB

At 8.15 a.m. on 6 August 1945, an American Superfortress aircraft dropped the world's first atomic bomb on Hiroshima. It killed approximately 80,000 people immediately and by the end of 1945 total casualties, due to injuries and radiation, had risen to 140,000. Approximately 70 per cent of the city's buildings were completely destroyed. The atomic bombing of Hiroshima, and later Nagasaki, brought death and destruction on an unprecedented scale but hastened the end of the war.

On 7 November 1951, Lieutenant Colonel John MacDonald, Commander of 28th British Commonwealth Infantry Brigade, issued a Special Order of the Day to 1st KOSB. In it he praised the achievements of the battalion on 4 November, and included these comments:

> The actions fought by you all, both collectively and individually on this day, were beyond praise, and it is true to say that your gallantry and sacrifice saved the divisional front from being penetrated.
>
> It is estimated that the enemy suffered well over 1,000 casualties as a result of your courage, skill and determination, together with that of our supporting arms.

Colonel MacDonald had, until very recently, been the CO of 1st KOSB and his selection of that battalion for special praise seemed to some, especially 3rd RAR, to be unduly generous.

Major Dennis Tadman, Commander of 1st Battalion KOSB, issued his own Special Order of the Day to his battalion on 11 November in which he thanked everyone for their magnificent efforts. Congratulations were also received from the Lord Provost of Edinburgh, where the regiment had been raised over 260 years ago.

Because of censorship restrictions, news of 'Charlie Chinaman's Gunpowder Plot' was not made public for almost a week. The newspapers of 10 November gave brief details, which were expanded upon over the following days. *The Times* reported on 10 November 1951(1):

Three companies of The King's Own Scottish Borderers, outnumbered

SPECIAL ORDER OF THE DAY
~~BY~~
By MAJOR D.H. TADMAN O.B.E.

COMMANDER 1st Bn THE KING'S OWN SCOTTISH BORDERERS.

(TO BE READ OUT TO ALL SOLDIERS OF 1 KOSB AT THE EARLIEST OPPORTUNITY)

From interrogation of recently captured prisoners and from other intelligence sources, it is apparent that on 4th November, 1951, the Battalion was attacked by virtually a complete enemy Division supported by another holding the line. This means that some 5,000 enemy were committed against us, supported by a great weight of artillery, mortars and self-propelled guns.

It is estimated that the enemy suffered well over 1000 casualties as a result of your courage, skill and determination, together with that of our supporting arms.

That the Battalion withstood and stopped this colossal onslaught, making only limited re-adjustments of company positions, is tribute to every one of you. I thank and commend you all from the bottom of my heart for your magnificient efforts, and this applies equally to those of you, not immediately in the front line, who gave and are giving such excellent and efficient support and service.

The Corps Commander and the Divisional Commander have requested me to convey to you their heartfelt thanks and congratulations, and I do this with great pride.

In this recent action, your courage, your tenacity and refusal to accept defeat in the face of innumerable odds will, I am sure, become an epic in the history of our great Regiment and of the British forces in Korea.

Korea,
11 Nov 1951.

D.H Tadman.

Commander 1st Bn The King's Own Scottish Borderers.

Major,

Major Tadman's address to the KOSB survivors on 11 November 1951. (*KOSB Museum*) by ten to one, suffered heavy casualties when 6,000 Chinese attacked their positions last Sunday after prolonged heavy shelling. News of the action, which took place on a ridge north-west of Yonchon, was withheld until today by the censorship …

The British troops stood firm until they were ordered to withdraw. British officers estimated that the Chinese killed and wounded numbered about 3,000.

In order to correct exaggerated Chinese reports of British casualties in the fighting of 4–5 November, the War Office made an announcement on 10 November about casualty figures for 1st KOSB. The figures quoted were 'Officers, 3 wounded, 1 missing; other ranks, 7 killed, 81 wounded'. The announcement also included casualty figures for The Royal Leicestershire Regiment and named several recipients of immediate decorations for bravery from several regiments. A further announcement on 17 November revised the number of KOSB other ranks wounded to 73, with 42 other ranks missing.

On 11 November, in his first letter home, Speakman wrote:

Well, I've been wounded, but it's OK now, and I am well on the way to recovery. I got it in the leg and shoulder, but doctor here got all the shrapnel out, and there's no need to worry as I'm quite all right.

In his second letter dated 17 November, Speakman only briefly mentioned the action:

You will have read of the Kosbies and how they fought on Hill 217. Well that's the hill I was on when I got wounded.

For many years Speakman assumed he was on Hill 217 but was, in fact, on United during his VC action.

NOTES

(1)   © *The Times*, 10 November 1951.

AWARD OF THE VC
NOVEMBER–DECEMBER 1951

Many people personally witnessed Private Speakman's heroic action on United hilltop, including Private S.L. Wilson, Corporal J. Supple and Major P.F. St C. Harrison. Their eye witness accounts, which later formed part of the VC recommendation (1), are detailed below.

Statement by No 2890080 Private S.L. Wilson, B Company 1st Battalion KOSB, dated 7 November 1951:

No 14471590 Pte W. Speakman

Pte Speakman was serving in B Coy Headquarters on the 4 Nov 1951 when the Company was attacked; at about 1600 hrs the company came under very intense artillery and mortar fire after which they were attacked by wave after wave of the enemy.

Pte Speakman made himself responsible for the left shoulder of the position and to see that it was kept clear of enemy. To enable him to do this he assembled a large pile of grenades and a party of six men over whom he assumed command, most of the NCOs by this time had became casualties, with disregard to his own safety he showed magnificent gallantry in leading charge after charge to shower the enemy with grenades as each successive wave appeared over the skyline, these charges and the casualties inflicted on the enemy showed the outstanding results of Pte Speakman's actions. Pte Speakman during these many assaults was wounded in the leg and although obviously in great pain would not give up his task to have his wound dressed, and only after extreme persuasion would he pause long enough for a first field dressing to be applied, he then returned to lead one assault after another to the time of withdrawal. Finally, at the critical moment of the withdrawal, he, under intense mortar, machine gun fire and grenades, led the final charge and showered the enemy with phosphorus grenades enabling the remnants of the company to withdraw with the minimum loss of lives.

His conspicuous gallantry, outstanding leadership and disregarding his own safety was an inspiration to all, he was personally responsible for great losses to the enemy and his final action saved many of his comrades lives. Pte Speakman's heroism is worthy of the very highest tradition.

Statement by No 22232559 Corporal J. Supple, B Company 1st Battalion KOSB, dated 9 November 1951:

No 14471590 Pte W. Speakman

On Sunday the 4th November 1951 at HILL 'UNITED', B Coy was attacked by wave after wave of communist troops, after a very heavy artillery barrage. The above-mentioned Pte Speakman was an inspiration to his comrades for sheer bravery, daring and disregard of his own safety, the first wave hit us at approximately 1700 hours, [sic] after a short battle the remainder of the company had to draw back to Company HQ, immediately Speakman took command of the situation, asking for grenades and taking a few men with him, he cleared the left shoulder of our hill, he done this time and time again. Eventually the enemy entrenched themselves in our MMG pits, seeing this, Speakman and Buchanan (2) advanced with hand grenades under intensive light machine gun fire and put our remaining MMG out of action, they both returned, immediately Speakman organised an attack on the shoulder he had cleared before, time after time and being wounded he led these attacks, it was through Speakman's conspicuous gallantry and utter disregard for his own safety that the remainder of the company were able to withdraw without further loss.

Statement by No 64605 Major P.F. St C. Harrison, Commanding B Company 1st Battalion KOSB, dated 7 November 1951:

No 14471590 Pte W. Speakman

This soldier of Company Headquarters distinguished himself beyond all praise when B Coy was attacked on UNITED on 4 Nov 51.

The Coy was heavily shelled and mortared and then attacked by vast numbers of the enemy.

Pte SPEAKMAN, showing magnificent powers of leadership, made himself responsible for keeping the left shoulder of the company position clear of the enemy.

This he did by assembling a great pile of grenades and organising a party of six men whom he repeatedly led forward to shower a hail of grenades as each successive wave of enemy arrived on the skyline.

The determination with which he led these charges caused great losses to the enemy who fell down in heaps on the crest.

Pte SPEAKMAN continued his task in the face of withering fire and although after half an hour he was shot through the leg and was in great pain he refused to return to have it dressed and carried on without ceasing.

Eventually he was made to pause to have a field dressing applied to his wound but returned immediately to lead charge after charge on the enemy as if nothing had happened.

At the critical moment of the withdrawal, he led the final charge to clear the enemy off the crest with a shower of phosphorus grenades which enabled the successful withdrawal of the remnants of the company off the position.

His conspicuous gallantry and inspiring leadership, after the NCOs had become casualties, his complete disregard for his own safety and his offensive actions undoubtedly saved the lives of many of the Company and he inflicted great losses on the enemy.

His great gallantry and heroic fighting quality is worthy of the highest recognition.

CSM Murdoch had also witnessed Speakman's actions on 4 November and had even mentioned to the padre at the CCS that if anyone deserved a VC it was Bill Speakman. Despite this, he was not one of the eye witnesses who gave statements for the VC recommendation as he was in Kure, Japan having his wounds treated. The eye witness statements were taken from unwounded soldiers who were present at the time and still with the battalion in Korea.

The Victoria Cross Warrant of 1856 stated that every recommendation should include 'conclusive proof as far as the circumstances of the case will allow and attestation of the act' although it did not specify the number of witnesses required. The eye witness statements of Speakman's actions formed the nucleus of his VC recommendation and were attached to a 'Recommendations for

Honours or Awards' form, which was signed by the Commanding Officer 1st KOSB, Major Tadman, on 11 November 1951.(3) It was then passed up the line to Brigadier MacDonald at Brigade Headquarters. He added the handwritten comment 'Most strongly recommended' and signed the form on 27 November. This level of approval was slightly awkward as in the recent past MacDonald had been the battalion's CO and his approval could be interpreted as bias in Speakman's favour. Nevertheless, at 1st British Commonwealth Divisional Headquarters, Major General Cassels had 'Most strongly recommended' typed on the form before signing it on 30 November.

EYE WITNESS STATEMENTS

Several phrases appear in all the statements – for example 'conspicuous gallantry' and 'with disregard to his own safety'/'utter disregard for his own safety'/'complete disregard for his own safety'. One eye witness says that 'Pte Speakman's heroism is worthy of the very highest tradition' while another says that 'his great gallantry and heroic fighting qualities is worthy of the highest recognition'. This may be just coincidence, but it is also possible that the eye witnesses were given some 'guidance' regarding the information that would be required by the War Office. In addition, there are so many similarities in the descriptions of the battle used by Major Harrison and Private Wilson that it is likely that these statements were not written independently. Phrases such as 'as each successive wave of enemy appeared over the skyline' and 'at the critical moment of the withdrawal' appear in both statements. There can be little doubt that Major Harrison had a part in the writing of all three statements, but there can also be little doubt that Private Speakman justly deserved the VC.

Major Harrison would have known that many recommendations for the VC in the Second World War were downgraded to another award because the stipulation for written signed eye witness accounts to support a recommendation were not met. It is clear in this case Major Harrison strongly believed Speakman deserved a VC and was not taking any chances.

From Korea the VC recommendation form went to Japan to be approved by Lieutenant General W. Bridgeford, Commander-in-Chief British Commonwealth Forces Japan and Korea. He wrote 'Strongly recommended' on the form and signed it and sent this and a covering letter, dated 7 December, to the Under Secretary of State at the War Office in London. It was received there on 18 December 1951. Unfortunately, it was not noticed at the time that Speakman's parent regiment was incorrectly listed as The Argyll and Sutherland Highlanders instead of The Black Watch.

Lieutenant General Bridgeford also forwarded a draft citation for the VC based on the eye witness statements. Minor amendments were made to the draft by the War Office; Coy was changed to Company, Pte was changed to Private and KOSB was changed to King's Own Scottish Borderers. A résumé was prepared by the Military Secretary, a soldier of lieutenant general rank, for the Chief of the Imperial General Staff and the Permanent Under Secretary at the War Office. He strongly recommended that the VC should be awarded to Private Speakman. Their response, dated 20 December, was 'Strongly supported'.

Before this had been confirmed by the King, a copy of the citation was sent to HMSO for including in *The London Gazette* of Friday, 28 December. The War Office pointed out: 'As I explained to you, the award has not yet been formally approved by the King but I expect to be able to phone you on the 27th on this ... If we do not have approval by the 27th, then the announcement will appear on the 1st January 1952.'

The War Office prepared the VC recommendation for the King on 21 December 1951. His Majesty King George VI approved it with the notation 'Appd. GR' but the date he approved it is not recorded. The Military Secretary wrote to HMSO on 27 December confirming that the King had approved the VC award.

It was not noticed until the day of publication of *The London Gazette* that the proposed announcement carried the wrong details of Speakman's parent regiment. The Army Records Office at Perth was requested to check the details, but it was only when the War Office telephoned for confirmation that the error came to light. It was noted that in correspondence from BRITCOM Japan, 'their recommendation also showed Speakman as A&SH, attached KOSB'. In a hastily written letter to HMSO, the Military Secretary at the War Office wrote:

> The regiment of this soldier should be amended from 'The Argyll and Sutherland Highlanders (Princess Louise's) attached to the 1st Battalion, The King's Own Scottish Borderers' to read 'The Black Watch (Royal Highland Regiment) attached to the 1st Battalion, The King's Own Scottish Borderers.' (4) It is very much regretted that, for reasons beyond our control, this amendment should have been necessary at such very short notice, and your ready co-operation in the matter is greatly appreciated.

With the amendments made, the VC announcement appeared in *The London Gazette* of Friday, 28 December 1951 (No 39418, page 6731), as previously arranged. The citation read:

The King has been graciously pleased to approve the award of the VICTORIA CROSS to:

14471590 Private William SPEAKMAN, The Black Watch (Royal Highland Regiment), attached to the 1st Battalion, The King's Own Scottish Borderers, in recognition of gallant and distinguished services in Korea.

From 0400 hours, 4th November, 1951, the defensive positions held by 1st Battalion, The King's Own Scottish Borderers, were continuously subjected to heavy and accurate enemy shell and mortar fire. At 1545 hours, this fire became intense and continued thus for the next two hours, considerably damaging the defences and wounding a number of men.

At 1645 hours, the enemy in their hundreds advanced in wave upon wave against The King's Own Scottish Borderers' positions, and by 1745 hours, fierce hand-to-hand fighting was taking place on every position.

Private Speakman, a member of B Company, Headquarters, learning that the section holding the left shoulder of the company's position had been seriously depleted by casualties, had had its NCOs wounded and was being overrun, decided on his own initiative to drive the enemy off the position and keep them off it. To effect [*sic*] this he collected quickly a large pile of grenades and a party of six men. Then displaying complete disregard for his own personal safety he led his party in a series of grenade charges against the enemy; and continued doing so as each successive wave of enemy reached the crest of the hill. The force and determination of his charges broke up each successive enemy onslaught and resulted in an ever mounting pile of enemy dead.

Having led some ten charges, through withering enemy machine gun and mortar fire, Private Speakman was eventually severely wounded in the leg. Undaunted by his wounds, he continued to lead charge after charge against the enemy and it was only after a direct order from his superior officer that he agreed to pause for a first field dressing to be applied to his wounds. Having had his wounds bandaged, Private Speakman immediately rejoined his comrades and led them again and again forward in a series of grenade charges, up to the time of the withdrawal of his company at 2100 hours.

At the critical moment of the withdrawal, amidst an inferno of enemy machine gun and mortar fire, as well as grenades, Private Speakman led a final charge to clear the crest of the hill and hold it, whilst the remainder of his Company withdrew. Encouraging his gallant but by now sadly depleted party, he assailed the enemy with showers of grenades and kept them at bay sufficiently long for his Company to effect its withdrawal.

Under the stress and strain of this battle, Private Speakman's outstanding powers of leadership were revealed and he so dominated the situation, that he inspired his comrades to stand firm and fight the enemy to a standstill.

His great gallantry and utter contempt for his own personal safety were an inspiration to all his comrades. He was, by his heroic actions, personally responsible for causing enormous losses to the enemy, assisting his Company to maintain their position for some four hours and saving the lives of many of his comrades when they were forced to withdraw from their position.

Private Speakman's heroism under intense fire throughout the operation and when painfully wounded was beyond praise and is deserving of supreme recognition.

General Sir Peter de la Billière wrote (5) that physical courage can be divided into two categories: hot courage and cold courage. He said that Private Speakman, when charging the enemy with no time to think or worry about the situation, displayed hot courage. Much has been written over the years about the nature of courage and what makes one man a hero and another man a coward. Speakman had his own view: 'All we did was fight like we were supposed to do.' A different view was put forward by Philip Niman (6), who defended Private Patrick Lydon at his court martial. Lydon had been charged with cowardice in the face of the enemy during the same action for which Private Speakman had been awarded the VC. Lydon was in C Company of KOSB. A psychiatrist, called to give evidence for the defence, stated that 'the distinction between cowardice and bravery is paper thin' and hinged on the individual's reaction to shock. It was suggested that many people had won gallantry awards because they were 'afraid of being afraid'. (For further details on Private Lydon see Appendix III.)

Further awards for the action on 4 November were gazetted, including DSOs for Major P. Harrison and Second Lieutenant W. Purves (see Appendix II for full list of awards to 1st KOSB). The DSO citation for Purves noted:

Although he was in great pain from a serious wound in the right shoulder, he fought an eight-hour battle on a partly overrun position under intense artillery fire. He later extricated his men with great skill and coolness. Not until he had received a direct order did he give any consideration to his painful wound. After another hour of fighting, the ridges of Hill 317, 400 yards from Second Lieutenant Purves's position, were in enemy hands and overlooked his position, which was now completely exposed. He fought on for almost five hours more.

Forced to attempt to extricate the two platoons under his command, Purves brought down a precipitous feature twelve wounded men and all the platoons' arms and equipment.

The outstanding leadership, bravery and resource of this young officer, together with his sense of responsibility, were an inspiration to all. The stubborn defence of this feature contributed materially in preventing the battalion from being overrun.

CSM 'Busty' Murdoch had to wait until 1st KOSB had completed its tour of duty of Korea before he was recommended for the DCM. The period of action covered by his citation is October 1951 to May 1952, and includes his involvement in Operation *Commando*. The citation, dated August 1952, also records Murdoch's actions during the fighting on United on 4 November 1951:

During the fierce enemy attack on 4th November 1951, CSM Murdoch gave further proof of his outstanding worth as a Warrant Officer. That the Company was able to hold for a period of four and a half hours, against the unceasing attacks of a vastly superior force of the enemy, was largely due to the calm and efficient manner in which he managed to keep up the ammunition supply to all the posts on the feature known as UNITED. This task was made most difficult owing to the whole feature being under constant heavy fire from SP guns, only 1,000 yards away, artillery, mortars and machine guns. In addition, the organisation and leading of the parties, required to take the ammunition from the ammunition dugout to the forward sections, with swarms of enemy constantly rushing the position, was a task requiring an individual with the highest personal qualities of leadership. He continued to do this throughout the action until he was severely wounded in the leg. Only when the Company was ordered to withdraw, did the Sergeant Major allow himself to be evacuated from the position.

The War Office made arrangements for Speakman's VC award to be announced in the press on the morning of Saturday, 29 December and for it to be broadcast by the BBC, but not before the 9.00 p.m. *News* on Friday night, 28 December. The War Office stressed that: 'This time restriction is imposed to prevent publication in the evening newspapers before the issue of the *Gazette*. This time bar must be rigidly observed.' (7) Brief biographical information was provided for journalists, including the name of Speakman's mother (which the War Office misspelt as Mrs Horton) and her address in Altrincham. She was notified of the VC award to her son by telegram on the afternoon of 28 December. The telegram was timed to reach Mrs Houghton just before *The London Gazette* was published that evening. It arrived on her 49th birthday; 'Nobody could have had a better birthday present,' she said.

On 29 December, the War Office wrote to Hancocks & Co, the London jewellers, asking them to supply a Victoria Cross with Private Speakman's details engraved upon it. Hancocks & Co, who had made every VC awarded since 1857, acknowledged the order, in a handwritten note, on 31 December 1951.

Arrangements were also made for Speakman to receive an annual annuity of £10 in respect of his VC award. This was payable quarterly in arrears and backdated to 4 November 1951. The annuity has been increased several times since then and is currently £1,495.

A telegram from British Commonwealth Forces Japan, regarding Private Speakman, notified the War Office that: 'He returns to 1st KOSB 29 December and GOC 1 Comwel [Commonwealth] Div has been asked to make official presentation of ribbon.'

Speakman had no prior knowledge of the VC award and was completely surprised when he found out. At the end of December Speakman was recovering well from his wounds and went into Kure:

> I wanted a samurai sword. I had some bucks coming to me so this guy who was working in the transit camp says to me: 'If you go to this shop you will find a samurai sword but it will not be as sharp as a proper sword.' Imagine getting one of those!
>
> I had just come up from the Japanese sword shop in Kure because we knew we were going back to the battalion soon. I bought the samurai sword but it somehow went missing in all the rigmarole that followed.

Samurai military traditions are based on the Japanese feudal system, when samurai knights were given land by local lords in exchange for military service. During the Second World War Japanese officers carried samurai swords, which became much prized souvenirs after the war.

Having purchased the sword, Speakman returned to camp:

> I didn't have a proper uniform, more a uniform with bits and pieces because I had just come out of hospital. All my gear had been burned, even combat

gear, so I had to wear whatever the hospital had to give me. I got back in the camp and was going for a cup of tea, when the camp sergeant major came running towards me: 'Speakman, Private Speakman?' I thought, 'Oh no, trouble again'. 'That's me', I said. He said: 'Are you 14471590 Private W. Speakman, Black Watch, attached KOSB?' I said: 'Yes'.

He said: 'Get dressed. You are wanted in the camp commandant's office'. I said: 'What for?' He said: 'I don't know, get dressed. Wear your boots and gaiters'. I said: 'I am dressed. I don't have boots and gaiters, I've just come out of hospital and this is what I've got and we will get re-equipped when we get back to battalion. The quartermaster will do this.' Just then an officer came up. He said: 'We have got to get him fitted out as we have someone here from the UK who wants to speak to him urgently and it is very, very important. We have to do it today because he is on the plane tomorrow to rejoin his battalion'. So they got me fitted up. He said: 'What have you been doing?' I said: 'I don't know. I don't know'. He said: 'Anyway, they want to see you'.

So they marched me to the camp commandant's office and I knocked on the door. 'Sir, 14471590 Private Speakman'. 'Come in', he said, 'This gentleman would like to see you'. There was a man standing in the corner, I think he was a brigadier. I didn't know who the camp commandant was because you don't normally see them. There were so many people coming out of hospital and passing through the transit camp, and others on their way to various regiments. The man with the red tabs said: 'Private Speakman? Well I am very pleased and very proud to present you with this; you have been awarded the Victoria Cross'. I will always remember this. He shook me by the hand and gave me this little matchbox sized box. 'Private Speakman, we are all very proud of you', he said. 'This is yours'. He said: 'Well, open it'. So I opened it and there was this little ribbon with a little cross on. I didn't know what it was.

He said: 'Do you know what it is, Speakman?' I said: 'No, sir'. He said: 'That is the ribbon of the Victoria Cross. You have been awarded the VC by His Majesty The King'. I said: 'What for, sir?' He said: 'Well, for what you did in Korea on 4th November'. I was so bewildered because all we did was fight like we were supposed to do; it took a while to sink in. Then he said: 'It's yours. You keep it. You are going back to your battalion tomorrow. Give this to the adjutant and he will take it on from there. There will be a parade and you will be decorated by Major General Cassels in front of the battalion'.

So I went back to Korea. The battalion at that time had been pulled back for a rest. The adjutant met me. Then he told me all about it. 'Well done, Speakman.

We're very proud of you. Major General Cassels is coming in a couple of day's time and Major Harrison and yourself will be presented with your ribbons'.

Speakman was surprised to hear of an unofficial honour shown to VC recipients: receiving a salute from officers. When he left Iwakuni airport in Japan to fly to Korea he was seen off and saluted by an Australian officer, Wing Commander Keith Hennock.

Speakman returned to Korea on 29 December with the ribbon of the VC wrapped in a handkerchief in his pocket. For nearly an hour after he arrived in Korea he forgot about the ribbon. He was talking to his company adjutant, Captain R.H. Oatts when he suddenly remembered. Speakman said, 'I nearly forgot to give you this, sir.' Taking the handkerchief from his tunic pocket, he removed the ribbon and handed it to the captain. 'They said in Japan that there mightn't be one over here,' he said.

In the corporals' mess, Speakman read the citation for the first time and then looked up saying, 'You know I didn't really lead anybody. There were lots of chaps who did what I did.'

Speakman officially received his VC ribbon from Major General 'Jimmy' Cassels, Commander of the 1st Commonwealth Division, on 30 December. Major Harrison received his DSO ribbon at the same ceremony. A parade was held in the courtyard of a Korean school, among the snow-covered hills, on the coldest day of the year. The kilted bagpipers had kept their bagpipes warm in front of a heater all night to ensure the instruments would play during the ceremony. Speakman, displaying typical modesty, asked his CO: 'Why me, sir? Am I the only one?' He said, 'Other decorations have been awarded to your mates: DCMs and MMs.'

Fifty men from Speakman's company and twelve each from other companies of the battalion and detachments from other units of the division were also on parade, forming a hollow square. Private Speakman's VC citation was read out by Lieutenant Colonel W. Vickers, Assistant Quartermaster General. Major General Cassels then congratulated him on the award and pinned the VC ribbon on his new tunic while the bagpipers played. Cassels then pinned the ribbon of the DSO on Major Harrison, to Speakman's right.

The War Diaries of 28th British Commonwealth Brigade (8) recorded on 30 December:

1000 hrs Comd [Commanding Officer – Brigadier MacDonald] attended the investiture by GOC of Victoria Cross to Pte Speakman, 1 KOSB at HQ 1 KOSB.

Speakman about to receive his VC ribbon from Major General Cassels, standing in front of table. (*Australian War Memorial HOBJ2811*)

Major General Cassels pinning the VC ribbon on Private W. Speakman VC. (*Australian War Memorial HOBJ 2812*)

1140 hrs Brig Gen Cross, Comd 3 US Infantry Div arrived by helicopter to accompany Comd to 1 KOSB luncheon party. The Brig Gen was most interested to hear the pipes and drums.

Lieutenant Colonel Tadman said, 'Speakman has always been an individualist. He does things alone and wants to be alone.'

Major Harrison, who had recommended Speakman for the VC, said of him: 'He did far more than can be put on paper. Everything needing to be done in an emergency he did, showing tremendous initiative.' He added, 'Apart from shouting at him not to charge into Manchuria, we left him alone to run his own show.'

Major Alan Jackson, the battalion adjutant, asked Speakman if he would like some leave. 'No, sir, I want to rejoin my company right away,' he replied. Speakman celebrated that evening with his mates, later recalling:

> They were all chuffed. They said, 'Well done.' There weren't many mates left actually. There were some from the other companies. But after the action there were not very many left. The guys who knew all about it said, 'Hey, this is the big one.' I said, 'All right, fine, all right.' I was very subdued when I finally found out what it was. No one goes out to win a VC. You just get on with doing the job. You are just too busy. Then someone taps you on the shoulder to tell you the news.

In one of the first of many press interviews, Speakman described the action which won him the VC as 'a fair old go' and went on to say:

Speakman on 29 December 1951 at Seoul Airport, the day after his VC was gazetted. (KOSB Museum)

Speakman after the ribbon ceremony. (© IWM KOR/U5)

Speakman being
congratulated by his
comrades after the
ribbon ceremony.
(*Bill Speakman VC*)

There was a bunch of us up near the crest of a hill. We had boxes of grenades
piled up in a ration tent behind us. We kept making trips to the crest and
tossing grenades as they [the Chinese] came. You know, I did not really lead
anyone. There were a lot of chaps who did what I did.

Although Speakman's action on United was the last of the four Korean War
VCs by date, his was the second to be announced. Major Kenneth Muir had
been awarded a posthumous VC in January 1951, but now the British public
had a living Korean War VC hero (9). The newspapers of the weekend of 29–30
December 1951 carried the story of Private Bill Speakman's heroic VC action;
many of them put it on their front pages. Most were content to quote from the
VC citation, but some sent reporters to see 'his widowed mother, Mrs Hannah
Houghton' in her 'four-room cottage at Altrincham' for more information. Her
address had been disclosed in a press release by the War Office.

On the night she heard the citation read over the radio, Hannah told a
reporter: 'To think he has gone through all that without giving me a hint of
what has happened. It is just like him. He never talked much about himself. But
he has always been a good son.'

She had recently collapsed at the hotel in Altrincham where she was a cleaner and was being treated as an out-patient at the local hospital. 'But I forgot my worries when I heard the news about Bill,' she was quoted as saying. 'I was so proud. It is the finest birthday present I have ever had.' Mrs Houghton was 49 on the day her son's VC was gazetted, although many newspapers quoted her age as 47. It is not known if she chose to take a few years off her actual age or she was subject to the same media misrepresentation which would follow Bill Speakman around for years afterwards.

She proudly showed a telegram which said: 'Dear Mum, am doing fine, not to worry, your son Bill.'

To the assembled newspaper reporters, she confided, 'You can imagine I'm right proud of Bill, but then I knew he would do well in the Army ... He is a very thoughtful boy. He sends 10s 6d home each week to pay for the rent.' Speakman told reporters, who were eager for news, that he was looking forward to some good home cooking; his favourite dish was said to be potato pie.

The Mayor of Altrincham sent a telegram saying: 'Altrincham is proud of you and eagerly awaits your homecoming.' Media interest in Bill Speakman VC continued throughout January 1952 and intensified at the end of the month when he returned to England.

At the end of December 1951 many national newspapers carried stories and interviews concerning the new VC hero, some of which included the alleged beer bottle throwing incident – although the 'beer bottle VC' tag did not appear until later. Not all the newspaper reports were based on fact. Many of the larger newspapers had their own reporters on the front line and Speakman got to know some of them:

There were certain reporters who would never come up that hill – they would never appear amongst you. Some reporters did, and we got to know those reporters very well. They would come in and get the CO's go-ahead because he knew they were proper reporters and they would actually report it and tell it as it was. But there were some who would wait until you got to the bottom of the hill and say, 'What's it like up there?' Of course, by that time they had got a story. They used to go and visit the wounded in hospital and they got stories.

NOTES

(1) The eye witness accounts, VC recommendation and VC citation are contained in National Archives file WO 32/14861.

(2) Private Edward Buchanan received the Military Medal for his part in the action.

(3) Tadman's recommendations for the 4 November 1951, dated 11 November, are held at the KOSB Museum. Of the 26 recommendations only 13 were granted. The 13 decorations not granted were: 1 MC, 1 DCM, 1 bar to DCM, 3 MMs and 7 MIDs. The list of those granted can be seen in bold in Appendix II. Busty Murdoch's DCM was not among Tadman's recommendation on 11 November but when his DCM was awarded later the citation covers 4 November action and therefore is also shown in bold, bringing the total granted to 14.

(4) On 3 December 1951 Speakman voluntarily transferred to the Lowland Brigade (KOSB).

(5) *Supreme Courage* by General Sir Peter de la Billière (Little, Brown, 2004). De la Billière, like Speakman, was a Korean War veteran and later served in the SAS.

(6) Letter to *The Times* 1 September 1983.

(7) It appears that time restrictions as to the release of information were not always rigidly observed. The War Office memo continued: 'Your attention is drawn to our loose minute of 2nd January 1951 in the case of the late Major K. Muir VC' (Major Muir was the first of the four VC awards for Korea to be gazetted). The loose minute (memo) referred to contained a reminder about the importance of preventing breaches of time restraints. When the VC for Lieutenant George Cairns (the last VC to be gazetted for the Second World War) was announced in May 1949, the BBC breached the 9.00 p.m. embargo and included the award in its 6.00 p.m. *News*. The media were reminded of this breach when the War Office announced the awards to both Muir and Speakman.

(8) Held in National Archives file WO 281/141.

(9) Lieutenant Philip Curtis and Lieutenant Colonel James Carne were awarded VCs in 1953 after the fighting had ended and Carne was released from an enemy prison camp. Curtis was awarded a posthumous VC.

HOMECOMING

JANUARY–FEBRUARY 1952

While Bill Speakman was still 5,500 miles away in Korea, and not expected home for some time, his mother was being treated as a celebrity in Altrincham. A British Pathé newsreel filmed Hannah Houghton at home – washing up at her kitchen sink and then reading the newspaper headlines about her son's VC in her living room.

Soon after the VC was announced, she was taken to the *Daily Express* office in Manchester to make a telephone call to her son and was very pleased to be able to speak to him. The headmaster of Wellington Road School wrote to her to say how proud the school was of her son's achievement. 'This is the kind of thing that makes a schoolmaster's life worth living,' said Mr Gooch, the

Speakman phones his mother.
(*KOSB Museum*)

headmaster. She also received a telegram from Mr F.J. Erroll, the Conservative MP for Altrincham and Sale (1), saying 'Please pass on to your son my sincere congratulations. You must be very proud of him.'

On 5 January she was guest of honour at the annual dinner of the Lancashire branch of The Black Watch Reunion Dinner in Liverpool, where she received a bouquet of flowers from Lord Wavell, the son of Field Marshal Archibald Wavell, 1st Earl Wavell. Mrs Houghton travelled to the dinner in the mayoral car.

The following week she was visited at her home by her local Member of Parliament, Mr F.J. Erroll, his agent and Councillor J.L. Warren, the Mayor of Altrincham. When asked how she was taking the publicity, Mrs Houghton replied that people were beginning to recognise her and she was constantly being stopped in the street. 'You will be able to give him a good ticking off for having caused you so much trouble,' the MP said.

Later in January, the family home at 27 Moss Lane had a 'make over'. A Manchester fireplace merchant saw the newsreel pictures of Mrs Houghton's old-fashioned fireplace and arranged to fit a new tiled fireplace at his own expense. Shortly afterwards, a local firm of decorators decorated her living room ready for her son's homecoming. While the decorators were busy in her house she took the opportunity to have a week's peace and quiet with her sister in North Wales.

Although grateful for all the gifts she had received, Hannah Houghton was unaccustomed to the media attention which came with them. As she said to one reporter: 'It was Bill who won the VC – not his mother.'

A 'Private William Speakman VC Testimonial Fund' Appeal was launched by the Mayor of Altrincham on 3 January 1952, less than a week after the VC was gazetted. Donations were received at an unoccupied shop in Railway Street, which was open daily until the middle of January. The mayor pointed out that if everyone in Altrincham were to contribute one shilling to the fund, more than £2,000 would be raised. The *Altrincham, Hale and Bowdon Guardian* later reported that a donation of £2 had been received from Mrs Mary MacDonald, the wife of Brigadier John MacDonald DSO.

In a Christmas 1951 letter to his mother, Bill Speakman advised her that he expected to be home in March 1952. Following his VC award, his leave was brought forward by two months so that he could receive his decoration from HM The King at Buckingham Palace. Speakman's Christmas card to his mother had been reproduced in several of the daily newspapers at the time of his VC award. Many reporters described Bill Speakman as the 'son of a widowed charwoman' so did not enquire why he had a different surname to his mother; it may have been assumed that his father had died and his widowed mother had remarried.

For most of January 1952 1st KOSB was in reserve, returning to the front line on 18 January. Before flying home to England, Speakman was given a short period of rest and recuperation in Japan. 'I went to Tokyo with Busty and we got entertained by a Japanese businessman,' he recalls.

He left for England, from Iwakuni in Japan, on board an RAF Hastings aircraft (2), on 21 January. It was originally planned to return Speakman to the UK by a scheduled BOAC flight but it was later decided that an RAF plane would be preferable to ensure he caught his Singapore connection. The eight-day journey involved stops at Manila, Hong Kong, Singapore, Ceylon (where Speakman bought a coconut for his 12-year-old brother Bert), Aden and Casa Benito in Libya, where the aircraft was delayed by engine trouble. Speakman recalls that 'by that time there was a circuit. There were circuits for the Middle East, for the Far East and there were RAF transport planes which carried the mail and diplomatic pouches.'

One of the RAF aircrew accompanying Speakman home later revealed that the new VC had been made an acting sergeant for the trip so that he would have a better class of accommodation on the regular stops. Another crew member asked Speakman: 'What made you do what you did?' He replied: 'I was bloody mad. They were killing my mates.'

At the last stop before the UK, in Libya, Speakman put on his new uniform. Shortly before landing he was given the news that the press were waiting for him, together with a reception committee including the Mayor of Altrincham. This was obviously something he was not expecting. 'I was so baffled that it was unreal,' he said. He later said that his life changed the moment he stepped off the plane.

The shy hero landed at RAF Lyneham in Wiltshire on Tuesday, 29 January 1952. Lyneham was constructed in 1939 and during the Second World War became the home of the RAF's air transport operations. When Speakman saw the large reception waiting for him he hesitated for a moment before coming down the gangway:

When I stepped off the plane at Lyneham and saw all those cameras I didn't know what had hit me. I just didn't know what to say. I really didn't know what to say. If I had known then what I know now, I would have got out the back door of that plane and got a bus to Altrincham!

'That's when it all started ...' Speakman faces the media as he leaves the aircraft at RAF Lyneham, 29 January 1952. (*British Pathé*)

He was greeted by the Mayor of Altrincham, Councillor James Warren, at the bottom of the gangway. Councillor Warren was also a war veteran, having lost his right arm during the First World War, and he and Speakman performed a rather awkward left-handed handshake in front of the cameras. 'We are really mighty proud of you in Altrincham,' the mayor told him. 'Your mother and neighbours are waiting for you.' Also waiting to greet Private Speakman were about seventy photographers and newspaper reporters, who fought for interviews. This was a large gathering for an operational RAF station during a war. One person who was not waiting to greet Speakman, however, was his mother:

> She didn't come because it was so sudden, but she knew about it. She was at home with the neighbours getting ready. They were painting the street, so the mayor said, 'We will get him and bring him back.'

Speakman is met at the foot of the aircraft at Lyneham by the Mayor of Altrincham, Councillor Warren. (*British Pathé*)

A new battledress was required for the journey home, Speakman recalls:

> So they gave me a lovely Canadian battledress, same as ours, but a finer cloth. Everyone was after it ... Someone scrounged this one. All my stuff, even when I was in the Army, was made to measure. So this uniform happened to fit me ... They gave me this nice battledress and a couple of nice shirts and a pair of shoes as well. They put the flashes on, the tartan patch and the commonwealth divisional sign. And they put some ribbons on. The VC ribbon must have been put on at that stage.

When he stepped down from the aircraft, Speakman wore six ribbons on his new tunic. He can clearly be seen wearing them in many of the photographs taken at RAF Lyneham, and some newspapers helpfully named the medals. (He also wore the same six ribbons when he went to Buckingham Palace to receive his VC.) The ribbons he wore were for the Victoria Cross, War Medal 1939–45, Defence Medal, General Service Medal (GSM), Korea Medal and United Nations Korea Medal. He was not entitled to wear three of these medal ribbons and despite speculation since then, Speakman was not 'cocking a snook' at authority (showing disrespect) by wearing them. (3)

From RAF Lyneham, Speakman was driven to the London Assembly Centre in Tottenham Court Road to meet Major General Eric Miles, colonel of The King's Own Scottish Borderers. After being recommended for the VC, Private

Speakman was transferred from The Black Watch to the KOSB. He was still in hospital in Japan when he decided to change from Highland to Lowland regiment. This was before the announcement of the VC but the officer who visited him in early December 1951 probably knew an announcement of the decoration was imminent. The change of regiment was noted on his Army record on 3 December:

> When I was in hospital an officer came to me and said 'Would you like to become a King's Own Scottish Borderer?' I said, 'Certainly.' The KOSB was a good regiment to be with. The other reason was that in The Black Watch you had to wear a kilt. Now, you need to be built to wear a kilt, but with me being so tall with skinny legs it was ludicrous. It really is an embarrassment to wear a kilt. You feel terribly uncomfortable and you are not allowed upstairs on a bus. So I thought 'KOSB' – they wear trews, but this was a bonus. You wore trews, so that was all right. It was the Leslie tartan. (4) What a regiment, it was fantastic. I never, ever, regretted joining the KOSB.

Major General Miles revealed to the waiting press another reason Speakman was sent home from Korea: his commanding officer was concerned that if he went into action again he might get killed. General Miles agreed with the commanding officer's concern and Speakman was brought home.

Speakman meets with Major General E.G. Miles, the Colonel of KOSB, in London. (*KOSB Museum*)

122

General Miles then outlined the regiment's plans for Speakman. It was proposed that when his leave expired he would not return to Korea as expected. He would, instead, be attached to the KOSB Depot at Berwick-upon-Tweed, where he would take a leadership course followed by promotion.

Speakman's reaction was predictable: 'This training plan is all right, but I want to get back to my pals as soon as I can.' He then drew pay and lodging allowance, totalling £13, for his five-week leave. That evening he watched a television show in the Nuffield Centre, London whilst sitting next to a Chelsea Pensioner; he did not realise at the time that one day he would join that select group of retired servicemen.

The following day, 30 January, Speakman returned to Altrincham to a hero's welcome. He was collected from London by the Mayor of Altrincham and driven home in the mayor's official car. He was reunited with his mother, Mrs Hannah Houghton, en route at Crewe. 'How are you, Bill?' she asked. 'Fine Ma,' he replied. At the Hale Road Bridge, the town boundary, the party transferred to an open car so that the estimated 15,000 people lining the route could see Altrincham's latest VC winner. (Captain Edward Bradbury VC was the first Altrincham-born man to be awarded the VC.)

Speakman accompanied by the Mayor of Altrincham. (*British Pathé*)

CAPTAIN EDWARD BRADBURY VC

Edward Kinder Bradbury, Altrincham's first Victoria Cross winner, was born in Altrincham in August 1881 and joined the Royal Artillery in May 1900.

On 1 September 1914, during the first month of the First World War, Captain Bradbury organised the guns of L Battery, the Royal Horse Artillery, against heavy odds at Néry, France.

That morning a German battery had opened fire on their camp, killing all the horses and killing or wounding many of the men. Captain Bradbury helped man the remaining guns, which were still under a fierce enemy attack. He directed the fire, even after one of his legs was taken off by a German shell. Though in great pain, he continued to give orders to his men until he was taken from the battlefield, mortally wounded. His posthumous VC was announced in *The London Gazette* of 25 November 1914.

Captain Bradbury's VC and medals are on display at the Lord Ashcroft Gallery at the Imperial War Museum, London.

The *Altrincham, Hale and Bowdon Guardian* reported in its edition of 1 February 1952 (Licensed by Newsquest Media Group):

> The police had a full-time job moving overeager youngsters, who clambered on to the bridge parapet … It was only by revving their engines and moving their vehicles inch by inch into the dense crowd that the police escort and outriders managed to avert what might have been a major hold-up.

Altrincham was ready to welcome Speakman when he arrived. Many of the streets displayed 'Welcome Home Bill' banners and all the town's 5,000 school children had been given a half day off school to join in the celebrations. Council workmen had erected flagpoles and fairy lights close to his house in Moss Lane and the neighbours painted welcome home messages in large white letters on the road and scrubbed the stone steps to his mother's house. Speakman was given an enthusiastic welcome by a town genuinely pleased for him.

The procession to the town hall was led by the Timperley Band, followed by a detachment of Altrincham Army Cadets and Royal British Legion veterans. A police car led the motorcade, followed by a newsreel car, then the open car with Bill Speakman and the mayor. At times the dense crowd spilled onto the road, holding up the procession. Speakman shook hands with many of the well-wishers who surrounded the car. After driving through the crowded streets, with many people waving Union flags, the cars headed towards the town hall, arriving there several hours later than planned.

The British Pathé newsreels of the occasion showed that Speakman had not fully recovered from the wounds he received almost three months before. He could be seen limping as he walked from the car to the town hall, shaking hands with the crowd as he went.

He was escorted by the mayor to his office and, with his mother, they then went on to the balcony to greet the crowds which had waited patiently to see the returning hero. 'I didn't realise it was so huge,' said Speakman, referring to the Victoria Cross, 'I really didn't.' He appeared to be overwhelmed by the welcome home he had received. With Speakman by his side, the mayor made a short speech of introduction from the balcony:

> This is indeed a pleasure, a unique occasion, and exceptionally pleasurable one that I have now to do, that is to introduce you to a local boy, a soldier, and indeed a very gallant soldier. One who has earned the most meritorious distinction that anyone can earn, the most coveted of all honours: the Victoria Cross.

The estimated 3,000 strong crowd cheered and Speakman made a short speech of thanks:

> There is not very much that I really can say to you people because words won't express my feelings at the way you have treated me today. But there is one thing I can say – it's good to be home and thanks a lot.

He looked very uncomfortable being the centre of attention, wringing his hands as he spoke. The civic reception in his honour was attended by Altrincham councillors and prominent local dignitaries. Thirty aldermen and councillors from surrounding districts had also been invited. Among the welcoming committee was Sergeant John Thomas VC, who had been awarded his VC for bravery during the Battle of Cambrai in November 1917.

SERGEANT JOHN THOMAS VC

John Thomas was born on 10 May 1886 in Openshaw, Manchester. In 1909 he enlisted as a private in the 2/5th North Staffordshire Regiment. After serving for three years he became a reservist and joined the merchant navy but returned to his regiment on the outbreak of war in 1914.

On 30 November 1917, when his battalion was close to the village of Fontaine-Notre-Dame, Lance Corporal Thomas left his trench and observed the Germans making preparations for a counter-attack. He shot several snipers and then began sniping at the enemy. After being away for three hours he returned to his trench with valuable information on enemy movements. Thomas received his VC from HM The King in March 1918 and was promoted to sergeant in March 1919.

He attended the VC Garden Party in 1920 and the VC Dinner at the House of Lords in 1929. Thomas died, after a long illness, at his home in Stockport on 28 February 1954.

Speakman shook hands with Thomas and examined the medals on his chest. He handled Thomas' VC and was no doubt thinking of the VC he would receive soon from the King at Buckingham Palace. In addition to the VC, Sergeant Thomas wore the 1914 Star and Clasp, British War Medal, Victory Medal and 1937 Coronation Medal. Despite looking very ill, Thomas was on the balcony when Speakman made his short speech.

Speakman examines the VC of Sergeant John Thomas VC. (*British Pathé*)

Welcome home
sign in Altrincham.
(*British Pathé*)

After the civic reception, Speakman returned to his home in Moss Lane.
His mother had gone in advance to welcome him. He waved to the crowds
gathered outside before embracing his mother and going indoors. Within days
of his arrival home, a newsreel recording of his homecoming was on show at
the local cinema.

The homecoming parade was generally well organised, but there are always
people who wish to complain. An anonymous letter to the *Altrincham, Hale and
Bowdon Guardian* protested against the arrangements for advising the waiting
crowd of the exact time the car bringing Private Speakman home would arrive
in Altrincham. This, the writer maintained, meant that 'many of the adults,
chilled to the bone, left disappointed'. However, another letter in the same
edition praised the mayor for 'his tireless efforts' in making the homecoming
such a success.

Such was Speakman's new-found fame that he was able to arrange things
which ordinary private soldiers could only dream of – such as organising leave
for a lifelong friend, Private Jack Atkinson, of Moss Lane, Altrincham, who was
serving with the Duke of Cornwall's Light Infantry when Speakman returned
home. Days later, Speakman sent a telegram to the commanding officer of
the regiment at Bodmin, Cornwall requesting that his friend Jack Atkinson
be given some leave. Two days later Atkinson arrived in Altrincham on nine
days' leave.

Speakman finally arrives at the family home in Moss Lane to embrace his mother. On the left is a relation called Savage. The Mayor of Altrincham is behind. (*British Pathé*)

It was officially announced, on the same day that he returned to Altrincham, that Private Speakman would go to Buckingham Palace on 27 February to receive his VC from HM King George VI. A week later the nation was shocked and saddened to learn of the King's sudden death. King George VI died peacefully in his sleep, at Sandringham, in the early hours of 6 February 1952. He was 56 and had reigned as King for just over fifteen years.

Princess Elizabeth and the Duke of Edinburgh were on a royal tour of Africa when they heard the news, and the new Queen Elizabeth II flew back to England as soon as she could. She was met at London Airport (Heathrow) by Prime Minister Mr Winston Churchill, who had returned to Downing Street the previous year. It was later announced that HM The Queen would present Private Speakman with his VC at the first investiture of her reign, to be held on the same day as originally planned to be held by the King.

Private Speakman was one of three men chosen to represent the Armed Services in a TV tribute to the King. The BBC programme, *The Commonwealth mourns its King*, was broadcast at 9.15 p.m. on 14 February. An aircraftman from Cyprus spoke for the RAF and a petty officer paid a tribute on behalf of the Royal Navy. Private Speakman, speaking on behalf of the Army, said:

> It is not only in Korea and places like that that a man can be asked to give everything for his country. The King could have let up on his official duties when he found things were not going too well for him, but he kept on with his job although he knew what it was bound to mean for him. Now he has paid the price, and there is not a man in uniform at home or abroad who could have done more for his country.

Speakman told a newspaper reporter: 'It's a great honour to pay a tribute to the King on behalf of the Army, and the boys in Korea in particular.' On 15 February he joined with the mayor, aldermen, councillors and representatives of public bodies in paying tribute to the late King at St George's Parish Church in Altrincham.

Many events in Altrincham, and the rest of the UK, were cancelled or postponed as a mark of respect following the King's sudden death. Among these events was the ACF Battalion Cheshire Regiment's dance in honour of Private Speakman VC, which took place a week later than planned. Speakman attended the dance at the drill hall, organised by his former cadet battalion, and was presented with a silver cigarette case.

The week before his investiture, Speakman broke his leave to go to the KOSB Depot Berwick-upon-Tweed to be fitted out for the ceremony. The kit was the diced Lowland Bonnet and regimental tartan trews. He was met at the platform by the KOSB adjutant and the RSM and although he slipped out of the station unobtrusively, he was hailed by dozens of townspeople who recognised his giant figure.

At the depot, eighteen newly joined National Servicemen were awed when Speakman strode into the cookhouse to join them for breakfast. He also met Pte John Jackson who had been with Speakman in B Company in Korea.

After the special kit parade, Speakman was taken to town to celebrate his award. His train back to Manchester was due to leave at 15.12. A taxi was called to rush to the barracks to collect his kit and then on to the station but he missed the train by two minutes. So the celebrations continued in a nearby tearoom until the next train at 16.30.

Speakman said, 'I'm sorry about missing the train, for I'm supposed to be going to a party in Manchester tonight. The whole thing has been too much for me. I haven't had a minute to myself. I am going to find it difficult to settle down to being an ordinary soldier again.'

Speakman received his VC at Buckingham Palace on 27 February 1952, at the Queen's first investiture. He was allowed to take three guests with him and took his mother, Mrs Hannah Houghton, the ubiquitous Mayor of Altrincham, Councillor James Warren, and the Mayoress. Councillor Warren had met Speakman at Lyneham, brought him from London to Altrincham, travelled through the streets with him before hosting a reception in his honour and was now escorting him to Buckingham Palace. It would appear, however, that this was because Speakman did not have any other relatives to take with him rather than the mayor being assertive. 'There was only my mother as Bert and Ann were too young – they were at home,' recalls Speakman.

There were over 100 recipients of orders and decorations that day, including fifty-five new knights, but Speakman was the first person to receive his award – the first award at the first investiture of the new reign (5). He was given some advice by a palace official before the investiture began:

'Don't you ever forget this, Private Speakman, you go in long before the officers go in – you have precedence.' They explained to me why. There was this officer, he got a DSO. I said, 'What about him?' The official said, 'No, you are the first one.'

As the guests were ushered into the State Ballroom, where they would watch the ceremony, the recipients of awards went through to the Green Drawing Room. They were then assembled in order and briefed on proceedings. Speakman, as the only VC recipient, was placed first in line. When the first group of recipients were led to the State Ballroom he was still in front of everyone else, something which made the shy hero very nervous:

Believe you me, for it to happen to a young soldier like me [he was 24 at the time] – it is overwhelming – you just don't know whether you are coming or going … You just don't know which way to turn. Luckily enough, I had friends.

He had been briefed on where to stand and what to do:

'When you go forward to meet the Queen, you will see a small stud. Look at it; that is where you stand.' I said, 'Do I kneel?' He said, 'No, you mustn't kneel. That is for those who get a knighthood. I'll take your hat.'

At just after 11.00 a.m. HM The Queen, wearing a black dress with a pearl necklace and a diamond brooch, entered the State Ballroom, and was followed by HRH The Duke of Edinburgh, wearing a naval uniform. The Queen wore black as she was in mourning for her father, King George VI, who had died three weeks earlier. When the Queen took her place on the dais she said 'Ladies and Gentlemen, pray be seated.' The ceremony then began.

Private Speakman, wearing the uniform of The King's Own Scottish Borderers, complete with tartan trews, was given the signal to enter the State Ballroom. He marched towards the Queen, stood to attention in front of her and bowed. Speakman was trembling and blushing deeply. His VC citation was read out by the Earl of Clarendon, the Lord Chamberlain, and the Queen attached the VC to a small hook which had been fastened to his tunic. Her Majesty spoke to Speakman and he recalls that she asked, 'How do you feel now? Are you better? Are you well?', 'I feel fine Ma'am,' he replied. The newspapers of the time reported that the Queen spoke to Speakman for several minutes. The Queen shook hands warmly with him and he bowed again, turned and marched stiffly out of the room. He whispered hoarsely to a court official: 'Give me a glass of water.' An official unhooked his VC, placed it in a box and handed

Obverse and reverse of Speakman's VC. (*National War Museum of Scotland*)

it back to him. Speakman was nonplussed to find that admirals and generals were saluting him, and that guards snapped to attention as he passed. 'Then it was all over. My mother was waiting for me,' he remembers. He then took a seat at the back of the ballroom to watch the remainder of the ceremony. His mother had watched the VC investiture with tears of joy in her eyes.

Outside the palace, a crowd of well-wishers had gathered, many of them wanting to shake hands with the new VC hero. The press were also waiting. Speakman told a reporter: 'The Queen asked me how long I had served with The Black Watch and how long I had been with my present regiment. It was a great experience and a great honour.'

He lived in his mother's house at 27 Moss Lane, Altrincham after returning from Korea. The constant attention, not just from the media but the general public as well, soon became unbearable. Speakman remembers that:

After about a week I put my civvies on. Wherever I went I was recognised. In pubs, they would say: 'Have a pint.' It was a bit overwhelming. As a boy I always liked being on my own. Then total strangers buying you pint after pint. It wasn't on. I wasn't used to it. A lot of VCs will tell you exactly the same.

Speakman and his mother were guests of honour at a dinner dance in Altrincham, where he received an inscribed silver cigarette case from his former workmates at Edward Holme & Co., the firm where he worked before

Outside Buckingham Palace after the investiture. Left to right: Mrs Warren, Speakman VC, Hannah Houghton, Mayor Warren. (*British Pathé*)

joining the Army. He also received a cheque for £50 from the directors. He was asked to present a Vernon's football pools winner, Miss Barbara Kelly, with a cheque for £75,000 (6), to which he readily agreed. 'Do you know,' she said, 'I am almost as thrilled to meet Private Speakman as I am to get the cheque.' He was also persuaded to kick off in a football match between Altrincham and Witton Albion. Braving the thick mud he ran to the centre of the pitch to open the match. He again found himself the centre of attention when he visited Altrincham General Hospital to present a television to the nurses, a gift from a local darts league. He arrived holding three red carnations, a gift from his mother to the Sister who was in charge of the ward where she was treated following a recent fall, and was soon surrounded by nurses.

He received a gold wristwatch from the masters and boys of Wellington Road Secondary School; the presentation was made by the headmaster, Mr A. Gooch. 'Thanks a lot for this watch … I will always say I went to the best school in Cheshire,' Speakman replied. A plaque at the school commemorates the courage of its former pupil. Headed by the words FOR VALOUR, and flanked by The Black Watch badge and the school badge, the plaque reads:

> PRIVATE WILLIAM SPEAKMAN
> KOREA 4TH NOVEMBER 1951
>
> UNDER THE STRESS AND STRAIN OF
> THIS BATTLE, PRIVATE SPEAKMAN'S
> OUTSTANDING POWERS OF
> LEADERSHIP WERE REVEALED AND
> HE SO DOMINATED THE SITUATION
> THAT HE INSPIRED HIS COMRADES
> TO STAND FIRM AND FIGHT THE
> ENEMY TO A STANDSTILL.
>
> HIS GREAT GALLANTRY AND UTTER
> CONTEMPT FOR HIS OWN PERSONAL
> SAFETY WERE AN INSPIRATION TO
> ALL HIS COMRADES.
>
> A BOY OF THIS SCHOOL 1939–1941

When not being followed by the press and admirers seeking his attention, he spent his time visiting his friends who had been wounded in Korea. One of them, Stewart Craig, who was blinded in action, was surprised when Speakman gave him all the money he received from the BBC for his television appearance. Speakman didn't mention this to anyone and it was only discovered by chance later.

His fame went beyond Altrincham; he had become a national hero, albeit a reluctant one. For someone of his exceptional height and build he was remarkably shy and tried hard to avoid all the publicity surrounding his VC award. He was not a good public speaker and found such occasions difficult to handle, but sometimes even more difficult to refuse. A sympathetic article in *The Sunday Express* of 2 March 1952 summed up his predicament:

> For Speakman, the postman's knock has filled him with dread ever since he arrived home. Each day to his mother's house in Altrincham piles of letters have come. The writers invite him to football matches, darts matches, shows, bazaars and contests. Some say they would be honoured to have him there. Others say candidly that if he came he 'would attract a crowd'. Bill Speakman answers his mail at the rate of about ten letters a day … He usually replies, 'I'll come if I can make it.'

At the many events he did attend he was surrounded by people wanting to buy him drinks and shake his hand, and was expected to pose for photographs and make speeches. It was an ordeal for him. 'I'm a quiet bloke,' he said at the time, 'I like to oblige these folk. They mean well and they are working for charity. But I can't work miracles and they get angry with me.'

He felt that he was expected to be on display at all times as the Army's latest VC winner and this was a role in which he did not feel comfortable:

> I got the VC at a time in 1951 when rationing was on. Everyone was down in Altrincham before I came home to see the Queen. When I got the VC it seemed to take people's minds off other things … That period in the 1950s was a rather bleak period I think in the history of Britain, it was terribly bleak. After the war you heard older people say, 'Who won the bloody war?'

Eventually, it all became too much for him. In a frank interview with *The Sunday Express* of 2 March 1952 he explained his feelings:

Look … I'm just one of the lads. I've been made up to lance corporal and corporal and I've been busted for not behaving myself. I'm an ordinary man. I can't behave like one now. The Victoria Cross gives you pride. I'm a regular soldier and I'm happy as one. I want to do my job as well as I can. That's why I'm in the Army … like my father was.

The bad side to winning the Cross is that people make you into something like a freak. They won't let you be normal. And all the time they are watching you to see if you are getting above yourself. You have got to watch yourself.

Speakman just wanted to get away from it all and return to Korea to be back with his regiment, but the Army had other ideas regarding his future. General Miles had spoken of plans to place him on a leadership course, followed by promotion. In the meantime, the Army was content to display to the nation their latest VC recipient, but the effect this was having on Speakman does not appear to have been taken into account.

NOTES

(1)   Frederick James Erroll (1914–2000) was the Conservative MP for Altrincham and Sale from 1945 to 1964. On leaving Parliament, where he held many ministerial posts, he was raised to the peerage as 1st Baron Erroll of Hale.

(2)   The Handley Page Hastings was a troop carrier and freight transport aircraft in use by the RAF during the Korean War. It had a crew of five or six.

(3)   He did not serve long enough to qualify for the two Second World War medals (War Medal 1939–45 and Defence Medal) and qualified for the GSM only after he had served in Malaya 1953–56. In view of the note on his Army record in 1947, he may have been entitled to wear the War Medal 1939–45, or thought he was entitled. The ribbons were sewn on before Speakman was given the tunic, so it must have been assumed by whoever put them on that he was entitled to all of them. Speakman is insistent that he did not put the ribbons on himself: 'I remember now, I had three ribbons. You can't put ribbons on yourself. You can't walk around wearing ribbons you are not entitled to.' Mark Adkin, in his book *The Last Eleven? Winners of the Victoria Cross Since the Second World War*, suggests Speakman was 'cocking a snook at the authorities' by wearing the ribbons but it is clear Speakman had no idea about his medal entitlement and was given a uniform with ribbons

attached and told to wear it at the investiture. It appears that someone had made an educated guess in a hurry and made an error.

(4) The tartan was named after David Leslie, 3rd Earl of Leven, who raised the KOSB Regiment in 1689.

(5) HM The Queen has since conferred honours on over 400,000 people during her sixty-year reign.

(6) £75,000 in 1952 is the equivalent of £1,770,600 today. Speakman used this opportunity to secure help for a friend. He only agreed to present the cheque if the pools company would send £100 to Stewart Craig, a New Zealand soldier blinded in Korea.

POSTINGS

1952–1953

In early March 1952, Speakman was posted to the KOSB Regimental Depot at Berwick-upon-Tweed. He drilled with National Servicemen and it was planned that he would be promoted to lance corporal with the Regimental Police. He was not happy, though, and longed to return to Korea to be with his friends and escape the media. With no wife or girlfriend – although there were unsubstantiated claims in the newspapers by women who said they were 'waiting for him' – he felt he had no ties in England. One newspaper report stated that he had received forty offers of marriage during the few weeks he was on leave in Altrincham. After being at Berwick-upon-Tweed for less than a week he requested a transfer back to Korea.

Despite the Army's initial reluctance to return Speakman to his regiment in Korea, his frequent requests and the difficulties he was having with the press in England made the Army reconsider. Consequently, he was attached to FARELF (Far East Land Forces), which included British bases in Japan and Korea, from 13 March until 12 August 1952.

Private Speakman sailed from Liverpool in the troopship *Empire Halladale* on 12 March 1952. In contrast to his triumphant return home less than two months earlier, there were few people to see him leave, although his departure was noted in the local and national press. His mother, Mrs Hannah Houghton, was upset at the thought of her son returning to the war in Korea but accepted that it was his decision. Speakman disembarked in Japan on 21 April and rejoined 1st KOSB on active service in Korea, but did not rejoin B Company as he had wished. Nor was he involved in any further action against the enemy. Nevertheless, he was pleased to be back in the Korean hills again and told a reporter: 'It's wonderful to be back among all my chums. It was awful being chased around England as though I was a film star.' He told another reporter: 'I feel very happy to see the East again.'

A letter from Bill Speakman VC appeared in the *Altrincham, Hale and Bowdon Guardian* (Licensed by Newsquest Media Group) on 14 March, just after he had left the UK. In it he wrote:

> May I take this humble opportunity of thanking each and everyone for their many kindnesses and gifts, which I appreciate more than any words can mention.
>
> I should like particularly to thank their Worships the Mayor and Mayoress, Councillor and Mrs J.L. Warren; the aldermen and councillors of Altrincham Corporation, and all friends and organisations, including also the children of the district, who gave my mother, family and myself such a wonderful reception on my return home.
>
> There were, it will be understood, many invitations which I could not fulfil, much to my regret, but at the same time I would like to take this opportunity on behalf of my mother, family and myself to thank everybody concerned from the bottom of my heart.

On the same Readers' Letters page (Licensed by Newsquest Media Group) a reader calling himself 'Old Contemptible' noted that:

> After all the trumpeting and feasting, Private Speakman, this A1 soldier, has packed his bag and is off again to Korea ... If one could read his thoughts on the subject they would furnish food for reflection by the sensation mongers. Bill Speakman did what a good soldier always does – his duty – and he is content to leave it at that without any fuss.

Speakman felt more relaxed being back among his comrades in his battalion and spent some time visiting his friends. He was able to resume his Army career and on 24 April, shortly after arriving in Korea, he was promoted to lance corporal.

Despite their success on 4 November 1951, the Chinese were unable to follow this up with a decisive victory and a prolonged period of trench warfare ensued. Over the next few months 1st KOSB moved back and forth between the front line and reserve positions. Although there were no major battles, enemy shelling and patrols probing their defences continued to be a problem. Ceasefire talks, which had begun in July 1951, dragged on for two years while the war continued.

Field Marshal Lord Alexander, Defence Secretary, shaking hands with Lieutenant Colonel Tadman, June 1952. Major General Cassels is to Lord Alexander's left. (© *IWM BF 10727*)

Field Marshal Lord Alexander (1) visited Korea in June 1952. He had been appointed Minister of Defence earlier in the year and went to Korea to see conditions for himself. After a tour of the front line he watched US aircraft deliver a napalm attack on a Chinese-held hill. 'That should give the enemy something to think about,' he remarked. He was met at the 1st Commonwealth Division airstrip by a guard of honour from The King's Own Scottish Borderers, and spotted a tall soldier in the line up. 'Isn't this Speakman, the VC?' Lord Alexander asked the commanding officer, Lieutenant Colonel Tadman DSO. He then spoke with Speakman, telling him that he 'did a magnificent job'.

Private Peter Fisher of the 1st Battalion, King's Shropshire Light Infantry recalls meeting Bill Speakman in Korea (2):

Our battalion marched into Britannia Barracks and onto the large parade ground there. We were just mingling around waiting to be shown where the barrack rooms were. One of my mates was feeling unwell so I was carrying his rifle and his small pack beside my own kitbag, and somebody else was carrying his kitbag. Then I heard a voice boom out: 'Where's that bloke with two rifles?'

Newspaper reporting Speakman's return to Korea. Speakman is on the right. (Bill Speakman VC)

The next thing I knew there was a hand on my shoulder. When I looked round I saw the hand was enormous – it must have belonged to a giant. And when I looked round and up it *was* a giant. Six foot six, enormous!

'Have a drink,' he said and thrust a bottle of beer in my hand. Whether he thought I had two rifles because I meant real business I don't know, but that was it. 'Have a drink,' he said and thrust a bottle of beer in my hand and then walked off. Immediately everyone was saying, 'That's Bill Speakman, Bill Speakman VC.' It was an interesting experience meeting him but I wasn't quite as brave as he thought I was. I was only carrying two rifles as my mate was unwell.

Peter Fisher and fellow Korean War veteran Patrick Lohan wrote a book, *Korean War: 25 June 1950 – 27 July 1953*, which included detailed lists of casualties and a history of the war as reported by *The Times*.

In early August 1952, 1st KOSB prepared to leave Korea having completed sixteen months of active service – although the last few months had been fairly uneventful. The battalion spent five days in Britannia Staging Camp, some 30 miles south of the divisional area, before departing on an uncomfortable journey by train to Pusan ready for the next posting. The battalion embarked at Pusan on 12 August 1952 in HM Troopship *Halladale*. The South Korean Minister of

Speakman outside a
bunker. (*KOSB Museum*)

Speakman examining
the graves of fallen
KOSB comrades at Pusan
on 12 August 1952.
(© *IWM MH31495*)

Defence and his staff waved the battalion farewell and a South Korean Navy Band played as the troopship left port. Although The KOSB had finished its tour of duty and was now leaving Korea, the war continued for almost another year – a ceasefire was eventually agreed on 27 July 1953. Chinese/North Korean and United Nations Forces each withdrew 2 kilometres from the ceasefire line to create a 4-kilometre-wide Demilitarised Zone (DMZ).

After the armistice, both sides exchanged prisoners. Private Patrick Lydon, RNF attached to C Company KOSB, who had refused to fight was taken prisoner of war by the Chinese. He was released on 7 August 1953 and arrested on his way home to the UK (See Appendix III). Private John Cowell, B Company KOSB, who was captured after the fierce fight for Hill 217, was released from captivity on 8 August (See Chapter 4).

South Korea went through an amazing transformation in the next sixty years, from aid recipient to aid donor, and now has one of the strongest economies in the region. Its GDP today is higher than many European countries. North Korea, however, under its isolationist communist regime, has stagnated and is one of the world's poorest countries. The communist-run economy is in a state of collapse; three-quarters of the factories are idle and there are virtually no cars on the road. Because of power shortages, electricity is cut off in most of the capital, Pyongyang, at night. It is estimated that in the 1990s, up to 2.5 million North Koreans died of cold and starvation. There is no medicine and children suffer from TB, polio and tetanus - diseases which have been eradicated in South Korea.

The Battle Honours *Kowang-San* and *Korea 1951–52* (Emblazoned on the Queen's Colour) and *Maryang-San* (Accredited Battle Honour) were later awarded to The King's Own Scottish Borderers. (Many Australians felt bitter about 1st KOSB receiving these battle honours as they believed that 3rd RAR had captured Kowang-san and the Borderers had failed to hold Maryang-san.) Lance Corporal Speakman was posted to Hong Kong with his battalion on 12 August 1952, and disembarked there on 16 August. The battalion stayed in Hong Kong, then still a British colony, for three months. At 6ft 6in tall, Speakman towered over the men in his own battalion, so in Hong Kong he must have seemed like a giant to the locals. He soon discovered that his size made him stand out in a crowd.

The VC ribbon he wore and his notoriety meant that he was even more conspicuous, and he found it difficult to avoid the wrong sort of attention. Like most young men of his age (he was 24 when he was posted to Hong Kong) he socialised in the many local bars, where he quickly gained a reputation, however unfairly, for getting into brawls. He was not a natural trouble-maker but somehow trouble always seemed to find him.

Speakman lost his lance corporal's stripe as a result of his often rebellious behaviour. On 2 September he went AWOL for over ten hours and consequently was demoted, confined to barracks for ten days and forfeited one day's pay. He was again in trouble at the end of the month when he went AWOL for three days and fourteen hours between 24 and 28 September. At the same time, he was improperly dressed, and was not wearing his headdress or waist belt. Private Speakman was sentenced to twenty-eight days' detention and forfeited four days' pay. Throughout his Army career, Speakman had always admitted his guilt when appearing before his commanding officer; he never made excuses, blamed others or tried to use his VC to get him out of trouble. This must have earned him a certain amount of grudging respect from his commanding officer.

Although in the same battalion as Second Lieutenant Purves, Speakman didn't know him well. As he recalls:

You could be in a company of the line and never know anybody from another company because that was the way it was. You couldn't move around. But we knew that what he did was absolutely fantastic. It was unheard of for a National Serviceman and a second lieutenant to get the DSO. He was a quiet guy and didn't stay to become a regular. He did his National Service and went back to banking.

Sir William Purves remembers Speakman (3):

I met Bill on a number of occasions. He was a great chap in the line but, sadly, couldn't handle it out of the line. People took advantage of him. He would go into a pub and somebody would say, 'Oh, you're Bill Speakman.' He's a great big man, six foot eight or something, you couldn't mistake him and people would say, 'Come on, Bill, I'll give you a drink' and, of course, very often they didn't pay for the drink and Bill would have one too many and he would get into all sorts of trouble. So Bill was promoted and then bust and then promoted again.

He missed the boat in Hong Kong, I remember. That would have been very embarrassing for the Army so somebody or other found them in a bar in Kowloon and got them out and got them into a boat and went careering down the harbour and caught up with the troopship and put him on board.

Shortly before the battalion was due to leave for the UK on 14 November, Speakman went AWOL. He was missing from 0100 hours on 13 November until 1015 hours on 14 November – a period of one day, nine hours and fifteen minutes. As a result, he was sentenced to twenty-eight days' detention and forfeited two days' pay. He admits that he deliberately went AWOL and was not just unavoidably detained in a bar:

> We were going home then but I didn't want to leave Hong Kong. I had just had an operation on my foot, to the side of my heel, and didn't want to go back to the UK. So I just went AWOL. I wanted to miss the boat and see it sail out. All of a sudden I was grabbed and I had to do jack on the troopship cleaning out the refrigerators.

The newspapers of the time recorded that his twenty-eight days in detention was spent 'spud bashing' in the galley of the *Devonshire,* which was homeward bound with troops and families from the Far East. When the *Devonshire* reached Port Said, the CO of the KOSB, Lieutenant Colonel Tadman, who issued the punishment, said, 'Speakman went absent for thirty-three hours and fifteen minutes at Hong Kong and turned up at the quayside just before the ship sailed. Speakman had apparently found the bright lights of Hong Kong too bright to resist and felt they deserved more of his time.'

1st Battalion KOSB returned to the UK on 19 December 1952, in time for Christmas with families. The troopship *Devonshire* was met at Liverpool by the Duchess of Gloucester, who was colonel-in-chief of the regiment. After inspecting the combined KOSB bands, accompanied by Major General E.G. Miles, colonel of the regiment, the Duchess boarded the ship. She made a short speech of welcome to the troops, who had been unable to dock for two days because of gale-force winds, and then spoke to several of the recipients of gallantry awards in Korea. Bill Speakman VC, returning from his second tour of duty in Korea, was one of the men presented to her.

On its return to the UK, 1st KOSB received a formal message from HRH The Duchess of Gloucester in which she welcomed the battalion home, congratulated it on its admirable record in Korea and thanked everyone for their loyal service.

Less than a week after returning to the UK, Speakman was granted Korean service leave from 24 December 1952 to 4 January 1953. His battalion was stationed at Shorncliffe, near Folkestone, after returning to the UK and in

March moved to Ballykinlar, Northern Ireland. The battalion remained in Ulster until August 1955, when it sailed for the Far East and did not take part in the Queen's Coronation. The Queen was crowned on 2 June 1953 and Speakman, together with all living Victoria Cross recipients, was awarded the 1953 Coronation Medal.

Bill Speakman's service with the Army expired soon after the battalion returned home. He had joined as a 17-year-old in August 1945 and after nearly seven and a half years thought it was time to try something new. One newspaper, in January 1953, reported that Speakman was unsure about whether to leave the Army and would decide within a fortnight if he wanted to remain in the Army or seek a civilian job.

Another article noted that the Deputy Mayor of Altrincham had presented him with a bank book in which £558 13s, given by the town's people, was credited to his account. He put the money, which would be the equivalent of £13,200 today, into a savings account. Whenever he went home on leave he would take some of it out, but most of it remained in the bank. 'That came in handy in later years as I still had a while to go in the Army,' he later explained. 'So the money stayed there and collected a bit of interest'.

Despite some reports to the contrary, he decided to remain in the Army. On 27 February 1953 he extended his service to twelve years with the colours, with a new expiry date of 9 August 1957. Having spent much of his young adulthood in the Army, he would have missed the reassuring routine of Army life and all his friends, with whom he had shared good times and bad. Finding a job in which he felt comfortable would not have proved easy; after the excitement of active service in Korea, any job would have seemed an anti-climax. He was granted an extension bounty of £50 for remaining in the Army.

Speakman told a regional newspaper in July 1953 that 'when I was at home at Altrincham I decided to get out of the Army, but I just couldn't find a job which really appealed to me'.

In the same month, an armistice was signed in Korea but this provided only a brief respite for the overstretched British Army. Before the last troops left the peninsular in July 1957, a series of conflicts ensued, all aimed at undermining the last vestiges of British colonialism. British troops undertook counter-insurgency campaigning in Kenya (1952–60), Cyprus (1955–60) and ill-fated operations in Suez (1956). Bill Speakman did not participate in any of these 'small wars' although he served in Malaya during 'The Emergency'.

Speakman being
interviewed
in Berlin. (*Bill
Speakman VC*)

He applied for a transfer to the Special Air Service (SAS), an elite unit
established during the Second World War, and was permanently attached
to the SAS Regiment in April 1953. He was taken on the strength of the
Airborne Forces Depot on 6 April and then struck off the strength of the
depot on 16 June when he proceeded to Far East Land Forces (FARELF).
After selection in Wales and initial training in Aldershot, he was sent
to Malaya:

> I applied for the SAS, was accepted, did my training in Wales and then I went
> to Malaya. The SAS, the jungle, Malaya; that was a lovely time, parachuting
> and all that.

146

THE SPECIAL AIR SERVICE (SAS)

The Special Air Service (SAS) had its origins in the small force raised by Captain (later Colonel) David Stirling in July 1941 to carry out raids on Rommel's army in the North African desert. This new unit, together with the Long Range Desert Group (LRDG), carried out daring raids on German airfields, destroying many aircraft. They later served in Italy and north-west Europe.

The regiment was disbanded in 1946 but was reconstituted as 21st Special Air Service Regiment (Artists' Rifles), a Territorial Army unit, the following year. In 1950, Lieutenant Colonel 'Mad Mike' Calvert formed the Malayan Scouts, recruiting from existing reservists and volunteers from the Far East and Rhodesia, for jungle operations in Malaya. In 1952, the Malayan Scouts were renamed 22nd Special Air Service.

After Malaya the SAS saw action in Aden, Radfan, Oman and Borneo. The regiment specialises in counter-insurgency and operating behind enemy lines and was involved in numerous reconnaissance activities, including the Falklands Conflict, the Gulf War of 1991 and in Afghanistan. The regimental motto is: WHO DARES WINS.

NOTES

(1)   Field Marshal Harold Alexander, 1st Earl Alexander of Tunis, was born in 1891 and joined the Army in 1911. He served with distinction in both World Wars and in 1942–43 was Commander-in-Chief of Middle East Command, playing a vital part in winning the Desert War. In 1952 he was created Earl Alexander of Tunis and in the same year became Minister of Defence, a position he held until 1954, when he retired from politics. He died in 1969, aged 77.

(2)   Interview with authors, 17 July 2008.

(3)   Extract from a tape (ref: 20471) held at the Imperial War Museum Sound Archive and reproduced with permission of the Imperial War Museum.

MALAYA
1953–1955

Speakman left the UK for Singapore to join his new regiment on 17 June 1953 and disembarked on 17 July. A regional newspaper reported on 18 July 1953 that Speakman 'was among 1,600 British troops who arrived at Singapore yesterday to join the Malayan campaign'. At Singapore, he attended a basic parachute course, in which he qualified, at Changi from 24 August to 19 September 1953. Some of his training took place in Sarawak, as Speakman recalls:

> During my training we were jumping over Sarawak – it was tough. I was the last in a stick of parachutists, on the final jump to get my wings. It was 'One, two out'. The PGI [Para-Glider Infantry] instructor was tapping us, saying, 'Go, go, go.' I got to the end and the plane lurched and threw me back. The PGI guy said, 'Don't jump, stop.' I said. 'Stuff you' and was out the door but when I was going out I straightened up, which I shouldn't have done. There was a red light and a green light and I smashed them. I staggered but went straight out of the door. I shook my head a bit, opened my canopy and heard it snap. By that time I was miles from the DZ [Drop Zone] so had to pull hard on the chute to get down to the DZ. There are storm drains out there, square and very deep, but I managed to avoid going into one of those. I was thinking: 'Thank God, I have won my wings.'
>
> But I was severely reprimanded when I got back. The PGI said, 'We would have gone round for you.' I said, 'No you wouldn't. So I jumped.' He said I should never do that again. I said, 'All right, I swear,' but I got my wings! A couple of days later I met an RAF mechanic who told me he was the aircraft mechanic for the plane I jumped from and he said they were going to charge me for busting the lights I hit on the way out. Fortunately, he was joking!

Speakman's ill-disciplined habits caught up with him in Malaya. Even before he had finished his parachute course at Changi, Singapore, in September 1953, he

Speakman, wearing SAS cap and shoulder badges in June 1953. (*Bill Speakman VC*)

was confined to barracks for fourteen days for being in an 'out of bounds' area in Singapore and failing to comply with an order.

When Speakman joined the SAS he was the most recent VC recipient and was still subject to a great deal of media interest. One newspaper published a photograph of him wearing his paratrooper helmet with a 'gung-ho' write-up describing him as 'a recruit whose name spells trouble for Red bandits in Malaya – Big Bill Speakman VC, who is out of his demob suit and back in the Army again' (1). By the time he arrived in Malaya the counter-insurgency campaign had just entered its sixth year.

Malaya became a British colony in 1824 when Holland exchanged its outposts there for British recognition of Dutch rule over the territories that now form Indonesia. Approximately 80 per cent of Malaya, including the mountainous areas, was covered with jungle. The development of the tin industry in the late nineteenth century resulted in large-scale immigration, mainly from China, and the introduction of rubber plantations saw a further influx of immigrants from India and China. Production was so high that in 1939, Malaya produced more than 50 per cent of the world's tin and 40 per cent of its rubber.

For almost 120 years the Malay States were ruled as British colonies, but the situation changed abruptly during the Second World War. Because of the increasing threat of Japan's naval power, Britain built a large naval base at Singapore, but it was never anticipated that Japanese forces would attack Malaya overland from the north. After Malaya was invaded in December 1941, Singapore was forced into a humiliating surrender to the Japanese in February 1942. While the Japanese invaders regarded themselves as liberators of the Malays, they treated the Chinese population with brutality. The Chinese-controlled Malayan Communist Party led the resistance against the Japanese and a great many Malays were also killed by the Chinese communists.

After the war, the Malayan Communist Party (MCP) planned to seize power in Malaya. The communist guerrillas who had fought the Japanese, with British arms and support, turned their attention towards ending Britain's colonial rule and establishing a communist state. Previous campaigns of civil unrest and strikes had not been successful in forcing Britain to include the MCP in any future government. The communist terrorists (CTs), calling themselves the Malayan Peoples' Liberation Army, returned to the jungle and carried out a campaign of killing rubber plantation owners and tin miners and attacking police stations to destabilise the country.

To counter this threat, troops were deployed to Malaya – the Brigade of Gurkhas and the Malayan Scouts being among the first to arrive. Contrary to some reports, Speakman was never a member of the Malayan Scouts. The Scouts arrived in Malaya fairly early in the conflict, before the arrival of Speakman and the SAS. In 1952 the Malayan Scouts became 22nd SAS Regiment; the regiment remained in Malaya until the end of 1958.

The CTs avoided major battles with the Army and preferred 'hit and run' raids, after which they retreated to their bases in the jungle. Their aim was to make the government abandon the countryside and retreat into the large towns. This unofficial war was known as 'The Emergency' and lasted for twelve years from the first terrorist killings in June 1948. In the first few years the Army was merely reacting to CT attacks and protecting the plantations and tin mines, while becoming used to the extreme heat and humidity of the jungle. The CTs did not have the long supply chain endured by the British Army and took their supplies from the local villagers.

A policy of depriving the terrorists of food and forcing them out of the jungle was implemented in 1951. This included the forced resettlement of all Chinese civilians, many of whom had been assisting the CTs, into 'New Villages' where they could be guarded and protected. The policy was devised by Lieutenant General Sir Harold Briggs, then Director of Operations, and was continued by General Sir Gerald Templer when he was appointed British High Commissioner and Director of Operations in 1952. Army, civilian police and intelligence services efforts were also reorganised to provide an integrated war on the CTs. British Army units were following the CTs into the jungle and ambushing them, with increasing success. It was not always easy to recognise the communist guerrillas (CTs) in the undergrowth, as Speakman remembers:

> You couldn't identify them because they were dressed as civilians, they were scruffy. These people had been under Japanese domination for a long time and they knew how to fight guerrilla warfare. In the SAS we had special tactics and we were trained by ex-rubber tappers and tin miners who showed us the way. We also had Sakai trackers who knew paths you would never recognise, so we would not get lost. To them it was like a big main road. Because we looked after them they would come back with news of CTs in the area and we would go out. We would get off a first burst and then they would disappear; they would not stand up and fight. We looked after the local people because without them we would have had a tougher job. We dropped big bags of rice and huge amounts of tinned corned beef.

The SAS made contact with the indigenous groups and gained their support. As part of the regiment's 'hearts and minds' policy, they provided the Sakai tribe with basic medical and construction needs and some of the tribesmen were employed as trackers. Iban tribesmen from Borneo were also brought

Speakman's Hill.
(*Bill Speakman VC*)

in because of their excellent tracking skills. Wherever possible, the bodies of killed CTs were taken back to base for identification. The Iban trackers were headhunters, as Speakman discovered, and had other ideas:

> They had been headhunters for thousands of years. Whenever the enemy were killed in an ambush all the Iban wanted were the heads, although we never actually saw this. For a while I lived in an Iban long house, with a very big pointed palm thatched roof, a fire inside and the smoke came out of a little hole in the roof. I was lying there one night and someone said: 'Look there; there are heads up there. They are heads, they are shrunk!' The shrunken heads had been pitched high on a stick. No one at the time knew how they shrank them.

Most of the jungle warfare skills employed by the SAS had to be learnt quickly. Navigation through the jungle was difficult as there were no roads and the dense vegetation meant that visibility was often no more than a few yards. Trees grew to about 200ft, forming a thick canopy, and the undergrowth which grew to about 10ft was impenetrable. The jungle canopy was so thick that the sun was seldom seen. SAS patrols, often no more than four men, avoided cutting through the undergrowth wherever possible as to do so might make their presence known to the enemy. Instead, they preferred to follow animal tracks or the many rivers. At the end of the day, it was not unusual to be covered in leeches. The SAS worked deep in the jungle, following the terrorists and killing them in ambushes, and established forts which could be resupplied by air. The British Army advanced with fixed bayonets, but not in the jungle, as Speakman recalls:

> In the jungle they even invested in a short version of the .303 rifle with a short bayonet so you could swing it round and drop the enemy. The trees used to get in the way of the rifle so the bayonet was not practical, but it is ideal for trench warfare.

The SAS carried out parachute drops directly into the jungle until this was discontinued in favour of using helicopters. High winds made jungle parachute jumps very dangerous and paratroopers sometimes found themselves stuck on the dense canopy of giant trees. They also risked breaking arms or legs, or being killed.

Lieutenant J.M. 'Johnny' Cooper, in charge of 8 Troop, B Squadron SAS, broke an arm jumping into the jungle and crash-landed through the jungle canopy, finally coming to rest dangling by his parachute from a tall tree. He was rescued by the rest of his troop and Freddie Brunton, the medical officer, scaled a nearby tree to secure a rope to lower him to safety (Brunton was awarded the MBE for his part in the rescue). After a period in hospital, Cooper was promoted to captain and given command of C Squadron. He was one of the original founders of the SAS when it was established during the Second World War. Bill Speakman served in C Squadron of SAS, when it was commanded by Captain Johnny Cooper. He still remembers Cooper with great affection:

> When I joined the SAS, Johnny was one of the first people I met. He said, 'Bill, you are here. Settle down now that you have done all your training.' He just welcomed me to the regiment. From then on it was just SAS training. Johnny Cooper was a guy who was always there for you, because he was that sort of man.

JOHN MURDOCH COOPER MBE DCM

John Murdoch Cooper MBE DCM, one of the founders of the SAS Regiment, was born in June 1922. He joined the Scots Guards in 1940 and volunteered for the Special Air Service when it was being set up by Captain David Stirling in 1941. He was one of the first to join the new unit and served in the Western Desert, where he received the DCM, and later fought in France and Germany.

After the Second World War the SAS was disbanded and Cooper adjusted to civilian life. He rejoined the SAS when it was re-formed and served with distinction in Malaya and Oman. He retired from the Army in 1962 and for several years worked for the Sultan of Oman's Armed Forces, achieving the rank of lieutenant colonel. Cooper published his memoirs, *One of the Originals*, in 1991 and died in July 2002, aged 80.

In October 1953, Cooper led his squadron into the mountains of Pahang to establish a fort deep in the jungle. After erecting screens to prevent any CTs observing their work, the squadron began felling trees and clearing the area. There was insufficient space for a landing strip so a helicopter landing area was prepared. By February 1954 Cooper's squadron had completed its task of building Fort Brooke, named after the commander of 22 SAS.

It was standard procedure to rotate squadrons after two–three months, but for this mission Cooper and his men spent 122 days in the jungle. Many men suffered from fever but the only fatalities were due to enemy action. On 26 November 1953, two SAS men on a patrol were killed in a terrorist ambush. The other members of the patrol returned fire but the CTs escaped deeper into the jungle. When the news was received at Fort Brooke, Speakman volunteered immediately to go into the terrorist-occupied jungle to recover the bodies so they could be flown out for a proper burial. He was not deterred by the fact that he did not have the right size jungle boots and that his feet were septic after being cut to ribbons on a previous patrol. He was laid up, doing administration duties, at the time but said to Captain Cooper, 'I'll go, sir, because I think I know where they are.'

With other SAS volunteers, he made two separate journeys into the jungle and located the bodies of Corporal K.B. 'Digger' Bancroft and Trooper F.W. Wilkins and recovered them one at a time. The bodies were brought back to camp on a bamboo pole, with Speakman taking most of the weight. The area where Speakman came out of the jungle with the bodies was called Speakman's Hill after him as he had organised such an impressive rescue party. (See Prologue for details of the two rescues.)

The two dead SAS men were flown out by Royal Navy helicopter and buried in Cheras Road Christian Cemetery, Military Annex, Kuala Lumpur. Trooper Wilkins was aged 20 and had previously served in the Army Catering Corps. Corporal 'Digger' Bancroft had served in the SAS during the Second World War, although his parent unit was the East Surrey Regiment. 'He was one of Stirling's men, like Johnny Cooper,' says Speakman. 'He was dropped behind enemy lines in France and helped place agents by submarine. Digger had survived France, Italy, North Africa, the LRDG, and then to Malaya where he was killed.'

On returning to base, Captain Cooper received a message from his commanding officer, Lieutenant Colonel Oliver Brooke. He said, 'Please convey to all ranks of your squadron my very hearty congratulations and thanks on a really splendid effort. C Squadron has acquitted itself extremely well over this long period from October to February and you should all be very proud.'

Trooper Speakman, with the rest of C Squadron, penetrated deep into uncharted parts of the country:

At times we were going high in the mountains, so high we went in where no one had been before. When you looked at the map it was all jungle and there was a blank space because no one had ever been there. When we got up there it was choking; it was eerie. There were lots of orchids growing there.

We were following in the footsteps of [Lieutenant Colonel] Freddie Chapman. He went into the jungle before the war and fought throughout the Japanese occupation. He was an outstanding guerrilla warfare soldier.

Even though Bill Speakman was overseas he was not forgotten at home. *The Daily Mirror*, at the time Britain's largest selling newspaper, ran a poll of teenagers in December 1953 to find out who they would like as an escort on a special evening. The Duke of Edinburgh came top of the poll followed by Dirk Bogarde and Max Bygraves in third place. Other contenders included ex-King Farouk, Bill Speakman VC, Sir Edmund Hilary and Sir Malcolm Sargent.

Back in Singapore, Speakman was sentenced, on 14 June 1954, to twenty-eight days detention by the commanding officer at Changi for 'creating a disturbance' on 10 June. There are no further details of the offence in his Army records but it is known from other sources that he was often encouraged by troublemakers to misbehave. This sometimes meant taking on the Regimental Police as they cleared the bars after the battalion had been paid.

After his previous disciplinary offences, this would appear to have been the last straw for the SAS. He was released from detention, with two day's remission, on 9 July, and on the same day struck off the strength of the regiment. He had served with the SAS in Malaya for just under a year. The following day he was taken on the strength of the 1st Battalion Royal Scots Fusiliers (1st RSF), the nearest Scottish regiment, and attached to D Company. (His former regiment, The King's Own Scottish Borderers, was in Northern Ireland at the time, later moving to Singapore.)

Speakman remembers the change of regiment slightly differently:

> I was seconded to the Royal Scots Fusiliers. I was very ill for a while – I nearly died with cerebral malaria. By that time things had gone on and I still had time to finish, so I stayed with the RSF until I rejoined the KOSB. That was a happy time as well because they were also a Lowland brigade regiment who wore trews. They treated me very well.

A 1st RSF platoon commander, writing home in August 1954, remarked that 'Speakman VC, having been flung out of the SAS, has elected to join us. He was zoomed off to D Company where, according to the latest reports, he is once more in the guardroom.' Another 1st RSF soldier remembers returning to his barracks at RAF Butterworth one day 'to find a very tall soldier lying on a cot reading a comic. He was longer than the cot and turned out to be Bill Speakman VC. He had finished a tour with 22 SAS and, as was the custom, had been posted to the nearest Scottish Infantry Battalion (1 RSF).'

Moving to a new regiment did not necessarily mean a new responsible attitude. Speakman was found in an 'out of bounds' area, after going AWOL for two and a half hours, on the night of 10 November 1954 and forfeited ten days' pay.

Like every other off duty soldier, Speakman enjoyed socialising in the local bars. He never drank on duty but off duty he enjoyed a few drinks. 'I never touched spirits,' he says. 'It was always a pint.' In today's parlance, he worked hard and played hard.

He was certainly not unique in this, but unlike other servicemen he could not expect any privacy, even when off duty. A soldier from a different regiment, for example, records seeing him leaving the NAAFI bar in Singapore, worse for drink, clutching the balustrade as he made his way down the steps. He was famous and everyone knew his name. The Victoria Cross had turned him into a celebrity and he was on display all the time. This was the disadvantage of fame, as Speakman discovered.

Colonel Michael Hickey served with the Army Air Corps in Malaya 1953–54 and recalls meeting Bill Speakman (2):

Flying at night was something I personally greatly enjoyed. I remember one particular evening, it sticks in my mind, that I arrived at 3,000ft over the airstrip at Kroh just as dark was falling. Down below I could see the camp with the Royal Scots Fusiliers in it. I could see that someone had very kindly lit a flare path for me on the airstrip which was in total darkness. Yet from the height I was, the sun was just setting down behind Penang Island, 50 miles to the west in a massive blaze of glory. And just out of sheer high spirits I looped and aerobated and did all the things you're not supposed to do with an Auster (3), out of sheer high spirits, before going down to land in the dark on the flare path to be received by Corporal Speakman VC whose job was to man the airstrip and provide me with cans of fuel.

He'd won his VC in Korea several years before and had drifted from regiment to regiment including the SAS, very briefly, and had landed up with the Regimental Police of the Royal Scots Fusiliers at Kroh and we got on famously. He was an enormous man and he could refuel my Auster without standing on a pair of steps by just holding a four gallon can in his mighty arms and pouring it through the funnel into the wing tank.

I long remember my association with Bill Speakman, who I last saw some years ago as a Chelsea Pensioner with a white beard. But he cropped up several other times in my career thereafter and we were always very glad to see each other. He was a gentle giant, a man who was easily prevailed upon by the 'bad hats' in the unit to misbehave.

But he was, as I said, an amiable man and had been an exceptionally brave one in Korea and it was very sad that ultimately he had to sell his VC. The one that he wore on parade at Chelsea was a replica.

COLONEL MICHAEL HICKEY

Michael Hickey was born in 1929. After being called up for National Service in 1947 he decided to make the Army his career. He attended the Royal Military College, Sandhurst and was commissioned into the Royal Army Service Corps in 1949. He served with the RASC in Korea 1950–51 and was seconded to the Glider Pilot Regiment in 1952. Hickey was attached to 656 Squadron Army Air Corps in Malaya 1953–54, where he flew Austers and also helped supply the SAS in jungle operations. He saw active service at Suez in 1956, and was transferred to the Army Air Corps in 1960.

After holding a number of operational and staff appointments in Britain and overseas, he retired with the rank of colonel in 1981. His final appointment was to the general staff of the MoD. In retirement he has become a successful writer and historian. Colonel Hickey is President of the Wessex branch of the Korean War Veterans Association.

Speakman recalls meeting Michael Hickey and refuelling aircraft at Kroh:

They landed at Kroh, a listening post right on the Thai border. I was so interested in flying, I said, 'I'm in charge of your planes.' Colonel Hickey was a great guy, I thought. He got peppered once or twice from the Indonesian side. I looked after his plane for him, refuelled it, and sometimes went on flying trips. That's when I said, 'I am going to learn to fly.'

On 4 May 1955, Speakman was again promoted to acting lance corporal and on 3 July promoted to acting corporal, before reverting to his previous rank of acting lance corporal two months later on 27 September.

The King's Own Scottish Borderers sailed from Belfast for the Far East on 25 August 1955, arriving in Malaya via Singapore. Later that year, Speakman requested a transfer back to his former regiment. 'I had to serve for three years', he explains. 'So I did my time and having done my three years I rejoined the regiment.' He would appear to have been attached to the KOSB as he was not officially taken on the strength of that regiment, although he retained his acting rank of lance corporal until after he returned to the UK in May 1956. On 11 December 1955 his Army file recorded that he 'sustained injuries of a trivial nature on duty – not to blame', without specifying the nature of the injuries. At the end of the year 1st KOSB received training in jungle warfare at a training centre in East Johore.

Lance Corporal Bill Speakman married Rachel Ann York Snitch, a private in the Women's Royal Army Corps, at St George's Garrison Church, Singapore on 31 December 1955. The couple had met at a dance in Singapore, when Rachel was working at the Singapore Garrison. Speakman was 28 at the time and Rachel was 22. Bill Speakman had been awarded his VC for fighting the Chinese and, ironically, Rachel's grandmother was Chinese:

> We met at a dance. She shared the same things as me and was a very intelligent girl. She was also into amateur dramatics. Rachel's grandmother was Chinese and Rachel had this ability to relate to the Chinese community although she could not speak Chinese – she didn't even look Chinese. Her grandfather was a missionary named Parker, who worked for the China Inland Mission.
>
> All the missionaries married locally to strengthen the local bond because they were converting them to Christianity. Parker met and married a Chinese woman, who was Rachel's grandmother and they had a daughter named Grace. Grace, who was half Chinese, met and married an Englishman named Eric Snitch and they had Rachel. The Chinese later chased all the missionaries out of China. I didn't like Eric very much as he was unsociable, but he was clever. He was an inventor and when there was no electricity during the war, Eric always had light in his house as he had his own generator. He used to build steam rollers out of motor bits in his spare time and he even gave me one of his motorbikes.

Speakman's marriage ended in divorce sixteen years later, but during their happier years together he and Rachel raised six children – three sons and three daughters: Colin William (1956), Jane Rachel (1958), Susan Helen (1959), Helen Rachael (1963), David William (1964) and Casper (1967).

NOTES

(1) At the time there were incorrect reports in the press that Speakman had left the Army but later rejoined.

(2) Extract from a tape (ref: 18732) held at the Imperial War Museum Sound Archive and reproduced with the permission of Colonel Hickey.

(3) An Auster is a single-engine light liaison/observation aircraft.

UK, GERMANY, MIDDLE/FAR EAST
1956–1968

'The Emergency' continued in Malaya, with 1st KOSB still involved in jungle operations and anti-terrorist patrols. In April 1956, the battalion moved to Selarang Barracks in Singapore to support the civil authorities in anticipation of threatened disturbances, which did not materialise. Following this, the Borderers moved to Johore on anti-terrorist operations in June.

Speakman did not accompany the battalion to Johore. He returned to the UK, embarking at Singapore on 5 May 1956 and disembarking on 26 May. Smiling at the cameras, Lance Corporal and Mrs Speakman were pictured in *The Evening News* just after they had arrived at Southampton on the troopship *Asturias*. He returned from Malaya ahead of the battalion as he and another NCO had been assigned recruiting jobs – Speakman had the Lowland regiments and the other NCO was responsible for the Highland regiments. He was taken on the strength of the permanent staff of The King's Own Scottish Borderers on 30 June – he had previously been attached to the KOSB from the Royal Scots Fusiliers.

The 1st Battalion KOSB remained in the Far East until October 1958, when it returned to the UK. The Malayan 'Emergency' officially ended on 31 July 1960, although the Malayan Federation was granted independence on 31 August 1957.

Marriage and family life had a stabilising effect on Speakman and provided a focus for him and, for a while at least, he managed to steer clear of the problems he encountered in the wild days of his youth. His first child, Colin, was born in Scotland in October 1956.

In response to the threat from the USSR during the Cold War, the government had established the Civil Defence Corps (CDC) in 1948. The new corps continued the excellent civil defence work undertaken by various organisations during the Second World War, but now took into account the problems posed by nuclear, biological and chemical warfare. The Central Office of Information made a number of CDC recruiting films for showing in cinemas, and in 1956 Lance Corporal Bill Speakman VC appeared in a two-minute black and white film.

In this recruiting appeal he read from a prepared statement in a studio, while film inserts showed current civil defence training, and ARP wardens and firemen at work during the Blitz. Speakman emphasised the need for prior training to help minimise casualties in a nuclear war. 'Civil defence', he said, 'is just as essential a part of our defence system as the armed forces, and in the event of war, trained members of the civil defence force would be working hand in hand with the armed forces'. The CDC was wound up in 1968, but a copy of this film is held by the Imperial War Museum.

The centenary of the Victoria Cross was celebrated in 1956. It had been founded by Royal Warrant on 29 January 1856 to be awarded to officers and other ranks of the Navy and Army who, serving in the presence of an enemy, should have 'performed some signal act of valour or devotion to their country'. There were various events and celebrations to mark the occasion, including the Victoria Cross Centenary Exhibition at Marlborough House, London from 15 June to 17 July, a thanksgiving service in Westminster Abbey on 25 June and a tea party for VC recipients in Westminster Hall the same day. The highlight of the celebrations was a parade in Hyde Park on 26 June 1956, when HM The Queen reviewed the assembled VC recipients.

The Victoria Cross Association was formed the same month with HM The Queen as the Association's Patron. Brigadier The Rt Hon Sir John Smyth VC MC MP became the chairman, and Sir Winston Churchill became the president. It was decided to hold biennial reunions, which would also include a memorial service at St Martin-in-the-Fields, London. Membership was extended later to holders of the George Cross.

Speakman was one of the approximately 300 VC holders, under the command of the senior VC, General Lord Freyberg VC, to be reviewed by HM The Queen in Hyde Park on 26 June 1956. The date was significant as the first VC investiture had been held in Hyde Park exactly ninety-nine years earlier.

Lance Corporal Speakman got the chance to meet Lieutenant Colonel James Carne VC DSO of the Gloucestershire Regiment, the only other surviving Korean War VC recipient. These two military legends were photographed at Wellington Barracks shaking hands before the parade and the photograph was published on the front page of the *Daily Telegraph* the following day. Speakman was also photographed standing next to James Woods VC, who was awarded his

Lance Corporal Bill Speakman VC shakes hands with fellow Korean VC recipient Lieutenant Colonel James Carne VC DSO outside Wellington Barracks, London during the VC centenary celebrations in June 1956. (*Bill Speakman VC*)

Speakman's invitation to the 1956 VC Centenary celebrations. (*KOSB Museum*)

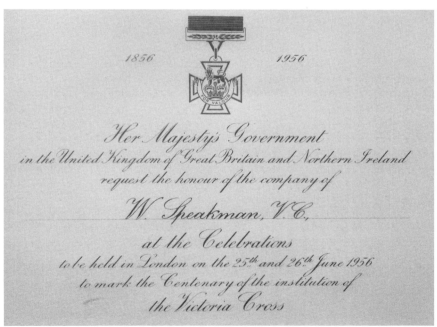

1856   *1956*

Her Majesty's Government
in the United Kingdom of Great Britain and Northern Ireland
request the honour of the company of

W. Speakman, V.C,

at the Celebrations
to be held in London on the 25th and 26th June 1956
to mark the Centenary of the institution of
the Victoria Cross

VC for bravery in France in September 1918 while serving with the Australian Imperial Force. At 6ft 6in, Speakman towered over the 5ft 3in Woods.

The Marlborough House VC Exhibition included photographs, citations, artefacts and, in a few cases, Victoria Crosses connected with over 600 VC recipients. Speakman was not one of the VCs featured in the exhibition, although Colonel Carne was. The Celtic cross he carved while a prisoner of the Chinese was on display, together with a framed presidential citation, a photograph, his VC citation and a communist bugle.

Bill Speakman VC attended the first Victoria Cross Association Reunion Dinner at the Café Royal on 24 July 1958. Field Marshal Earl Alexander of Tunis was the guest of honour at the dinner, which was attended by more than eighty VC recipients and forty GC recipients. Speakman was pictured wearing the War Medal 1939–45 and the Defence Medal – neither of which he was officially entitled to. He also attended the second reunion dinner, also held at the Café Royal, on 7 July 1960. In May the following year the Victoria Cross Association became the Victoria Cross and George Cross Association.

Speakman was awarded the Army Certificate of Education (ACE) 3rd Class on 11 December 1956. He continued his studies and passed English, maths and general map reading on 30 November 1957. After passing the written

Speakman at the Café Royal, 24 July 1958. Left to right: Viscount De L'Isle VC, Speakman VC, Major D S Jamieson VC and Major Nigel Macdonald. (*VC & GC Association*)

Speakman with Air Commodore Freddie West VC at the Café Royal, 24 July 1958. (*VC & GC Association*)

map reading examination on 22 February 1958, he was awarded the Army Certificate of Education 2nd Class.

On 8 February 1957, while at Berwick-upon-Tweed, he extended his length of service to twenty-two years with the colours and was granted a bounty of £100. Speakman had shown his commitment and the Army responded by promoting him to acting sergeant on 25 March. Less than two months later, on 10 May, he was attached to the Army Recruiting Staff at 119 Recruiting Centre, retaining his acting rank. In September 1957 he was promoted to the substantive rank of corporal, this promotion being backdated to 1 April, while still acting sergeant. He was later attached to the Army Information Office, Dumfries, before being posted back to 1st KOSB on 26 January 1959.

The 1st Battalion KOSB returned from a three-year tour of duty in Malaya and Singapore in October 1958 and was stationed at Milton Bridge, Edinburgh until its next posting. On 31 January 1959 the battalion, preceded by the military band and the massed pipe bands of three KOSB Battalions, marched down Princes Street, Edinburgh with bayonets fixed and colours flying. The salute was taken by the Lord Provost, who was accompanied by the colonel of the regiment. One of the other dignitaries taking the salute was the general

At a recruiting table at a country show. Left to right: Sergeant Speakman VC, Sergeant Fraser, Sergeant Johnstone. (*Bill Speakman VC*)

officer commanding (GOC) 52nd (Lowland) Division (TA), Major General John MacDonald DSO OBE, who had commanded the 1st Battalion in Korea in 1951.

Speakman relinquished his acting rank of sergeant and reverted to corporal on 26 January 1959, the day he rejoined 1st KOSB from the Army Information Office. His second child, and first daughter, Jane, was born in March 1958.

After a stay in the UK of almost thirty-three months, Speakman was posted, on 15 February 1959, to West Germany as part of BAOR (British Army of the Rhine). In April he was again promoted to acting sergeant, backdated to 8 March, having held the acting rank for thirty-five days. His wife gave birth to their third child, Susan, in August, and made plans to join him in Germany. On 10 October, Rachel Speakman and the three children (Colin, Jane and Susan) disembarked at the Hook of Holland and moved into married quarters two days later.

Acting Sergeant Speakman went AWOL for one and a half hours on the morning of 28 May 1960 and failed to attend the Queen's Birthday Parade rehearsal. He was severely reprimanded for this lapse.

Speakman at Leith in 1961 with Lieutenant General W.R.F. Turner CB DSO. (*KOSB Museum*)

When Lieutenant Colonel R.C. Robertson-Macleod (1) was appointed commanding officer of the battalion in 1960, he remembered Speakman and gave him some advice. Speakman recalls his new CO saying, 'Settle down. Settle down and just go about your business.' He was clearly impressed by Robertson-Macleod:

In a Scottish regiment you get attached to an officer because he leads you. Take Robertson-Macleod of the Macleod family, for example. Two families united. The times he's been bombed and shot at and had to dig himself out and he became the CO of the regiment. He's a big, tall guy like me – you would follow him anywhere. A good officer will say 'We go' or 'We don't go'. That's all a soldier wants. But there is no point having an officer who dithers. When he knows he is going to go, a soldier starts to get himself ready but when the officer says 'We don't go' a soldier can stand down and unwind a bit.

Speakman, with the rest of his battalion, left Berlin and returned to the UK in March 1961. They embarked at the Hook of Holland on 23 March and disembarked the following day. Rachel Speakman and the children took up permanent residence in the UK, while the battalion remained at Redford Barracks in Edinburgh until the next overseas posting on 5 February 1962. During this period, Acting Sergeant Speakman was involved in public duties at Edinburgh Castle, including the Changing of the Guard ceremony. He returned to South Korea, briefly, in 1961 to attend the opening of the United Nations War Cemetery at Pusan and laid a wreath in memory of all the KOSB men buried there. On 1 July 1961 Speakman was promoted to the substantive rank of sergeant.

In June of that year Speakman acted as an escort at a ceremony in Edinburgh. The battalion provided the guards at the installation of Lieutenant General W.F.R. Turner CB DSO as 88th Governor of Edinburgh Castle and GOC, Scotland. General Turner was presented with the keys of the castle by his son, Second Lieutenant W.S. Turner 1st KOSB. As the governor took the salute, 1st Battalion KOSB marched past, followed by the other units on duty.

In November 1961, on the tenth anniversary of the battle for Hill 317, seven soldiers in battledress and carrying sten guns climbed a hill in Dunbartonshire, in the central Lowlands of Scotland. All were KOSB veterans of the Korean War, who had taken part in the defence of Hill 317 and the surrounding hills

HM The Queen inspects a guard of honour, Edinburgh on 27 June 1961. Speakman is on the right. (*Bill Speakman VC*)

Speakman's uniform on display at KOSB Museum. (*John Mulholland*)

on 4 November 1951, and included Lieutenant Colonel R.C. Robertson-Macleod and Sergeant Bill Speakman VC.

After the Second World War Britain was no longer a world power and gradually withdrew from the empire that had once spanned the globe. The post-war programme of granting independence to many of its colonies gathered pace. One such colony was Aden in the South Arabian Peninsula. It had been a British protectorate since 1839 and later became a Crown Colony. Aden's natural harbour lies in the crater of an extinct volcano and its position at the entrance to the Red Sea made it an important refuelling port for the Suez Canal and a link to India. In 1963 the colony was incorporated, with a number of small sheikdoms, into the Federation of South Arabia. The following year, Britain announced its intention to grant independence to the federation in 1968, but that a British military presence would remain in Aden.

There had been an Egyptian-backed coup in neighbouring Yemen in 1962 and a People's Democratic Republic was established. Armed tribesmen infiltrated the border into Aden from Yemen and the threat of an organised guerrilla war against the proposed independent federation concerned the British government. A terrorist campaign by the National Liberation Front (NLF) began in December 1963. In addition, Egypt's President Nasser had large numbers of well-armed troops in Yemen and his intentions were considered 'unfriendly' at best. A state of emergency was declared on 10 December 1963, when a grenade was thrown at the British High Commissioner. British troops, including the SAS, were sent to Aden to help deal with terrorist attacks against government targets.

By this time, 1st KOSB had already been in Aden for almost two years on a routine posting. The Borderers had left Southampton aboard the troopship *Oxfordshire* on 6 February 1962 and arrived in Aden harbour on 19 February. Their departure from England was memorable as RSM W. Murdoch of the 4th/5th Battalion was at the dock to bid farewell to his brother RSM J. 'Busty' Murdoch MBE DCM of the 1st Battalion, the only two brothers to have both served as RSM in the KOSB at the same time. On arrival, the battalion became part of BFAP (British Forces Arabian Peninsular). The intense heat in Aden made working conditions difficult but, fortunately, the battalion was quartered in air-conditioned barracks at Khormaksar. Speakman's fourth child, Helen, was born in the UK in February 1963, while he was stationed in Aden.

Most of 1st KOSB's work involved garrison and patrol duties, and watching the Yemeni border from a hill station. Aden was not a glamorous

On the deck of troopship *Oxfordshire* at Southampton on 6 February 1962. Left to right: Lance Corporal Brown, Lance Corporal McCormick, Lance Corporal Tennant, Sergeant Speakman VC, Lance Corporal Hunter, Lance Corporal Henderson. (*KOSB Museum*)

posting and most British servicemen were pleased when it was time to leave. It was considered little more than a barren rock, which was once an important refuelling stop, on the edge of the desert. 'Aden was patrolling and trying to contact the terrorists,' says Speakman. 'They can appear and then suddenly disappear.' While in Aden, Speakman carried out public relations and photographic work for the battalion:

> I rather liked doing that job. When we arrived in Aden it was on a two year stint and I wanted to show what the battalion was doing. So they gave me a camera and I went on all the operations to see them chasing bandits and the Radfan rebels, and I did my share of patrols in between. It was not all camera work but I made sure I always carried a camera and got some good footage.
>
> Whenever I took photos they went back to the regiment as a permanent record of its part in a campaign. I was using an 8mm cine-camera – double sided thing where you had to change the tape around. With this type of camera you could use both sides of the film. After using one side you could turn the film over and use the other side. I had a good camera and developed all my own pictures.

British Forces in Aden published a newspaper, *The Dhow*, which was edited by Major P.H. Middlemiss, a retired officer serving at GHQ Middle East Command. Middlemiss used Speakman as his public relations man and said of him:

> Speakman was a huge success; his large frame, coupled with his notoriety and happy manner made him very welcome everywhere, he seemed to know everyone and he could arrange anything.

Middlemiss used Speakman to produce eye-catching headlines. Sergeant Speakman VC was at Khormaksar Airport to meet the first BOAC VC10 when it landed and the headline in *The Dhow* was 'VC greets VC10'.

The battalion's time in Aden ended on 23 January 1964, just over six weeks after the start of the state of emergency, when it left by aircraft for the UK, arriving there the next day. Speakman served in the UK from 24 January to 3 May 1964. After returning from Aden, the battalion was stationed at Shorncliffe where it formed part of the United Kingdom Strategic Reserve.

However, it was not long before 1st KOSB returned to the region, at short notice, as a rebellion had broken out in Radfan, a mountainous area 50 miles to the north of Aden. The Radfan tribes, armed with Egyptian and Yemeni weapons, joined the armed struggle against British rule in Aden by attacking travellers on the main roads.

Less than three months after leaving Aden, the battalion flew back from RAF Lyneham on 3 May 1964, arriving the next day. They took over garrison duties in Aden to allow troops already there to be used as reinforcements in troubled areas as the situation worsened and also to support counter-insurgency operations against rebel Radfan tribesmen. There were relatively few rebel tribesmen but they moved about, mainly at night, while the soldiers searching for them did so during the day, in the dust storms and under the burning sun. The situation improved when British troops adopted guerrilla tactics and hunted for the rebels at night.

Britain had about 12,000 troops in Aden at the time. A second terrorist group, the Front for the Liberation of South Yemen (FLOSY), was set up in 1966 and fought the NLF as well as the British troops trying to keep the peace. In June 1967 British-trained local police mutinied and attacked a British military convoy, killing eight British soldiers. The mutiny was crushed, but it hastened the end of British rule and plans for a continued military presence were quietly dropped. Britain abandoned Aden to the rival factions in November 1967 and, after a short but bloody civil war, it became part of the People's Democratic Republic of Yemen.

Speakman had left Aden several years before the loss of this former Crown Colony. 1st KOSB returned to the UK on 28 July 1964, where it remained until the following year. The battalion was again stationed at Shorncliffe and was an important part of the United Kingdom Strategic Reserve from 1964 to 1967. Speakman's fifth child, David, was born at Shorncliffe Military Hospital in August 1964.

More overseas postings followed, and 1st KOSB emplaned for Hong Kong on 16 April 1965, arriving there two days later. The battalion remained in Hong Kong until 20 May 1965, when it departed for temporary duty in South Korea. After arriving by aircraft at Seoul, the battalion was attached to UN Command Korea and flew back to Hong Kong on 25 May. Two months later, on 25 July, the battalion was again on the move, on the troopship *Sir Lancelot*, and disembarked in Singapore on 30 July. It then received two months training at the Jungle Warfare School in Johore to prepare the men for their next posting. Having served with the SAS in the jungles of Malaya, Speakman was already familiar with the problems of jungle warfare. On 29 September 1965 1st KOSB embarked for Borneo, disembarking on 1 October.

The Federation of Malaysia, comprising the former British colonies of the Malay Peninsula, Singapore, Sabah (formerly North Borneo) and Sarawak, was officially recognised in 1963. (Singapore left the federation later.) Malaysia shared a 1,000-mile-long common border with Indonesia on the tropical island of Borneo, with the British colonies of Sabah and Sarawak and the small protectorate of Brunei on the northern seaboard. The rest of the island was part of Indonesia, which opposed the new federation and attempted to destabilise it. President Sukarno planned to extend Indonesian rule over the whole island and authorised cross-border terrorist raids and, later, regular army attacks from Borneo on Sabah and Sarawak. The main target for Indonesian attacks was Sarawak. British and Commonwealth forces were deployed to the area and later fought Indonesia in the jungles of Borneo. As war was never declared the fighting became known as 'The Confrontation' (2), but was, nonetheless, full-scale guerrilla warfare.

Arriving in Borneo on 1 October 1965, 1st KOSB remained there for five months, until 28 February 1966. By the end of this tour of duty, it was the only battalion to have served in Korea, Malaya and Borneo and as a result was battle-hardened. In Borneo, the Borderers had been organised into a headquarters company and three rifle companies; Speakman was in B Company. By the time they arrived, Gurkha units and the SAS were already in action, using all the jungle warfare tactics they had learned in Malaya.

Speakman arriving in Singapore on board *Sir Lancelot* on 30 July 1965. (*Bill Speakman VC*)

All the Blue Bonnets: The History of The King's Own Scottish Borderers (3) describes the arrival of the regiment in Sarawak:

> Battalion Headquarters disembarked at Sibu, the second largest town, forty miles up the Rajang River. From Sibu the rifle companies were taken a further sixty miles upstream by the same ship, specially designed for river navigation, in which they had sailed from Singapore. Reaching Song, an important transit post, the companies disembarked and dispersed to their respective bases by a combination of longboat, speedboat and helicopter.

Once in position in their company bases, the battalion patrolled the border area with Indonesia for the next five months. Led by their Iban trackers, 1st KOSB (and other Commonwealth units) patrolled the jungle. They would be taken to a cleared patch of jungle by helicopter and would then live in the jungle for two weeks, searching for signs of Indonesian incursions. Terrorists or enemy soldiers discovered by these patrols were ambushed and killed. There were few roads in Sarawak and often the only means of travel was by river. The humidity of the jungle was made worse by the full packs the British units carried and they encountered the same problems they had in the jungles of Malaya. At the end of their patrol a new landing area was cleared and a helicopter flew in to collect them. 'In Borneo it was just patrolling, patrolling,' says Speakman. 'Patrolling is all we did.' Patrols sometimes went out by boat, but to get close to the Iran Mountains, which separated Sarawak from the mainland Borneo, helicopters were deployed.

The British Army frequently crossed the border into Indonesian Borneo, although this was kept secret at the time and there were restrictions on how far units could go into enemy territory. Cross-border raids were carried out, initially, by the Gurkhas and the SAS, with other regiments patrolling the jungles and border areas of Sarawak and Sabah. Speakman recalls his time in Borneo:

> We were trying to kick the Indonesians out because they were causing so much trouble. Borneo was a British mandate with important oilfields and we did a very good job there. The battalion was always in the jungle, building forts and following Sir Gerald Templer's example in Malaya. We were billeted up near the Indonesian border and crossed it a couple of times but didn't have any contact with the enemy – the other guys did, the ones who got lucky.

Because of the excellent relationship which existed with the local tribes (mainly Ibans and Dyaks), many of them chose to serve in the British Army. A local unit, the Sarawak Rangers, had been formed as long ago as 1872 and after the Second World War it became a colonial unit under British control, later joining the Malaysian Army. The Rangers served in Malaya during 'The Emergency' and in Borneo during 'The Confrontation'. The Iban were headhunters, although this practice was officially frowned upon.

Regrettably, Speakman lapsed into rebellious habits while in Borneo and was disciplined on several occasions. On 1 November 1965 he failed to return to camp before 0100 hours, failed to be in possession of means of identity and did not return to his unit when ordered to by a staff sergeant of the Royal Military Police. As a result he was severely reprimanded.

The following month, on 10 December, he went AWOL for eight hours, disobeyed a lawful command and failed to book out of camp. He was fined £32 18s, which was taken from his pay.

On 9 January 1966 he again failed to return to camp before 0100 hours. He was fined £32 18s, which was taken from his pay. Incredibly, after being disciplined on three separate occasions in three consecutive months, Speakman was not demoted. This may have been due to his seniority and the fact he was a VC holder. He was also a very experienced NCO with a lot to offer the Army. It is also the case that throughout his Army career, Speakman had a less than impressive disciplinary record and a fearsome reputation (whether deserved or not) for hard drinking and getting into bar brawls.

In Indonesia, an abortive communist coup in 1965 led to an army takeover and the downfall of President Sukarno the following year. 'The Confrontation' ended in August 1966 when Indonesia finally ceased hostilities and signed a peace treaty. By any standards, 'The Confrontation' was a small war. There were only about 17,000 Commonwealth servicemen in Borneo at the height of the fighting and Commonwealth casualties over a five year period were 114 killed and 181 wounded.

Having completed its time in Borneo, 1st KOSB flew to Singapore on 28 February 1966. Two days later (1 March), the battalion departed Singapore by air and arrived back in the UK on 2 March 1966. There followed a period of disembarkation leave and in June the battalion reassembled at Shorncliffe, where the families had remained during the Borneo tour.

From the mid-1960s, Sergeant Speakman was spending more time on administrative than operational duties. He was the battalion's photographer and public relations sergeant. 'The PR work was in recruitment,' he says. 'I used to talk to people and say: "If you are going to join the Army, why not join the KOSB? You could also win one of these (the VC)".'

Once back in the UK, the battalion remained there until 13 September 1967. Speakman completed his twenty-two years' service for his Army pension on 20 September 1967, but in March 1967 he had been permitted to continue in the Army until 11 December 1967, which was later extended a further twelve months to 11 December 1968. His youngest son and sixth child, Casper, was born in January 1967.

Whilst stationed at Edinburgh in 1967, Speakman was appointed as a recruiting sergeant. He was also part of a guard of honour at Balmoral and met the Queen, who instantly recognised him, on many occasions. By April 1967, Speakman was stationed with KOSB at the Lowland Brigade Depot at Penicuik, less than 10 miles from Edinburgh. His portrait was painted for the officers' mess at Berwick-upon-Tweed. 'It was commissioned by the officers', says Speakman, 'and was painted while I was still in uniform.'

In the portrait there is only one clasp on his General Service Medal: the *Borneo* clasp was not authorised till October 1967, so it is likely that the portrait was made in late 1966 or early 1967.

Speakman's service in Malaya earned him the General Service Medal 1918–1962 (the ribbon of which he had inadvertently worn at his VC investiture) with the clasp *Malaya*. He also received the Campaign Service Medal, with clasps for *Radfan* and *Borneo* (4). Despite his long service he did not qualify for the Long Service and Good Conduct Medal. Active service had prevented

Speakman's portrait now in the Officers' Mess in Dreghorn, Edinburgh. (*KOSB Museum*)

174

him from attending any of the Victoria Cross and George Cross reunions since 1960 but he continued to take an interest in the VC and GC Association and his fellow recipients. During the 1950s and 1960s he served as a member of the Association's committee.

In April 1967 he was charged with stealing a purse from a house in Edinburgh and found guilty of the offence, although he does not have a criminal record. This period marked a low time for Speakman; his family life was not as happy as it had been and he did not view with any enthusiasm the prospect of being discharged from the Army the following year.

Edinburgh Sheriff Court has not retained the paperwork relating to his court case, but the newspapers of the time provide useful background information. If the case had involved anyone but Sergeant Bill Speakman VC it would probably have been forgotten long ago, but his Victoria Cross, together with his notoriety, has kept the story alive.

On Saturday, 29 April 1967 he appeared at Edinburgh Sheriff Court on a charge of stealing a purse containing £104, together with a key and key ring, from a handbag in a house in Magdala Crescent, Edinburgh. Speakman and a woman companion had gone to the house for drinks on 30 March after meeting the occupiers, Mr and Mrs Donald Banks, in a hotel bar. Mrs Banks had £104 in a purse in her handbag and when she returned home she left the handbag on a sofa in the living room. (£104 would be equivalent to £1,550 today.) She later discovered the money and the key were missing. Mr Francis Keane, prosecuting at the Sheriff Court, said, 'Speakman then said he would have to leave as he did not realise how late it was. His friend said they should stay and look for the money but Speakman insisted that they left.'

The next day Speakman telephoned Mr Banks and asked if the money had been found. He called in at the house later that day and was told that the police had been informed about the missing money. Speakman was seen by the police on 1 April and denied the theft. He offered to admit it if his female companion was not involved but although the police initially refused, it is interesting to note that she was not charged.

In court, on 29 April, he pleaded guilty to the charge and asked to be allowed to repay the missing money. The sheriff deferred sentence until 5 June to allow time for the money to be paid back. At his second court appearance on 5 June, by which time the money had been repaid, Speakman was given an absolute discharge – the legal equivalent of 'a slap on the wrists' which does not involve a criminal record. In giving this verdict, the sheriff noted that Sergeant Speakman 'has never been in trouble before' and no doubt recognised the courage which had earned him the Victoria Cross in Korea.

In between the two court appearances, Speakman was, somewhat unfairly, in trouble with his battalion for 'improperly using' an Army vehicle on 16 May 1967, for which he was reprimanded. Some of his disciplinary offences were not real offences but technicalities. On many occasions he had to travel to farms to see people after normal hours to recruit them because they were working during the day. Although good at recruiting, Speakman was less conscientious when it came to procedures and form filling and, as a result often took vehicles for Army work without completion of the necessary forms, although verbal permission was often obtained, thereby committing an offence.

The battalion was posted to Osnabruck in West Germany, in June 1967, as part of a BAOR contingent defending the UK and Western Europe from attack from the East. It would have been a relief to Speakman when he followed the 1st Battalion to Germany on 14 September and was able to escape the attention of the press. The Borderers were converted to a mechanised battalion and equipped with armoured personnel carriers; the first stages of conversion had begun while 1st KOSB was still in the UK in early 1967.

Speakman on guard duty at Edinburgh Castle. The boy was the son of Steve Milner, a KOSB soldier who liked to dress him in uniform. (*Bill Speakman VC*)

Speakman had served in Berlin before, but things had changed dramatically since his last visit. Berlin was always likely to be a potential flashpoint in the Cold War as East and West met in this divided city. In August 1961 the East German Army had sealed off the border between East and West Berlin and closed the Brandenburg Gate to stop people fleeing to the West. Barbed wire entanglements and fences were erected and the first concrete blocks of a permanent barrier were in place later the same month. The Berlin Wall split Berlin in half and separated West Berlin from East Germany. Watchtowers were placed at regular distances along the Wall and East German guards shot anyone trying to escape to the West. The Wall remained the symbol of the Iron Curtain until November 1989, when restrictions were lifted on travel to the West. The Wall was dismantled soon afterwards and the two Germanys were reunified. As Speakman later recalled:

> Before the Wall was up you could go into East Germany and buy all sorts of lovely cutlery, crystal glass and cameras. Then the Berlin Wall went up and we were hemmed in.

During the posting, the battalion undertook specialist training in armoured warfare and took part in many exercises, but saw no active service. Sergeant Speakman remained in West Germany as part of 1st KOSB until 15 October 1968, returning to the UK without his battalion the following day. (1968 was a quiet year for the Borderers, and the rest of the British Army, and is the only year since 1945 when no British servicemen have been killed on active service.) He had been transferred from the Lowland Brigade to the Scottish Division in July 1968 in readiness for his imminent retirement. Speakman returned from Germany with his family, who had been there with him. He came home early pending his discharge in December and was posted to the Scottish Division Depot at Glencorse, Edinburgh on 16 October. His former battalion remained in Germany until May 1970 when it was posted to Belfast on peacekeeping duties.

In July 1968, Speakman attended a luncheon for VC and GC recipients at Buckingham Palace. This would be the last official VC event he would attend for twenty-two years. Footage of this event can be seen on the British Pathé News website.

Speakman arrives at the lunch for VC and GC recipients at Buckingham Palace, 1968. (*British Pathé*)

NOTES

(1) Major R.C. Robertson-Macleod DSO MC TD commanded D Company on Hill 317 on 4 November 1951, when Speakman won his VC. He was later commanding officer of 1st KOSB from 1960 to 1962.

(2) One VC was awarded for the Malaysia–Indonesia Confrontation, to Lance Corporal Rambahadur Limbu 2nd / 10th Gurkha Rifles.

(3) *All the Blue Bonnets: The History of The King's Own Scottish Borderers* by Robert Woollcombe (Arms and Armour Press (now The Orion Publishing Group), 1980.) © Robert Woollcombe, 1980

(4) The clasp for service in Aden was *South Arabia* and was awarded for continuous service of thirty days or more between 1 August 1964 and 30 November 1967. 1st KOSB just missed qualifying for it.

CIVVY STREET: ENGLAND AND SOUTH AFRICA

1968–1980

Although Speakman would have preferred to remain in the Army, this was not really an option. He reached his forty-first birthday on 21 September 1968, while still in Germany, and was now considered too old for active service. His engagement with the Army officially came to an end on 11 December 1968, when he was discharged from the KOSB Depot at Berwick-upon-Tweed. He had, in fact, left his unit on 13 November 1968 and was granted twenty-eight days' terminal leave from 14 November to 11 December. His Army records reveal that he joined the reserves on 11 December 1968 but was never recalled. He was 'discharged with no further reserve liability on 21 September 1982', his fifty-fifth birthday. When he left the Army he was required to sign a declaration under the Official Secrets Act.

In addition to his weekly pension and a Gallantry Award of 3s 6d, he also received a terminal grant of £967 4s. Speakman joined the Army in August 1945, making his service in the Army 23 years and 124 days. 'When you leave the Army you are given six months compulsory leave,' he explains. 'You don't get paid for it but you get assisted.'

Speakman had no job when he left the Army, although he had his Army pension, and no career plans. He had loved Army life and would miss it. In an interview with the *Sunday Express* of 17 November 1968, Rachel Speakman commented:

> The Army is the only life he has known since he was a boy. I don't know what he can do. He has no qualifications for any other job. Really he doesn't want to leave the Army, but twenty-two years is the longest you can serve now.

The *Sunday Express* article stated that Speakman had left the Army unannounced four weeks ago, which would have been a reference to the twenty-eight days' leave he was granted after his actual leaving date. His Army file contains a testimonial, which would no doubt have been used as a reference for future employment:

> Sergeant Speakman is a most excellent NCO with a distinguished military career behind him. His winning of a well-deserved Victoria Cross under extremely adverse conditions in Korea brought great credit on him and on his regiment. In peace he has proved a capable organiser with a particular flair for public relations and security work. Very highly recommended.

Like many VC recipients before him, Speakman found it difficult to find employment and settle into post-service life. He tried a variety of unskilled and semi-skilled jobs and for a time was a night cleaner, a gas conversion fitter and the manager of a warehouse. None of these jobs really appealed to him. After twenty-three years in the Army nothing offered the same job satisfaction. 'When I left the Army,' he says, 'I was told: "Don't work for six months. Get used to being a civilian". So I started work on the house.'

At the time the Speakman family were living at *Allandale*, Wyton, near St Ives, Huntingdonshire (1) in a detached house owned by Rachel's mother Grace. Eric Snitch had died before Speakman left the Army but Grace was still alive when the family moved in. It was tight in terms of space, but everyone managed. Grace died shortly afterwards, leaving the house to Rachel.

The house was in very poor condition and required a lot of renovation, including a new roof and treatment for condensation. Speakman remembers that the house was close to Wyton airfield and 'we had a nice patch of ground at the back, on the River Ouse. I made a small stream at the back so that the children would not get into trouble at the river.' Without a job he couldn't see how he would be able to complete the necessary repairs. He had a wife and six children and also needed a job in order to support them:

> Every bit of money I had I spent on the house; that was going to be our home. The roof started to leak so we had to do something. I had to pay for central heating as the house was terribly damp. For the first time in my life I went on the dole.

He decided the only alternative was to sell his VC and medals. In 1968, Speakman sold his VC group to John Hayward, a London medal specialist, for a

Speakman's VC group as purchased in 1968 by John Hayward and now on display in the National War Museum of Scotland. (*National War Museum of Scotland*)

Speakman wearing his medals in the summer of 1968 shortly before they were sold. (*British Pathé*)

sum reported to be £1,500 (2). This was about average for prices realised at the time. John Hayward was then one of the main buyers of VCs and at one time owned fifteen VCs. He would not confirm the price he paid for Speakman's VC group because of customer confidentiality and Bill Speakman cannot remember. Speakman recalls the sale, although not all the details:

> I didn't really try to keep it quiet. I went to this medal dealer in London and I said, 'What can I get for these?' He said, 'I know you – you're Bill Speakman. I have seen you.' I said, 'What can you get me?' He told me the going rate and said, 'That's what I can give you.' It was about £1,500. That was a lot of money in those days.
>
> People only sell VCs because they have to, otherwise they are not going to do it. Some people who have won the VC would rather starve to death than sell it. I never regretted selling my VC because the money came in handy to do up the cottage and then sell it.

One rumour about the reason Speakman sold his VC suggests that the decoration had caused him nothing but problems since he received it and, as he no longer had to wear it after leaving the Army, he wanted to be rid of it. Speakman says there is no truth in this story:

> The VC has never caused me any problems whatsoever. The only thing it causes is over-popularity, with people wanting to meet me and asking me to explain how I won it. But no one has ever been nasty about it. When I won the VC it was not for me alone but for all the guys who were there with me and I made sure everyone knew that. I still tell people that because I could not have won it on my own.
>
> I hate wearing medals and they make holes in my suits, but the VC is a medal to be proud of. I sold it because I had come out of the Army and couldn't find a job. I made up my mind to sell my VC and got on a bus and went to London. When I came back I renovated the cottage and it benefited me because we later sold it at a good price.

With the funding secured, Speakman set about carrying out the renovations to his house. The roof was the main problem but he also had to deal with the poor state of the brickwork, mainly to the side and back of the property. 'I pointed as best I could and then I put a brand new fence round the place.' Renovating the house was not an easy task, but finding a job which appealed to him proved even more difficult. In fact, finding any sort of job was becoming increasingly difficult for many people; in 1970 there were 603,000 people unemployed and

Allandale, Wyton, St Ives, Huntingdonshire. Speakman's VC was sold to re-roof the property in 1968. (*John Mulholland*)

by 1972 the unemployment figure reached one million and would continue to rise. Speakman recalls the problems he faced after leaving the Army:

All I wanted was a job and I couldn't find work in my own country because I was 42. I did odd jobs in the village and then worked for Tesco in Alconbury; it was probably my first job. I spoke to the manager of the store and he said, 'I could do with a receiving manager but you also have to be able to deal with receiving goods.' I said, 'Well, I have done that before.' But I had to leave there because there was no money in it.

I was offered a civilian cleaning job working for the US Air Force at Alconbury Air Base for a while. It was nights but they said, 'You will get good money, we will feed you and you will be in charge.' So I was working in the NCOs club, the officers club, organising people from outside and this colonel in the US Air Force was retiring. He was my boss and he said, 'I want you to help me.' Everywhere they go they have to employ a certain number of local people. Alconbury was the largest US air base in the UK – so I am told. I had to scrub pots and pans and I didn't worry about it one little bit. I had my car, I had food, I had wages, and was looked after. It was a good, well-paid job. Working nights suited me as I could work on the house during the day and work at the base at night.

To add to his problems, he was still being followed by the press and TV. On one occasion a reporter noted a long ladder propped against a wall where some pointing was needed and Speakman nearby mixing cement. Years later, Bill Speakman recalled the media interest while he was working on pointing a wall on the family home:

I was pointing. The BBC and ITV came and followed me. I said, 'I'm pointing. Go away. I'm a civilian now.' I tried to get them to move away. They had no right to be there. Sitting down there in their truck and taking photos. I said, 'What are you interested in?' 'We are trying to find out what you are doing in Civvy Street,' they replied. I said, 'Yes, but you are embarrassing me. The bloody neighbours are looking.' So I got on my bike and rode off. You can't hit them or anything like that. Like children. You can't spank them.

Speakman is very protective of his family and has tried to spare them the media attention he has endured for so long:

We were just an ordinary family and lived ordinary lives but I made sure the children didn't go through what I went through with the media. Many times people, when they could not get to me, have tackled Suzie, Jane, any one of my children. They would say, 'Your father is not here, what do you remember of him?' Once or twice the kids said 'We remember this and that' and they should never have done that. I said to the kids, 'You do not answer questions, otherwise they are going to quote you. You will have talked about your dad and it is not actually true.' Then these reporters get a bit intimate: 'How are your mother and father getting on?' They were doing this. When we went to Aden for three years, the family came with us. But then they dragged us back again when the Radfan rebel business started, all the families stayed home at Shorncliffe.

I remember one holiday with the family; we were at a place called Hunstanton on the north coast of Norfolk. We were in a bungalow which had a TV set. It was in July 1969 when they landed a man on the moon. We were watching the TV and I went out onto the beach and the moon was up. I said to the kids: 'Come here, come here. That's the moon where the guys have landed. It's on TV but that is where they have landed.' You could see the moon from the beach. 'This is where the men have landed on that moon up there.' The kids wanted to know how they got there. 'By rocket,' I said. The kids had not heard of a space rocket before – just a firework rocket. I remember the moon occasion, that was really something.

The Speakman family home in Avenue Road, Torquay, purchased with the proceeds of the sale of *Allandale*. (*John Mulholland*)

Speakman eventually found employment in Southampton and commuted from Wyton. 'I had a car – an old banger,' he says. 'It was then I had good money coming in and we decided to move.' They sold the house in Wyton and used the sale proceeds to buy a former guest house in Avenue Road, Torquay, in Devon, large enough for Speakman and his wife and six children. The new property had six bedrooms and each child had hot and cold water in their room:

> The kids were getting older and by this time I was in the merchant service but I wanted to be a master-at-arms. I saw an advert in *Farmers Weekly* for a large guest house in Torquay and thought 'That's what I want'. It is amazing how many people read *Farmers Weekly* when they want to get away from the city – it is not just farms for sale. Torquay was in the Southampton area so I went down to have a look at 40 Avenue Road, Torquay and bought it. Everything for me has always fallen into place because I believed in what I could achieve. Sometimes you can get a job through a medal but sometimes you can't. People just don't like it – the jealousy you have to put up with!
>
> I had to go to sea to make a living because there was no work in the UK. By that time I had bought the guest house in Torquay, to give the kids a room each. It had plenty of accommodation but needed a few things doing to it.

By that time I was earning money so we could do that. I had a very good, well-paid job and I was very well thought of.

On 19 August 1970 Speakman obtained a post as an assistant master-at-arms on the Union-Castle Line, sailing between Southampton and Cape Town, South Africa. The Union-Castle Line operated a fleet of lavender-hulled passenger liners and freighters between Southampton and South Africa. Speakman was promoted from assistant to junior master-at-arms within the first two or three voyages while serving on RMS *Windsor Castle* from August 1970 to February 1971. RMS *Windsor Castle* was the largest ship operated by Union-Castle and was noted for its high standards, which included air-conditioning throughout all areas.

THE UNION-CASTLE LINE

Formed in 1900 with the merger of the Union Shipping Line and the Castle Mail Packet Company, the Union-Castle Line operated a fleet of passenger liners and freighters between Europe and South Africa. In 1956, the Union-Castle Line was taken over by the British & Commonwealth Shipping Co but retained its trading name.

The Union-Castle Line named their ships with the suffix *Castle*. Bill Speakman served in two of these ships: RMS *Windsor Castle* and RMS *Pendennis Castle*. At 38,000 tons, RMS *Windsor Castle* was the flagship of the Line and was launched by HM Queen Elizabeth, The Queen Mother in June 1959. The ship was in service between 1960 and 1977. She departed from Cape Town for the last time on 6 September 1977, arriving at Southampton on 19 September, and was sold.

RMS *Pendennis Castle* was a smaller passenger/cargo liner of 28,500 tons, built by Harland & Wolff in Belfast in 1957. There was no launch ceremony as the shipyard was on strike at the time. She was in service between 1959 and 1976 and was the fastest mailship in the Union-Castle fleet. On her final arrival at Southampton on 14 June 1976, the ship was sold.

The increasing usage of container ships for freight and air travel for passengers and mail, together with the huge increases in the cost of fuel oil, meant that by the late 1970s Union-Castle's operations become unviable.

Speakman later served as junior master-at-arms on RMS *Pendennis Castle* from 9 July 1971 and during one voyage he was acting senior master-at-arms.

Although built as cruise liners, *Windsor Castle* and *Pendennis Castle* were also Royal Mail steamers.

The master-at-arms on a ship is the senior rating, of chief petty officer rank, responsible for maintaining discipline among the crew and carrying out administrative duties. He is also responsible for security and the safety of passengers and cargo. This would have been similar to Speakman's position as sergeant in the KOSB, and a job that appealed to him. He always wore his medal ribbons on his uniform, so passengers and crew would have been aware that he was a VC holder. He was in a position of authority, with a certain amount of autonomy, and it gave him the opportunity to travel. While serving as master-at-arms, Speakman met George Horsfall, with whom he later worked in South Africa.

One of his roles as master-at-arms was to keep watch on passengers. Sometimes 2nd and 3rd class passengers 'strayed' into 1st class areas and he had to gently send them back to their areas. This was done with quiet diplomacy as no one wanted an incident; it is difficult, however, to imagine anyone arguing with him. There was a bullion room in RMS *Windsor Castle* and he also had responsibility for this. Any stowaways discovered on board were held under guard by the master-at-arms. He made a point of not drinking on duty as he was in charge of discipline but passengers would often leave him drinks which he did not touch.

To equip him for his new role he attended a number of specialist courses. In August 1970 he attended the Merchant Navy Officers Fire Fighting School at

RMS *Windsor Castle* sailing from Cape Town for the last time. (*Bill Speakman VC*)

HMS *Phoenix* and in August 1971 attended a Training in Naval Establishments Fire Fighting Course at HMS *Excellent*. He received certificates for passing both Navy courses. Speakman also attended local fire brigade courses twice a year to keep up to date with new developments. In Cape Town, in February 1971, he received a certificate of qualification as a lifeboatman. More training in the UK followed, and he received the Merchant Navy Training Board Certificate for attending and passing the Supervisor's Course at West Cliff in March–April 1971. Speakman describes his role as master-at-arms:

> My job was the patrol, safety and security on ships and for passengers because we carried gold and diamonds and foreign currency. I never drank when I was in service as a master-at-arms. I made a point of that and I had the respect of the crew on the *Pendennis Castle* and the *Windsor Castle*. I had the crews behind me and we transformed the ships. It was a lovely job. Union-Castle gradually phased the ships out because everyone started flying to South Africa. We used to carry a lot of motor parts they couldn't manufacture in South Africa, but eventually they opened their own factories.

The long absences at sea inevitably put a great strain on his marriage and in 1971 Bill and Rachel Speakman separated. They divorced in June 1972. 'She was a wonderful woman,' says Speakman, 'but we got divorced because eventually we couldn't see eye-to-eye.' Rachel Speakman later explained in the *Sunday Express* of 10 November 1974:

> He was away most of the time, sailing to South Africa and back, just coming home for a few days at a time. I could see that things were not going to improve between us. We moved to Torquay but it was just the same. There was nothing between us and so I asked him for a divorce.
>
> We parted in 1971 and we were divorced in June 1972 on his petition. He said it was on the grounds of two years' separation and irretrievable breakdown. I did not contest his grounds.

In early 1972, Speakman emigrated to South Africa, a country he had visited many times with Union-Castle. On hearing that the mail ships were to be discontinued he decided it was time to emigrate and left the Union-Castle Mail Steamship Company on 4 March 1972. He received excellent references from the masters of both ships he served in and the owners of the Union-Castle Line.

The staff commander of RMS *Windsor Castle* wrote in a letter to Speakman in January 1972:

Your sobriety on board, whether on or off duty, was beyond reproach, and your general ability and interest in the job has led me to recommend you for promotion to junior master-at-arms within the first two or three voyages. I am sorry that you may be thinking of leaving the company, as I would be pleased to have you sail with me again and wish you all success in the future.

South Africa, despite apartheid, must have seemed an exciting place to be and one with a much warmer climate than England. He decided to make a fresh start there and cut himself off from his family and former regiment. At last he found the freedom and privacy he had long sought.

Before emigrating, he took an intensive course on security, loss control, crime prevention and fire, man management and surveying and advising on detection and prevention systems at the EMI Training College at Chalfont St Peter, Buckinghamshire.

Rachel Speakman continued to live in the house in Avenue Road, Torquay with her six children. Bill Speakman's entire Army pension was sent to his former wife each month to help support the family. She told the *Sunday Express* in its edition of 10 November 1974:

He just hated being a hero. He didn't want the VC … He said he wanted to make a complete break. I do not know exactly where he lives. I have only got a Post Office box number in Cape Town and the money he sends is sent by his bank … I have no regrets. It was not a marriage as I would have liked but I have six wonderful children.

In the early 1970s, Bill Speakman changed his surname to Speakman-Pitts to allow a relation to maintain the Pitts family name. The exact relationship is unclear — it is known that his grandfather William had married twice and so there could be a connection on that side of the family. Speakman had first been approached about the name change before he left England:

I was in Southampton at the time on a fire course, while still working for Union-Castle. A woman phoned and came to see me. I forget her name, but she was a solicitor from the Isle of Wight. She said, 'We have a request from a lady who would like to meet you.' We didn't meet and the solicitor handled the request. She asked, 'Is there a Pitts in your family?' We found out the Speakmans were related to the Pitts — very distant relatives. I'm also related to another Altrincham family named Venables (3).

Then I got to meet the lady concerned, a very nice lady. She asked: 'Would you mind adding our name to yours?' The Pitts had no males to carry the name down the line so I agreed. I said, 'Put it on.' Just like that. It was not for wanting a double-barrelled name, I just agreed to it. I refused to change my name so the solicitor just added the word 'Pitts'. The change to Speakman-Pitts was made by deed poll in the Isle of Wight. It was a favour, but a good favour. But now everything has died, so I am getting rid of the Pitts name.

I remember there was a big Pitts' book but we never got that again. I don't know if Grace had it or if Casper has got it. My mother's two sisters, Mary or Emily, may have it.

I asked the children if they wanted to change their name but they said: 'We don't want the name Pitts.' There is only one child who has got the name and that is Kate. Kate Speakman-Pitts, but when she marries she will take another name. My wife Jill became Speakman-Pitts. We went into it very carefully and the reason was good – otherwise there would be no succession. My name is still officially 'Speakman-Pitts' and will remain that until I change it again by deed poll. I have to renounce it. In Altrincham I am Bill Speakman to everyone.

In South Africa, he went into business with George Horsfall, a Yorkshire man he had met on board RMS *Pendennis Castle*. He had said to Speakman, 'I want you to join me. You and I are going to open a security business.' Speakman recalls:

Because I had been on an electronics course, I was doing the burglar alarms and we had the blacks as security guards. We had a good company going – a British company at the time. From there, while I was working installing burglar alarms and electronic equipment in various factories, I was offered jobs.

I went to Cape Town to do the security job with George Horsfall. Then we went to live in Boksburg, five miles east of Johannesburg. We did a lot of work for a company called Pick 'n Pay. They are a big supermarket, a bit like Tesco are today. I worked for them for a while and my last job was down in the Cape.

He applied for and received security clearance from the South African Government. His next job was as a security adviser and surveyor to EMI-Cape Nightwatch Service and EMI-Cape Burglar Alarms in Cape Town in April

1972. He remained with EMI for four years and left in March 1976 after being offered another job. He received an excellent reference from EMI when he left the company.

He was employed by Pick 'n Pay Wholesalers (Transvaal) (Pty) Ltd at their Boksburg and Durban hypermarkets from March 1976 to May 1978. In his letter of reference, the general manager of the company commented that Speakman was 'totally trustworthy, very loyal and possessed with tremendous leadership and management potential'. While at Pick 'n' Pay, Speakman was responsible for, amongst other things, factory and store detection, prevention of theft, loss control and TV security viewing.

On 1 May 1978 Speakman was employed as group security and fire adviser by Murray & Roberts (Natal) (Pty) Ltd, based in Durban in Natal. They are South Africa's leading engineering, contracting and construction services company and Speakman's area of responsibility covered Natal, Swaziland and Transkei. He continued to attend courses and pass examinations, and in November 1978 passed the National Occupational Safety Association examination and practical test on fire protection. He advised on the training and administration of security officers, watchmen and dogs, and arranged the vetting of personnel to be employed in high risk areas. His work took him to Angola, as well as Swaziland and as chief security and fire adviser he had a helicopter at his disposal. During this period, Speakman achieved his long-held ambition to learn to fly:

> I have a pilot's licence and can fly a microlight and a light aircraft called a Kuda. It's a South African spotter plane. When I worked for Murray & Roberts I helped serve in 105 Squadron of the South African Air Force. It was like a territorial unit – Commando Squadron. Because I was interested in flying I became their warrant officer. The pilots were mainly sugar barons and they flew their own planes – all Kudas. They knew the areas along the borders where the terrorists were coming in. We used to go looking for them, the pilots were the spotters and because they knew the area they could fly without maps. I was the squadron warrant officer and knocked them into shape. You have to put something back into Africa for what they give you.

While working for Murray & Roberts in Natal he often visited Rorke's Drift, where eleven VCs were awarded for the famous defence of the mission station in January 1879:

I didn't live very far from Rorke's Drift when I was working in Natal. I went down there many, many times. There are still reminders of the battle there.

Speakman remembers that he was working for Murray & Roberts when the company built a Holiday Inn at Ulundi (the battle which ended the Zulu War in July 1879). During excavations for the foundations they discovered military hardware from the battle, including bullets, helmets and even a bugle. Some of these items were put on display in the hotel. Speakman owned some of the artefacts but he gave them away over the years.

Back in the UK, HM The Queen celebrated her Silver Jubilee in 1977. A Silver Jubilee Medal was issued and distributed to, *inter alia*, all living Victoria Cross holders, including Bill Speakman VC, even though he had already sold his VC.

In 1980 Speakman applied for South African citizenship. He had fallen in love with the country and its people and later explained:

A lot of my service was done where the sun is. I belong in the sun. I fell in love with South Africa. I don't care what people say about South Africa – it is a great country.

He became a naturalised South African citizen but did not give up his British passport and had dual nationality:

I had a South African passport and a British passport, both still valid today. If I am resident in Britain I can travel to South Africa on a British passport going in for six months and then leave on a British passport. If I am resident in South Africa I must enter the country on a South African passport and leave on the same passport. I also have an ID booklet, which everyone in South Africa has, and this means we don't have all this fraudulent business.

He married Jill Whitelaw in the early 1970s. Jill was South African although her father, who had served in the Royal Engineers, had emigrated from Scotland:

We had one daughter, named Kate, who now lives in Australia. Jill was told she could not have any more children. She was a radiographer and had been for a long time. We took a chance with Kate but the doctor told her that she couldn't have other children as she had been subjected to radiation. Jill said, 'Let's be on the safe side.'

The marriage later ended in divorce and he married again in 1995.

Speakman has often described his interests as light aircraft pilot, climbing, swimming and skiing. He was able to take an active part in all these interests in South Africa and learnt to fly while he was there. He says that his interest in flying came from living close to Ringway (now Manchester Airport) as a child:

I always wanted to fly and I got the opportunity in South Africa. I started with microlights. They used to call them wheelies because they flew so close to the ground. I did well at that and then did a bit of instructing. I went on from there to light aircraft and started taking courses. You could afford a microlight but you couldn't afford a plane. But it was flying, pure flying. A tubular frame around you and you could fly for two hours at a time and I got such joy from this. I flew over the game reserves in a microlight. We used to fly at five o'clock in the morning and flew into the sunrise, over the sea to Robin Island, across the veld and the bush. It was wonderful. We had paraplegics – we taught them how to fly microlights.

NOTES

(1)   In 1974 Huntingdonshire became part of Cambridgeshire.

(2)   £1,500 in 1968 would be worth £22,000 today. However, in recent years VCs have appreciated greatly in value and if auctioned today the VC group would be worth up to £350,000. (See Chapter 12).

(3)   Speakman's connection with the Venables family can be traced back to 1919 when his stepfather, Herbert Houghton, married Lily Venables. She died in 1928.

SOUTH AFRICA AND ROYAL HOSPITAL CHELSEA

1980–1997

On 8 July 1982 Sotheby's had Speakman's VC group (minus the 1977 Silver Jubilee Medal) up for auction. He had sold the VC and medals privately to London medal specialist John Hayward in November 1968, shortly after leaving the Army. John Hayward later sold the group to a client, who sold it in the summer of 1974 to an anonymous buyer. Details of the auction vendor were not disclosed.

The VC group, mounted court-style, comprised:

- Victoria Cross (engraved *Pte. W. Speakman, Black Watch, att'd KOSB 4 Nov. 1951*)
- Korea Medal 1950–1953
- United Nations Korea Medal
- General Service Medal 1918–62 (one clasp, *Malaya*)
- Campaign Service Medal 1962 (two clasps, *Radfan* and *Borneo*)
- Coronation Medal 1953

The reverse arms of the Victoria Cross had been lightly engraved *Hill 217* by Speakman himself and the auctioneers recorded of the group that 'some [were] lacquered and with contact wear but otherwise good–very fine'.

This award – perhaps one of the most historically important of recent times – was received from the hands of Queen Elizabeth II during her first official investiture since accession to the throne.

It was estimated that the VC group would sell for between £20,000 and £25,000. John Hayward acted as agent and intermediary for the auction vendor.

It was reported that Bill Speakman's VC group sold for £20,000 'after just 90 seconds of bidding' and was later acquired by Jack Stenabaugh, a Canadian

Speakman's VC (National War Museum of Scotland)

medal collector. *Medal News* noted that the VC group sold only just on estimate, and suggested that the price may have suffered from the controversial publicity it had received over the years, but a 'more important factor was the absence from the bidding of two major VC specialists through whose collections the award had already passed'.

In 1986, the Scottish United Services Museum, Edinburgh, purchased the VC and medals from Jack Stenabaugh for the same price he had bought it. The amount of this generous transaction was not disclosed but was thought to be in the region of £20,000 (1). The Scottish United Services Museum later became the National War Museum of Scotland and Speakman's VC group is now on permanent display in Edinburgh Castle. Displayed next to it is the wristwatch given to him at a homecoming reception in Altrincham in 1952. 'The Museum asked me for certain things', says Speakman. 'There was a wristwatch which I could not wear as it was too delicate for me, so I gave them that.'

It is unlikely that the VC group will ever be sold again, but it is estimated by John Hayward, now a medal consultant at Spink, that at auction it could fetch up to £350,000. (The VC and medals of Flight Lieutenant W. 'Bill' Reid sold at auction in November 2009 for £348,000.)

An unfounded rumour, mistakenly reported as fact in *Medal News* in June 1982, stated that after Speakman had sold his VC group there was an outcry in the popular press and that the general public sent in donations to buy it back, only for him to sell it again. There was possibly some confusion between Speakman and another VC hero whose decoration was sold twice – James Magennis VC (2). In Speakman's case there is no truth in the story and in 2009 the editor of *Medal News* said he believed the correspondent, was 'either ill-informed or had a rather fanciful imagination'. In 2010 Bill

Speakman, keen to put the record straight, wrote to the editor pointing out the facts. His letter and an unreserved apology appeared in the September 2010 edition of *Medal News*. To the magazine's credit, this is probably the only example of an apology to Speakman by the media for a misrepresentation of the facts. 'I'm pleased this myth has been laid to rest,' he commented.

The provenance of Speakman's VC is documented from when he sold it in 1968 to when it came up for auction in 1982. It is apparent that the VC was sold honourably by the recipient and held in private collections for many years before emerging at auction.

The VC group was loaned by the Trustees of the National War Museum of Scotland to Sotheby's in 1992 for an exhibition of 'Important British Gallantry Awards 1800–1950' (notwithstanding that Speakman's VC was awarded for an action in 1951). Held between 26 May and 5 June 1992, the exhibition at Sotheby's New Bond Street showroom marked the occasion of the 50th anniversary of the Orders and Medals Research Society.

After emigrating to South Africa, Speakman had cut himself off from the Victoria Cross and George Cross Association and turned down expenses-paid invitations to visit London for reunions. The last reunion he attended was in 1968 but as a VC holder he still received the invitations.

He also, rather surprisingly, shunned his own family. An article in the *Sunday Express* of 30 March 1980 reported that Speakman's mother, Mrs Hannah Houghton, had 'not seen or heard from him for years'. Suggesting a communications breakdown, Speakman claimed to be puzzled by the fact that for many years his family said they did not know his whereabouts. The article continued:

> After being told where he is, Mrs Houghton said yesterday: 'It's good news to hear he is safe and well. But living in Durban? That's quite a shock really since we always believed he was in Cape Town.'
>
> His sister, Mrs Ann Stringer, said yesterday: 'I had no idea he was in Durban. I'll send him a letter. Maybe this time he will reply.'

Despite his desire for a quiet life, Speakman found he was still the subject of media attention – probably reawakened by the auction of his VC in 1982. He had a particular dislike of newspaper reporters:

What you tell them, they twist it and cause an awful lot of unhappiness. I was once in South Africa and a guy interviewed me and I said, 'I don't feel like being interviewed. Go away.'

In April 1983 he left the employment of Murray & Roberts (Natal) (Pty) Ltd, where he had worked since 1978. The climate in Natal had proved unsuitable for his daughter and this necessitated a move to a more suitable climate, hence his resignation. His daughter Katie had a respiratory complaint which was made worse by the hot and humid climate. In a letter of reference, Murray & Roberts recorded that Speakman was a 'thoroughly reliable hard-working person of sober habits and dress and whose integrity is beyond doubt'.

He joined the Divisional Council of the Cape, in Cape Town, on 1 August 1983 as deputy chief security officer. After holding this position for six months he was promoted to chief security officer:

Then finally I was offered the job of chief security officer, Cape Town. I was first a deputy and when the chief security officer was declared unfit for the job I took over the position. I did a good job. I had a Rhodesian guy with me who had been an RSM in the South African Rifles.

Speakman's wide range of experience and knowledge of security procedures proved him a competent officer in the council's security section. Within the next five years, under his leadership, the Law Enforcement Section expanded to more than 100 officers and men and had a budget of several million rand. He recalls some of the problems he encountered:

My job as chief security officer for the Cape Division covered an area of 100,000 square miles. I was there during the troubles. That was when I got petrol-bombed on my back. They were throwing petrol bombs all over the place. I had a jacket on and I was getting a guy out of a truck because we had to move as the tyres were burning. A petrol bomb came over and it splattered. Some of it caught me on the back. It never healed, but it is just one of those things. I later had that one cut out and another piece of skin grafted on. I had that done in South Africa. They cut it out because it was forever weeping; it would never heal otherwise. I also had the scars on my leg from Korea operated on.

The riots weren't anything to do with apartheid. It was all inter-tribal clashes. They wouldn't even let fire engines into locations, the tin shanty towns, if there was a fire because the firemen would get stoned. We used to have to go in there and escort them so they could fight the fire. There were thousands of these shacks. Someone would set fire to a shack and there would be a blaze. I had men and horses on the beaches. We did everything; it was an interesting job and we had a good unit there.

He was appointed building superintendent of the council in 1987. He again excelled in this highly responsible position and made the council's head office complex a safe and pleasant work environment. He had resigned as chief security officer after the injury at work (described above) curtailed his activities in this role. He was proud to have succeeded in a job which should have been given to a South African:

Mr de Klerk, the future President of South Africa, said, 'I want you because I can trust you. You have a medal and you know what to do.' So that was good. Having the VC has helped me at times and yet at other times it has stopped me from doing what I wanted.

In his spare time, Speakman continued to fly microlights and small aircraft, as well as climbing, swimming and canoeing:

I did a lot of that in my day and became good at it. I did a lot before my leg problems and often went to the Drakensburg Mountains. You can walk in and the Drakensburg Choir sing in there. There were drawings on the walls of the caves that had been done by men thousands of years ago. On one occasion I was up at the caves not far from where a farmer lost one of his sheep down a hole in the ground. He went down to rescue it by lowering himself on a rope and discovered an underground cavern containing stalagmites and stalactites. He told his friend and they went potholing down there. They had tallow candles in their helmets and from the smoke from the candles they would write their names on the walls. That was seventy or eighty years ago and the names are still there. Certain sections have been closed to stop souvenir hunters breaking off stalagmites and stalactites – they won't let you touch anything. It is amazing to go into these caves in the mountains and look at something which is millions of years old. That's the sort of thing you have in Africa – it is so vast.

Speakman is not a religious man and admits that he is 'not much of a church person'. He believes in karma and says that what will happen, will happen:

I learned that a long time ago when I started seeing things in the Army. I don't believe in religion anymore – in fact I am a bit of an atheist and rely on my karma. I don't hold a philosophy, I hold a belief. I am very fond of the way the Japanese live because they live a pure and simple life, like other people who lived ages ago. They believed in what they saw, like the sun and the rain because it benefited the crops. They believed in the results they saw; they didn't believe in something you couldn't see and couldn't hope to see. In the British Army we never criticised what other people believed. No matter where he served abroad the British soldier would never interfere with that country's religion. Some people take umbrage when you say: 'I don't go to church' but I just don't believe in it. I am what I am and I believe in my karma. If I can help anybody I will help.

For the first time since 1968, Speakman attended a Victoria Cross and George Cross Association reunion in 1990 and was welcomed back by his fellow Association members. The 16th VC and GC reunion was held in London in October/November that year and began with the traditional Service of Remembrance and Re-dedication at St Martin-in-the-Fields in memory of former holders of the Victoria Cross and George Cross who have died. Speakman took two of his daughters, Jane and Katie, with him to the reunion events. The formal dinner was held at the Café Royal on 1 November 1990, in the presence of HRH The Princess Royal, and there were receptions for the VC and GC holders and their guests at Buckingham Palace and St James's Palace.

Speakman had not attended a reunion for twenty-two years; it was the expense of flying to and from England which had deterred him from attending the VC and GC Association Reunions more regularly:

If I remember rightly, when they started having these reunions every two years you had to pay a certain amount to get from wherever you lived in the world to London. I remember getting a letter saying that they would like me to attend a reunion. I thought, 'I'm not going because it means I have to pay the air fare.' Luckily enough I turned the letter over and it said, 'We will get you there and pay for the transport there and back.' And that is when I started going again, because otherwise it would have been an awful strain on my finances.

HM The Queen Mother converses with Speakman and two of his daughters at St James's Palace, November 1990. (*IWM/VC & GC Association*)

HRH The Duke of Edinburgh converses with Speakman. On the left is Rear Admiral Place VC DSC, Buckingham Palace, November 1990. (*VC & GC Association*)

He did not attend VC and GC Association reunion events in 1993 or 1995, and the next occasion he was present was in 1997.

Following his sixty-sixth birthday on 27 September 1993, Speakman decided it was time to retire from the Divisional Council of the Cape:

> From there I turned 66 and they asked me to work on until I was 70. I said, 'No way, I've had enough.' They had all the right guys down there so everything was fine. But at 66 I thought the grass is greener on the other side. I was only coming back to the UK every so often to go to the palace. So in 1993 I returned to England to become a Chelsea Pensioner for a year.

He became an In-Pensioner, living in the Royal Hospital Chelsea, on 1 November 1993. Soon afterwards, on 13 November, he took part in the annual Festival of Remembrance at the Royal Albert Hall. Wearing the Pensioners' distinctive scarlet coat and tricorn hat, he was part of a group of Chelsea Pensioners who marched down the steps and across the arena. Aged 66, he would have been one of the youngest Pensioners present (the minimum age is 65) and was still an imposing sight.

THE ROYAL HOSPITAL CHELSEA

The Royal Hospital Chelsea was founded in 1682 by King Charles II as a home for veterans of the regular Army, which had been established twenty-one years earlier. Veterans had to be unfit for duty, either through wounds or twenty years' service to the Crown. The hospital is still located in the original building, designed by Sir Christopher Wren, and houses up to 400 retired soldiers. Eventually, it was not possible to accommodate everyone who applied, so cash pensions were paid to those veterans who could not be taken. They became known as Out-Pensioners to distinguish them from the In-Pensioners living in the Royal Hospital.

An In-Pensioner receives board, lodging, clothing and full medical care in return for surrendering his Army pension. In-Pensioners must be single and have no dependent relatives. They are organised on military lines, with a governor and other officers, and have numerous on-site facilities, including a library, billiards room, bowling green and even a hospice. Women have recently been admitted as In-Pensioners.

Speakman in his Chelsea Pensioner's uniform at a social event in 1994. (*Bill Speakman VC*)

Speakman looks back on his time as a Chelsea Pensioner with mixed feelings:

> It was very good and we were well looked after. They were all ex-soldiers. You have to have done twenty-one years in the Army before you can become a Chelsea Pensioner. It doesn't matter if you were a private or a sergeant as long as you have done your twenty-one years.
>
> I heard such a lot of moaning and groaning. They did not know how well off they were. When you become an In-Pensioner you hand over your Army pension and you get five-star treatment. So I could not take all this moaning and groaning. I said: 'You don't know when you are well off.' And, of course, I got the pull of Africa again; I missed it. So I packed my bags and went back to South Africa.

An In-Pensioner may revert to an Out-Pensioner by leaving the Royal Hospital and returning to civilian life. Speakman reverted to an Out-Pensioner after just twelve months, at his own request, on 4 November 1994.

After leaving the Royal Hospital he returned to South Africa and, after being unemployed for a while, settled down again. He was offered employment by the Cape Town Divisional Council:

> They offered me a position as a maintenance manager because they already had a chief security officer. Then I worked as maintenance manager in the property department and was responsible for about six high-rise buildings. I did the administration of the blocks.

When Speakman emigrated to South Africa in 1972 the country was still under white minority rule, enforced by strict apartheid laws. In 1990, President F.W. de Klerk, bowing to the inevitable, announced an end to apartheid, and by the end of 1991 all apartheid laws had been repealed. The first multiracial elections were held in April 1994 and won by the African National Congress. There was a peaceful handover from white to black rule and the country avoided the bloodshed seen elsewhere in Africa. Nelson Mandela was sworn in as the first black President of South Africa in May 1994. He had been released from prison only four years earlier, at the age of 71, having spent twenty-seven years in custody.

Speakman in Sweden in 1994.
(*Bill Speakman VC*)

Speakman was in England at the time of the historic change of government, but met Nelson Mandela on several occasions and thought highly of him:

> He and de Klerk got together and said, 'We are going to lose South Africa if we don't get it right.' I was working for Cape Town Divisional Council then; I attended a lot of meetings in parliament and in the council chambers to sort out security.

He had the relevant security clearance and professional qualifications and was a member of the Security Association of South Africa, the Fire Protection Association of South Africa and the National Occupational Safety Association. He married Heather Rooken-Smith, neé Griffin (3), on 25 September 1995 but the marriage ended in November 1997.

> When I got divorced from Jill, I married Heather. She was a Kenyan girl of Welsh descent. Her family were ex-pats who worked for the civil service in Kenya but left the country for South Africa when the political situation worsened. Unfortunately, that marriage did not last long either. She wanted this and she wanted that and there was such a difference between us I got a divorce. I have been married three times.
>
> I was on my own for a while. Then I met Marylyn. We decided not to get married but we became partners – very good partners. We've always seen eye to eye. She's strong and I'm strong. She has got four daughters and is well in with my family. I'm also well in with her family.
>
> Marylyn came from Southampton. Her husband, Len, was an engineer on Cunard liners, an oil lubrication expert. When Len died of leukaemia, Marylyn and I looked after each other.

In 1995, Speakman was flown from Cape Town to England, at the BBC's expense, to appear on *This Is Your Life*. The subject of the programme was Lieutenant Colonel John (Johnny) Cooper MBE DCM, who had served with Bill Speakman in the SAS in Malaya. One of the other guests introduced by Michael Aspel was Captain Freddie Brunton MBE, who, as an SAS medical officer, had helped rescue Johnny Cooper when he was dangling by his parachute from a tree in the Malayan jungle. Cooper and Speakman had not met for forty-two years and both appeared very pleased to see each other. Speaking on the programme, Bill Speakman said of Johnny Cooper:

Marylyn Jones at the 2005 VC & GC Reunion held at the Royal Hospital Chelsea. (*VC & GC Association*)

> Johnny is one of the finest SAS men I know and his exploits prove it. He is a great inspirer of confidence. When I first arrived in Malaya from Korea, he got hold of me and we had a good man-to-man chat. He said: 'Bill, you are going to be alright.' That has stood me in good stead and I appreciate that. I am pleased to be here – you are one hell of a guy. I am pleased and proud to know you and have one thing to say, 'Go well and take care.'

Years later, after Cooper's death, Speakman paid a further tribute to his former SAS leader:

> Johnny Cooper was a man who had come up through the ranks. When you talk about charisma, he had more than charisma. He had this ability to put himself across to people and make them at ease. He was also an extremely competent soldier. We had an extremely good relationship; his relationship with everyone was absolutely superb. He was that sort of man.

The BBC had approached Speakman in South Africa to invite him to be a guest on *This Is Your Life*:

They telephoned me when they found out where I was and then wrote to me to ask if I would appear. I said, 'Yes'. They got hold of me and brought me home, paid the air fare, and we did it in the studios along with Johnny. As soon as I finished I went back to South Africa.

NOTES

(1)　£20,000 in 1982 would be equivalent to £59,800 today.

(2)　James Magennis (1919–86) was awarded the VC for his part in a midget submarine attack on a Japanese cruiser in July 1945. He sold his VC for £75 in 1952 and when the press reported the story the VC was bought by a benefactor and returned to him. The authors have been told on good authority that he then sold it again. Following his death in 1986 the VC was sold at auction and realised £29,000. It was the first of many VCs to be bought by Lord Ashcroft KCMG. Since 1986 Lord Ashcroft has collected over 170 VCs which are on public display in the Lord Ashcroft Gallery of the Imperial War Museum. The gallery combines the Ashcroft Trust VC Collection with the VCs and GCs already held by the IWM and a special wing, funded by Ashcroft, was opened in November 2010.

(3)　Heather and her first husband, Ian Rooken-Smith, were involved in African tourism and once operated the Mount Kilimanjaro area before moving to Namibia. She married Bill Speakman a year after the death of Ian Rooken-Smith.

RE-EMERGENCE

1997–2013

Speakman's mother, Mrs Hannah Houghton, died on 23 April 1998, aged 95. She died at Wythenshawe Hospital, Wythenshawe, from bronchopneumonia, and prior to her death she was living at the Southbank Nursing Home in Bowdon. Her husband, Herbert Houghton, died in 1949 and she had been a widow for forty-nine years. Hannah's daughter, Mrs Ann Stringer, was present at the hospital at the time she died and later registered the death. Bill Speakman was then living in South Africa and was unable to return to England for his mother's funeral.

He attended the 19th Victoria Cross and George Cross Association Reunion held in London in May 1997 and was accompanied by his third wife, Heather. The reunion began with a Service of Remembrance and Re-dedication at St Martin-in-the-Fields, in Trafalgar Square on 27 May. In the afternoon there was a reception for the VCs and GCs and their guests at St James's Palace, hosted by HM The Queen Mother. The following day, members of the Association and their guests visited Penshurst Place, Kent, for an informal tour of the house and gardens and lunch in the Baron's Hall. That evening there was a visit to the Imperial War Museum for the official opening of the Victoria Cross and George Cross permanent exhibition by HRH The Prince of Wales.

The biennial reunion dinner was held at the Locarno Suite of the Foreign and Commonwealth Office, on 29 May, with HRH The Duke of York as the guest of honour.

Speakman did not attend the VC and GC Association Reunions in 1999 and 2001, but did take part in HM The Queen's Golden Jubilee celebrations in 2002. The 50th anniversary of the Accession of HM The Queen to the throne was celebrated throughout the UK and the Commonwealth; Golden Jubilee Day, 4 June 2002, was declared a bank holiday. That day, Colonel Stuart Archer GC and Mr Bill Speakman VC represented the VC and GC Association at the National Service of Thanksgiving at St Paul's Cathedral. Her Majesty

Speakman outside St Martin-in-the-Fields, Trafalgar Square at a VC & GC Memorial Service. (*Erling Breinholm*)

Speakman with his wife Heather with the Duke of York at Locarno Suite, Foreign and Commonwealth Office, May 1997. (*VC & GC Association*)

would have recognised Speakman as the recipient of the first award at the first investiture ceremony of her reign.

In the afternoon there was a carnival pageant in The Mall. Three holders of the VC, one of whom was Bill Speakman, and nine holders of the GC travelled in open-topped vintage Rolls-Royce cars as part of the services parade. Speakman was in the back of a Rolls-Royce with Jack Bamford GC, who had received the George Cross for saving the lives of two of his brothers in a house fire in 1952. Word was passed along the line to stand up as they approached the Queen. This presented a problem for Speakman:

I was so wonky on my legs I could hardly stand. Fortunately, I had always got on well with Jack, who was in the Rolls-Royce with me. I said to him, 'Jack, I'm going to grab hold of you. You have to keep me upright.' He was hanging on to me and said, 'Are you all right?' The car turned a corner and I nearly went over, but he held on to me. He had me tight – he was a really good guy to be with.

They saluted the Queen and Prince Philip, The Duke of Edinburgh, who were on a special stage on the Victoria Memorial in front of Buckingham Palace. 'The Queen waved to me and she had a few words with me after that', says Speakman.

The Queen said, 'How is the Rolls?' Then we talked and I said, 'It is wonderful to see you again, Ma'am.' We get on quite well and we had a chat, but she never puts you on the spot. Then she went on to speak to the other people. What a wonderful woman. If the world could have leaders like that it would be a better place. People who want to see the Queen never push forward: she goes to people to talk to them. I also spoke to Prince Philip, mainly about military things.

Speakman received the 2002 Golden Jubilee Medal, his second new medal since he sold his VC group in 1968; he had previously received the 1977 Silver Jubilee Medal. Although the VC he now wears is a replica and the Korea Medals are not the ones issued to him, the two Jubilee Medals are genuine and give value to his new medal group. Both medals were issued unnamed but with documents to prove provenance they would be worth £2,000–£3,000 each to a medal collector.

On 14 May 2003, HM The Queen paid special tribute, on behalf of the nation, to recipients of the Victoria Cross and the George Cross when she unveiled the first national memorial at Westminster Abbey. The memorial ledger is engraved in nabresina stone, with enlarged bronze and silver crosses, inlaid with enamel ribbons. Beneath is the simple inscription:

REMEMBER THEIR VALOUR AND GALLANTRY

The Queen unveiled the memorial and then asked the Dean of Westminster to dedicate it. Bill Speakman VC was one of the eleven out of fifteen living VC recipients who were present at the ceremony.

Speakman outside the entrance of Westminster Abbey at the ceremony to unveil the VC & GC Memorial, 14 May 2003. (*Erling Breinholm*)

A week later, on 20 May 2003, he unveiled a plaque on a bridge named for him in his hometown of Altrincham. A sixty-strong crowd of family, friends, well-wishers and civil dignitaries assembled at 11.00 a.m. at the Cresta Court Hotel and braved the rain to walk to the nearby bridge, a flyover across rail lines, carrying the dual carriageway linking two main roads. The party was led by a piper from The King's Own Scottish Borderers. Trafford Council's mayor, Councillor Mrs Harney, praised Speakman's bravery in what had been a very difficult conflict.

After the unveiling of the plaque, Speakman, aged 75, but still an erect 6ft 6in, made a short speech in which he said he was overwhelmed and honoured by the civic tribute in his hometown. He said:

> It's good to be home and I'll take these memories back with me to Cape Town. I feel good about it and I'd like to thank everyone for doing this – it's wonderful. Nobody's comfortable with all this attention. Being an ordinary person, it's a bit overwhelming.

The idea for the *Speakman's Bridge* plaque came from a local woman, Mrs Rose Jones, who persuaded the council to have a memorial to their local hero. The plaque, costing £160, was paid for by Trafford Council.

Apart from the plaque, Speakman was further honoured by naming him a Freeman Burgess of the Borough and an honorary member of the Altrincham Civic Society. After forty years away from Altrincham, he announced plans to return to his hometown. 'I've had my share of being abroad and away from home.

The plaque on Speakman's Bridge, unveiled 20 May 2003. (*John Mulholland*)

Speakman unveils plaque at
Speakman's Bridge, Altrincham,
20 May 2003. (*Bill Speakman VC*)

It was exciting and it was a challenge,' he said. He also stated another reason
for returning. Like many ex-pats, he was suffering from the failure of successive
British governments to increase his state pension while living abroad.

Speakman returned to South Africa but returned to live in Altrincham
in 2005 to have an operation on his leg. He was living at 13 Old Mill Lane,
Altrincham. He then went back to South Africa and returned again to the UK,
living in Torquay and Paignton until December 2008, when he again returned
to South Africa. In 2009 he finally settled in Altrincham permanently. Marylyn,
who Speakman had known well in South Africa, decided not to leave her home
and return with him to the UK.

Speakman is also honoured on a plaque in the National Memorial Arboretum
near Lichfield, Staffordshire. Established in 1997, the Arboretum comprises
150 acres of trees and memorials. In the British Korean Veterans Association
(BKVA) section there is a circular plaque named to Private William Speakman
VC, next to a rowan tree. There are four plaques in the BKVA plot – one for
each of the VCs awarded for Korea. (1) The plaque for Speakman mentions the
Hinge, although his VC action actually took place on United Hill.

The 23rd Reunion of the VC and GC Association was held in London in
September 2005. Bill Speakman was there, in addition to two new members of

Speakman's plaque at the National Arboretum, Staffordshire. (*www. militaryimages.net*)

the Association – Private Johnson Beharry VC of the Princess of Wales's Royal Regiment and Trooper Christopher Finney GC of the Blues and Royals. They had both received their decorations for service in Iraq.

Their Royal Highnesses The Prince of Wales and The Duchess of Cornwall were present at the traditional Service of Remembrance and Re-dedication at St Martin-in-the-Fields on 13 September. HRH The Princess Royal attended the Association's reunion dinner at the Royal Hospital Chelsea on 15 September. Despite the two new VC and GC members, the years continued to take their toll and Speakman was one of the seven out of only thirteen living VC recipients who attended the reunion.

A Service of Commemoration was held at Westminster Abbey on 26 June 2006 to mark the 150th anniversary of the institution of the Victoria Cross and the 50th anniversary of the Victoria Cross and George Cross Association. HRH The Prince of Wales, President of the VC and GC Association, and HRH The Duchess of Cornwall attended the service.

HM The Queen talks with Speakman. In the middle is Maureen Richardson, widow of G. Richardson GC, and her partner, Charles Telling. (*IWM/VC & GC Association*)

Eight of the twelve surviving VC holders and twenty-two of the twenty-four surviving GC holders attended. Bill Speakman VC was one of the VC holders present at the Abbey on that historic occasion.

A reception was held in St James's Square Gardens afterwards for the living holders of the VC and GC and their guests and the descendents of past holders. The Prince of Wales met all the VC and GC holders at the reception and addressed the 1,700 strong gathering.

Later in 2006, Speakman took part in the Channel 5 TV programme *Victoria Cross Heroes*, based on Lord Ashcroft's book of the same name. The programme celebrated the 150th anniversary of the Victoria Cross, and HRH The Prince of Wales introduced the three-part series, which offered a mixture of archive film, reconstructions and interviews with VC holders. In it, Speakman discussed the situation on United Hill in November 1951 and how he was awarded his VC.

Nearly forty years after the end of 'The Confrontation' with Indonesia, the Malaysian government decided that a medal would be awarded to all Commonwealth personnel who served in Malaya–Borneo between 1957 and 1966. The Pingat Jasa Malaysia (PJM), or Malaysian Service Medal, was announced in 2004, and in early 2005 HM The Queen approved the PJM for wear by Australian and New Zealand citizens.

The British government proved less flexible, however, and announced in 2006 that British citizens would be allowed to receive the medal but not to wear it. It was pointed out that PJM recipients had already received either the General Service Medal or Campaign Service Medal with clasp for *Malaya* and under long-established rules could not receive more than one medal for the same service. Bill Speakman received his PJM in 2007 and said of the government's decision:

The award of the PJM Medal by the Malaysian government is a timely honour to those who served. We are privileged to receive it with good grace and respect and should wear it with the dignity it warrants.

We have all decided, all of us in the regiment [KOSB], the battalion and even the Korean veterans who were there, to wear the PJM medal. That was a tribute to us by the Malaysian government and Malay people for liberating them. When I attended the Minden Day Parade at Berwick-on-Tweed in July 2008, all the guys there who were with us in Malaya and Borneo wore the medal. One guy said to me, 'Bill, that's one medal I wear.' We were told by the British government not to wear it but this is a medal I am proud to wear.

On 8 August 2007 Her Majesty granted permission for the PJM to be worn during the main independence celebrations in Malaysia, from 15 August to 9 September 2007, but not at any other time. This was a contentious ruling among veterans who largely ignored the ruling and lobbied the government. Eventually, in 2011, the government relented and the PJM may now be worn at any time.

In 2007, Bill Speakman VC wrote the foreword to *A Party Fit For Heroes* (2), about the 1920 VC Garden Party at Buckingham Palace, which was the first VC reunion. Although he is much in demand, this is the first book for which he has agreed to write a foreword.

Speakman returned to England from South Africa, with the intention that this would be a permanent move, in 2005 and stayed for three years while his consultants tried to arrange the operations on his knees.

For a while he lived with his daughter, Susie, in Torquay before moving into sheltered accommodation in nearby Paignton. He has seven children – three sons and four daughters – and is not sure how many grandchildren he has:

ALTRINCHAM

Bill Speakman was born in Altrincham, Cheshire, in September 1927. He left his hometown, after living there for almost eighteen years, to join the Army in 1945. Wherever he was in the world his thoughts were with Altrincham, where his mother still lived until her death in 1998, and he often returned to the town. His most memorable visit was in January 1952 when he was given a hero's welcome after he had been awarded the VC. 'The whole town turned out to meet me,' he says. 'It was overwhelming.'

Although the house where he was born has been demolished and there is no plaque to record his birthplace, he has been honoured by having a local bridge named after him. He unveiled the plaque on Speakman's Bridge in May 2003.

He returned from South Africa to live in Altrincham in 2005 before moving to Devon. He returned to his home town again in 2009. In addition to having the bridge named after him, Speakman was further honoured when he was named a Freeman of the Borough and became an honorary member of Altrincham Civic Society.

In 2010, a block of retirement flats was opened near Speakman's Bridge and they were named *Speakman Court* in his honour.

Of my daughters, Susie works for Network Rail in Torquay, Jane and Helen live in Sweden, and Katie (from my second marriage) lives in Australia but is shortly moving to New Zealand. Katie is a radiographer like her mother. Of my sons, Casper is an expert in heating arrangements – he has a very good job – Colin, my eldest son, works in theatre as a technician and David is a tree surgeon. David lives in Chudleigh, Devon. Colin plays in a band and they give all the money from their gigs to old people. My ex-wife, Rachel, still lives in Torquay. The girls look after their mother and the boys look after me. I am more than proud of them all.

Speakman soon settled into the local community and became patron of South Devon's Turning Point Heritage Trust, which helps preserve wartime sites. 'There's a lot of history here, but not a lot of people know about it. People need to wake up and be aware of it,' he told the Torquay *Herald Express*.

He was guest of honour, in the directors' box, at a football match in February 2008 between Torquay United and his hometown of Altrincham. This might have proved a test of his loyalties, but fortunately the match ended in a 1–1 draw. Afterwards he said, 'As long as you see a good clean game, that's great – and it was very fair between Torquay and Altrincham. I had a really memorable evening.'

Minden Day is celebrated every year by the British regiments which took part in the decisive victory at Minden in Germany during the Seven Years' War (1756–1763). On 1 August 1759 six British regiments, supported by Hanoverian regiments, defeated France and her Allies and prevented a French invasion of Hanover. Among the British regiments present was the 25th Foot, later to become The King's Own Scottish Borderers (3).

On 26 July 2008 Bill Speakman VC was one of the 250 KOSB veterans who joined the annual Minden Day parade in Berwick-upon-Tweed. The numbers attending the parade were increased by a reunion of KOSB veterans who had served in Aden and Radfan. 'It has been a fantastic day and a wonderful turnout,' commented Speakman afterwards. He did not march in the parade as he was too frail and travelled instead in a KOSB Jeep. He wore his medals for the occasion, including the War Medal 1939–45 to which he was not officially entitled. Afterwards, he met many former colleagues, including 'Busty' Murdoch MBE DCM who had served with him in B Company on United in Korea.

In August 2008 he attended a memorial service at a monument erected by Turning Point Heritage Trust. The memorial monument in Torquay is to members of the local Home Guard who died when their gun exploded in 1941. Speakman said of the service: 'It was marvellous. Those men deserve to be remembered and we will always remember them.'

On being asked if he suffered from post traumatic stress he said:

No. People wake up with nightmares and screaming. Not me. I just thank my lucky stars I'm here. I've done my bit. I may be from another planet. I don't know. I don't have nightmares. I don't pretend to have them. I don't want them. But I don't get them.

For many years he has suffered from painful knee joints and NHS operations planned for January and September 2008 had to be cancelled for various reasons. He did not attend the 25th Reunion of the VC and GC Association in September 2008 as he was due to go into hospital at the time. Speakman required treatment for osteoarthritis in his lower legs and feet and had no feeling in his feet:

I kept coming back to the UK, trying to get my legs done. I was getting promises, having to wait and getting cancellations. A lot of people said to me: 'Bill, why

Minden Day, Berwick-upon-Tweed, 28 July 2008. Three decorated Korean veterans, left to right: Bill Speakman VC, James 'Busty' Murdoch MBE DCM and John Common MM. *(KOSB Museum)*

don't you use your VC to put yourself forward and jump the queue? You are famous.' I said, 'No way.' I don't want fingers pointing at me. If I do that, then I've betrayed the VC. I am extremely proud to say that I have never used my VC to jump the queue. Other VCs have done it but not Bill Speakman. And so I waited and waited.

The last anaesthetist I saw in the UK frightened me. He told me that once I have had the operation I could get an infection when I left hospital. I could finish up in a wheelchair. You would not get an infection in a South African hospital. Then the anaesthetist asked me to sign another piece of paper about blood clotting. He said, 'It is bad but we have got to warn you.' They don't talk to you about the operation on your knee. The first thing they hit you with is what can happen.

I wanted to have both knees operated on at once but the doctor said I would have to learn how to walk with one. He said that if they operated here it might interfere with the healing process and I might not be able to walk again. I saw another doctor, a South African, and we discussed this. During the apartheid period a lot of young students and doctors left South Africa to work in the UK, but they are a special breed of doctors. He agreed that somehow we will manage to get the operation done in South Africa. 'Bill, we will sort something out,' he said. So I'm going back.

219

Bill Speakman returned to the sunshine of South Africa in December 2008. After living there so long he found the climate in England too cold and damp and longed to go back permanently. 'December is our hottest month,' he says. 'November, December and January are hot':

> The heat is going to help my knees. I will be able to walk again. They've looked after me here [in England] but I am going back and will stay in South Africa – that's where I will die. I just could not take the weather here. My leg was getting worse and worse.

After less than six months in South Africa, Speakman returned to England in May 2009 for the long-awaited operation on his knees, and was given accommodation in Altrincham by Trafford Council. His half-brother, Bert, lived in the council bungalow next door, so they saw each other frequently. Without a trace of irony, Speakman said that he got his favourite meals from the Chinese takeaway, two doors away. He now lives in a retirement sheltered housing flat in Timperley. His decision to return to the UK for his knee operations was prompted by financial considerations:

> I couldn't get them done in South Africa as it would have wiped me out financially – it was terribly expensive. There is no NHS in South Africa. They have a scheme for local people, but that is mainly for coloureds, Indians and blacks. They have nothing like our NHS.

In September 2009, he attended the unveiling of a blue plaque in Chapel Street, Altrincham, to commemorate the 'Bravest Little Street in England' (see Chapter 1). During the First World War, 161 men from the 60 houses in the street answered the call to arms. The plaque was unveiled by the Mayor of Trafford, and Speakman, as special guest of the organiser, read the Kohima Address. The organiser of the event, Peter Hennerley, was an old friend of the Speakman family and his brother, when he was a teenager, dated Bill's sister.

Because of ill health, he was unable to attend the service for the passing of the First World War generation at Westminster Abbey on 11 November 2009 but had recovered sufficiently to switch on the Christmas lights in Altrincham on 21 November. He was not impressed when he was introduced to the waiting crowd as the person 'who threw beer bottles at the enemy'. He performed the switching-on ceremony with Sergeant Mark Taylor, who had recently completed his third tour in Afghanistan. 'It was a privilege to be asked to switch the lights on with Mark in my home town,' he said. 'Everyone has been really great and I hope they have a wonderful Christmas and wish them all the best for a happy and peaceful new year.'

He is still in demand for newspaper, magazine and television interviews and gladly gives his time. After sixty years of avoiding the press he is now happy, and confident enough, to talk, if only to correct some of the inaccurate stories written about him in the past. When asked why he never considered suing for defamation for some of the nonsense that has been written about him, he replies:

What can you do? How can you prove it? For a start the Army won't let you; even an officer can't sue a civilian. I never even thought about it before and what would you fight with? The Army are not going to back you up. When you are a soldier you don't have a leg to stand on; you have

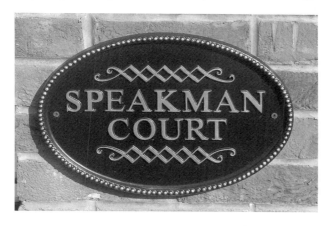

Speakman Court at the junction of Barrington Road and Gaskell Road, close to Speakman's Bridge. (*John Mulholland*)

to ride with it. It didn't bother me at all. Even in civvy street, what could I do? It would go on and on.

A new housing development in Altrincham in the spring of 2010 was named after Bill Speakman, with his permission. The construction company named their blocks of one- and two-bedroom retirement apartments, which are situated close to the town centre, *Speakman Court*. It is located at the junction of Barrington Road and Gaskell Road, close to *Speakman's Bridge*. The developers had a small prize for whoever came up with a name for the development. An Altrincham resident, Josephine Reynolds, 66, who remembered Bill Speakman's homecoming in 1952, suggested *Speakman Court*. She won the £200 prize and Speakman gave permission for his name to be used. Speakman was invited to formally open the development but was not available on the opening date.

When Josephine Reynolds collected her prize she said:

As soon as I saw the competition to name the new development in the local paper, I immediately thought of Bill Speakman. I was around 10 years old when he was awarded the Victoria Cross for gallantry and we all went down to the town hall in Altrincham to welcome him home from Korea. It was such an exciting day as everyone was waving flags and clamouring to shake hands with our local hero. I am absolutely delighted to find out that I won the competition to name the development after Bill Speakman. I am proud to live in Altrincham, where this brave man was born, and I am thrilled he has been honoured in this wonderful way.

On 9 April 2010, Bill Speakman returned to South Korea to take part in a series of events to commemorate the 60th anniversary of the start of the Korean War, in June 1950. He was with 200 other Commonwealth veterans from the UK, Australia, Canada and New Zealand who had been invited back by a grateful South Korean government to visit old battlefields and pay their respects to their fallen comrades at military cemeteries. One of the other decorated war heroes on the tour was Derek Kinne GC, who was awarded the George Cross for the courage he displayed in withstanding torture by his Chinese captors while in a POW camp.

The veterans gathered for an emotional wreath-laying ceremony at the UN Memorial Cemetery. Bill Speakman rose from his wheelchair and with the help of two other veterans laid a wreath with his personal inscription:

222

Wreath and note laid by Speakman at Busan. (*Bill Speakman VC*)

Bill Speakman at the UN Memorial Cemetery. To his left in the light coat is Derek Kinne GC. (*Bill Speakman VC*)

Here in this land 'Brave Borderers' fought and fell so that its people could be free.
'Rest in Peace my Brave Borderers.' We will never forget you. Bill Speakman.

The veterans visited an observation post on the edge of the Demilitarised Zone
(DMZ) which still separates North and South Korea. From there, Speakman
pointed out Hill 217 and other positions in the action for which he was awarded
the Victoria Cross fifty-nine years earlier. 'There it is, right there,' he said, pointing
to the spot where waves of enemy soldiers attacked his battalion. Many newspapers
reported that his VC action was on Hill 217, a myth partly perpetuated by
Speakman himself. He travelled around the various sites by wheelchair, with an
ex-Parachute Regiment veteran as his helper, as he still had severe knee problems
and was due for an operation when he returned home. Before leaving Altrincham,
he said that he hoped to see Hill 217 again, although he would not be able to
climb it this time. (4)

'I'm glad to be back in Korea,' he told a group of reporters and South Korean
military cadets. 'You are a part of me. This is a wonderful country.' He said he
was pleased to see the impressive changes to South Korea since the war ended
and it confirmed his view that the war had been worth fighting. Speakman
laid a wreath, which he took to Korea with him, when the veterans visited
the United Nations Memorial Cemetery in Busan (formerly known as Pusan),
where most of Britain's war dead are buried.

Flights back to England after the official end of the tour on 19 April were
cancelled as clouds of ash from an Icelandic volcano closed all UK airports. The
South Korean government came to the aid of Speakman and the other UK
veterans who were stranded in Korea by covering the cost of their hotel bills until
flights recommenced four days later. The South Korean government also presented
each veteran with a DVD recording of the highlights of their visit. On his return
to England, Speakman said that they had been treated like celebrities. This will
probably be the last time Bill Speakman VC visits Korea and he did not attend any
of the events in the UK to commemorate the Korean War.

Speakman had a four-hour operation on one of his knees in May 2010, shortly
after his return from Korea, but still finds it difficult to get around. An operation on
the other knee, planned for November 2010, was not carried out because of the
problems with the first operation and the risks involved in further surgery.

Despite his mobility problem, he attended a ceremony at the Cenotaph in
St Helier, Jersey at the start of Armed Forces Week in June 2010. Two other British
VC recipients, John Cruickshank VC and Johnson Beharry VC, also attended the
same ceremony. However, Bill Speakman did not attend the 26th Reunion of the

KOREA IN CONFLICT IN 2010

On the sixtieth anniversary of the outbreak of the Korean War (25 June 2010), Lee Myung Bak, the President of the Republic of Korea, looked back on the special relationship between his country and the United Kingdom. In a letter published in many UK newspapers, he concluded: 'I offer my heartfelt gratitude for the selfless friendship that the United Kingdom showed us sixty years ago. The Korean people will never forget the valiant UK warriors who fought in defence of freedom in the Republic.'

Despite these celebrations there was conflict between North and South Korea in 2010. In March that year a South Korean naval vessel, the *Cheonan*, was sunk, no doubt by a North Korean submarine. A total of forty-six sailors lost their lives and, rejecting military action, which could have sparked a wider conflict, South Korea instead settled for economic sanctions: trade with the North stopped temporarily and all but the most essential welfare aid ended.

On 23 November 2010 North Korea launched a three-hour artillery bombardment on the island of Yeonpyeong, which is a civilian fishing village and military outpost close to North Korea. Two civilians and two South Korean marines were killed. Sixteen people were injured and the entire population fled to the mainland. Since the attack only half have returned. South Korea's response to the attack was swift and 80 shells were fired into North Korean territory. But some in South Korea are critical that only 80 shells were fired compared to the 170 fired at Yeonpyeong. This episode was the first military land assaults between the two countries since 1953.

Some analysts suggest the assault was caused by Kim Jong-Il to usher in his youngest son and heir-apparent, Kim Jong-Un, who a few weeks earlier had been promoted to the rank of a four-star general and made second in command of the military. In December 2011 Kim Jong-Il died and was succeeded by his son. Kim Jong-Un is continuing the provacative policies of his father.

VC and GC Association in November 2010. His name is included with other VC recipients on the VC Roll of Honour at the Union Jack Club, London, where many VC and GC recipients stay when attending their biennial reunions.

On being asked if any of his fellow VCs had stood out he said:

No. Every VC I ever met has stood out. Some are gentlemen, others are rough and ready like myself: a bit of a rough diamond. But they all had to do something to win the VC. They will tell you, if they are honest, they did not do it for the chance of winning a VC. But when they won it they might have said 'That's nice. I won a VC.' But they had to fight for it. It was earned. You showed me those three recommendations for my VC. I didn't know how it worked. But I knew the King approved the award. It is a big decision for someone to say: 'He is going to be awarded the VC.' I think everyone who fought with me should have got a VC. When I first found out I was to be given the VC, I looked at the ribbon and said, 'What about the other guys?' You do feel that.

Speakman relaxes at home in 2010. (*John Mulholland*)

Bill Speakman is now firmly settled back in Altrincham. On 25 March 2011 he was guest of honour at the opening of a development of retirement sheltered housing in Timperley where he now lives.

In May 2011, he contributed to the making of *Finnigan's War – A Documentary on the Korean War*. The director, Conor Timmis, flew to England from the USA to meet Bill Speakman and filmed an interview with him at his home on 7 May. The film is a non-profit project, with all the proceeds going to support the construction and maintenance of a new National Korean War Museum in Illinois, USA. *Star Wars* actor Mark Hammill narrated the citations for the US gallantry awards. The name of the film comes from Conor Timmis's grandfather, Sergeant Finnigan, who won the Silver Star for bravery in evacuating wounded soldiers during a Chinese attack on 2 November 1951, just two days before Speakman's VC action. The documentary includes a re-enactment of Speakman's VC action.

He attended the 27th Reunion of the VC and GC Association, which took place in May–June 2012, and at a reception at the Naval and Military Club (better known as the In and Out Club), London, he received his Diamond Jubilee Medal from the Prince of Wales.

In November 2012, Speakman attended a ceremony to open a soldiers' accommodation block in his name at Catterick Garrison, North Yorkshire, where a plaque was unveiled by the Colonel of the Royal Regiment of Scotland.

At 85, Speakman's hearing is not as good as it used to be but his mind remains sharp and active and he is an avid reader. He has recently read T.E. Lawrence's *The Seven Pillars of Wisdom*, Anthony Farrar-Hockley's two volumes on *The British Part in the Korean War* and a book by Roy Hattersley on British foreign policy since 1945. He also reads novels, particularly books by Wilbur Smith who he says 'really captures Africa'. He also thinks highly of Sean Bean in the TV series *Sharpe*.

In the sixty-two years since Speakman's award, official recognition has now been made of the difficulties which face new VC recipients who suddenly have to meet royalty and politicians, attend ceremonial dinners, deliver speeches and speak to the media. For example, in January 2011, it was announced that Corporal Ben Roberts-Smith of the Australian SAS had been awarded the Victoria Cross for Australia for his part in charging three Taliban machine gun posts in Afghanistan. On the day of his investiture it was reported that Roberts-Smith VC would be coached on how to handle his new life in the public limelight. Bill Speakman would have welcomed that level of support when he returned from Korea.

Today, as Speakman looks back over his life he wonders whether events might have taken a different course if he had not volunteered for Korea:

The day I got off that plane at RAF Lyneham it all started and life has never been the same since. I didn't know what hit me; I was just a country lad from Altrincham. I had so many requests to attend functions and help organisations, they asked this and that and sometimes expected too much. At times it felt that I was being thrown from pillar to post but I tried to please them. The Army helped by giving me special leave.

I was so pleased when Johnson Beharry received his VC. It took the heat off me now they have a new guy. I was getting so much mail every week and still being asked to attend various functions. Now I'm looking forward to a nice normal life. I have no regrets. If I could do it all over again I would.

NOTES

(1)   The British Korean Veterans Association was formed, from other veterans associations, in 1981. Its aims are to offer comradeship to those who fought in Korea 1950–53 and to give comfort to less fortunate members and widows of veterans.

(2)   *A Party Fit for Heroes* by Derek Hunt and John Mulholland (Naval and Military Press, 2007)

(3)   In 2006, The King's Own Scottish Borderers was merged with The Royal Scots (The Royal Regiment) to form The Royal Scots Borderers, 1st Battalion Royal Regiment of Scotland.

(4)   Hill 217 was adjacent and connected to United Hill where Speakman won his VC.

APPENDIX I

DECORATION AND MEDALS AWARDED TO

WILLIAM SPEAKMAN VC

The full medal entitlement of Bill Speakman is:

Victoria Cross
Korea Medal 1950–53
UN Korea Medal
General Service Medal, 1918–62 (Clasp *Malaya*)
Campaign Service Medal, 1962 (Clasp *Radfan* and *Borneo*)
EIIR Coronation Medal, 1953
EIIR Silver Jubilee Medal, 1977
EIIR Golden Jubilee Medal, 2002
EIIR Diamond Jubilee Medal, 2012
Pingat Jasa Malaysia Medal

When Bill Speakman left the army and sold his VC and medal group in 1968 his group at the time consisted of:

Victoria Cross
Korea Medal 1950–53
UN Korea Medal
General Service Medal, 1918–62 (Clasp *Malaya*)
Campaign Service Medal, 1962 (Clasps *Radfan* and *Borneo*)
EIIR Coronation Medal, 1953

When Speakman received his VC from HM The Queen in 1952 he wore the ribbons of:

Victoria Cross
Defence Medal
War Medal, 1939–45
General Service Medal, 1918–62
Korea Medal, 1950–53
UN Korea Medal

At the time, Speakman was not eligible to wear the Defence Medal, the War Medal or the General Service Medal ribbons. This was not an error by Speakman himself but by the person who prepared his uniform for the investiture.

Speakman's record of service says he was eligible to the War Medal 1939–45 but this was a clerical error as Speakman had not served the twenty-eight days required to qualify during the Second World War up to 2 September 1945. Speakman was also not entitled to the Defence Medal but he subsequently was awarded the General Service Medal 1918–62 following his service in Malaya in 1953.

Speakman after receiving his VC ribbon from Major General Cassels in Korea on 30 December 1951. (*Australian War Memorial HOBJ2809*)

In a 1953 photograph of Speakman in his SAS uniform (see Chapter 9) he wears the ribbons in the following order:

Victoria Cross
Defence Medal
War Medal, 1939–45
General Service Medal, 1918–62
UN Korea Medal
Korea Medal 1950–53

Again, he was not entitled to wear the Defence and War Medals. At the time he may have been eligible for the General Service Medal for service in Malaya. The UN Korea ribbon should been worn after the Korea Medal 1950–53 as this was a British medal which takes precedence. Later that year, Speakman would have added the ribbon for the Queen's Coronation Medal.

In July 1958, Speakman attended the first VC Association Dinner at the Café Royal and wore miniatures. Among them were the Defence Medal and War Medal 1939–45. These two medals were not included in his full-size group when sold in 1968, which reinforces the fact he was not entitled to them.

Speakman did not qualify for the Army Long Service and Good Conduct Medal. He qualified for the long service element but not that for good conduct. Although Speakman served in Aden in troubled times, 1st KOSB just missed qualifying for the clasp *South Arabia,* which required continuous services of thirty days or more between 1 August 1964 and 30 November 1967.

Since selling his VC group, Speakman has received four more medals:

EIIR Silver Jubilee Medal, 1977
EIIR Golden Jubilee Medal, 2002
EIIR Diamond Jubilee Medal, 2012
Pingat Jasa Malaysia

Speakman is one of only two VC recipients to have received the Coronation Medal, 1953 and the Silver, Golden and Diamond Jubilee Medals. The other is John Cruickshank VC who received his VC in the Second World War. Since 1937, all living VC holders automatically receive Jubilee and Coronation Medals.

In 2006, the British government announced that veterans who served in Malaya and Borneo between 1957 and 1966 could receive but not officially wear the Pingat Jasa Malaysia (PJM) medal. Most veterans, including Speakman, chose to ignore government advice and wear this medal along with official medals.

In 2011 the government relented to lobbying by veterans and recipients are now officially to wear the PJM. In addition the government of South Korea have issued the Korean War Service Medal to the veterans of twenty-one countries who served in Korea. This medal has not been sanctioned by the British government as an official medal. Speakman received this medal and has worn it but chose not to on his visit to South Korea in April 2010. On Speakman's visit to South Korea in 2010, his group consisted of the following:

Victoria Cross (replica)
Korea Medal, 1950–53 (replica)
General Service Medal, 1918–62 clasp *Malaya* (replica)
Campaign Service Medal, 1962 clasps *Radfan* and *Borneo* (replica)
EIIR Coronation Medal, 1953 (replica)
EIIR Silver Jubilee Medal, 1977
EIIR Golden Jubilee Medal, 2002
Pingat Jasa Malaysia Medal

Speakman's actual VC and medal group, as it was in 1968, is currently on display at the National War Museum of Scotland in Edinburgh Castle.

APPENDIX II

AWARDS AND CASUALTIES FOR KOREA TO THE KING'S OWN SCOTTISH BORDERERS
APRIL 1951 – AUGUST 1952

(Those in bold were awards for 4–5 November 1951)

AWARDS

VC
Pte W. Speakman

DSO
Lt Col. J.F.M. MacDonald OBE
Lt Col. D.H. Tadman OBE
Major P.F. St C. Harrison
Major R.C. Robertson-Macleod MC TD
Second Lt W. Purves

OBE
Lt Col. D.W. McConnell

MBE
Major A.E.S. Jackson MC
Captain K.W. Milligan

MC
Captain R.H.S. Irvine
Lieutenant J.A. Foulis
Second Lt E.R. Mudie
Second Lt R.A. Brooks
Second Lt H.N.C. Patterson

DCM
WOII J.D. Murdoch
Sgt J.M. Lancaster
Cpl A. Laidlaw

MM
Sgt J. Haye
Sgt R.F. Mitchell
Cpl J. Common
Cpl P. Devenney
Cpl E. Wood
Pte R. Bryson
Pte E.S. Buchanan
Pte D. Carstairs
Pte D.B. Dalziel
Pte T. Johnstone
Pte M. McCurdy
Pte J.R. Pender

BEM
WOII G.J. Grant

MENTIONED IN DESPATCHES
Major K.D. Bright
Major T. Little MC
Major A.D. McKenzie
Major A.M. Thorburn
Captain A.B. Cran
Captain D.C.R. Ward
Lieutenant J. Dalrymple-Hay

Lieutenant J.A. Foulis MC
Lieutenant C.I.K. Innes
Lieutenant A.H.F. McMillan–Scott
Lieutenant P.B. de T. Rooke
Lieutenant K.W. Wilson
S Sgt G.E. Gray
C Sgt R. Lyal
Sgt J. Dorward
Sgt J.J.A. Forster
Sgt D. McLellan
Sgt A.R. Munn
Cpl J. Castles
Pte T. Bell
Pte D.F. Kelly
Pte G. McCrossan
Pte N. Robertson
Pte S. Wilson
Fusilier D. Whalley
Staff Sergeant G.E. Gray

TOTAL

VC	DSO	MC	DCM	MM	OBE	MBE	BEM	MID
1	5	5	3	12	1	2	1	24

BATTALION BATTLE CASUALTIES

(23 April 1951 – 12 August 1952)

Killed in Action	37
Died of Wounds	2
Wounded in Action	214
Missing in Action	21
Prisoner of War	23
Died on active service	3
Returned from enemy lines	1

APPENDIX III

22538361 PRIVATE P.E. LYDON, RNF ATTACHED C COMPANY, KOSB

In the same action that Bill Speakman won his VC, another soldier attached to the KOSB became famous for the opposite reason: Private Patrick E. Lydon refused to fight the enemy and became a POW for twenty-one months. After being released by the Chinese, he was arrested on the troopship *Asturias* on his way home to the UK. Lydon was court-martialled for cowardice, convicted, sentenced, jailed and dismissed from the Army with ignominy.

Lydon, 24, volunteered for the Army and was sent to Korea and posted to the Royal Northumberland Fusiliers (RNF). On 3 October 1951 Lydon received minor shrapnel wounds to the head whilst serving with the RNF in Operation *Commando*. Soon afterwards, the RNF returned to the UK having completed their tour of operations but Lydon had to stay on in Korea to complete his tour. He was later released from hospital and on 1 November was attached to C Company, KOSB.

The court martial took place at Catterick, Yorkshire on 20 October 1953. Lydon, a tall well-built man, was marched into the bare, hot courtroom. His brother and sister were present. The President of the Court was Brigadier L.F. Martin and the Judge Advocate was Lord Russell of Liverpool (1). The prosecutor was Captain G. Lomer and Lydon's defence lawyer was Mr Philip Niman.

The prosecution alleged that during the Chinese attack on 4 November 1951 Lydon refused orders to fight the enemy and lay at the bottom of the trench saying, 'I cannot. I am afraid.' Military authorities at the time said it was the first occasion such a charge of cowardice had been heard for more than thirty years. The formal charge was: 'Misbehaving before the enemy in such a manner as to show cowardice.' Lydon pleaded not guilty.

The prosecutor, Captain G. Lomer, described how the KOSB held back a full divisional attack on 4 November 1951. He said Lydon was in a trench as the shelling became very heavy. Captain Lomer said, 'Lydon was in a slit trench with Corporal Braid and two other soldiers. One man in each trench had his head up, looking for the enemy. Braid will tell you that Lydon did not perform his duty satisfactorily and that he had to reprimand him for lying down in the trench and not keeping a proper lookout for the enemy.'

'Then Lydon left the trench and sidled off', said Braid, 'saying something that cannot be remembered now and went towards Platoon HQ.' Braid ordered him back but he did not return. Lydon left his rifle, grenades and equipment behind. After an interval in which we don't know what happened to him, Lydon arrived in Lieutenant Bateman's trench. Bateman was single-handed and using a Bren gun. Lydon laid down in the trench. Bateman ordered him to get up and fight and look for some grenades, but he could not get up. At this time and for a further 15 minutes or so, when his comrades were putting up a desperate resistance, Lydon was cowering at the bottom of the trench and refusing to fight. Finally it was decided to fall back, form another 'box' and carry on the fight. Private Burgess, of Bateman's platoon, could not move Lydon, who had not fired a rifle or thrown a grenade. The more Burgess tried to shift him the more he got no answer except that Lydon muttered 'Tow Shong', which is the Chinese for 'I surrender'. Lydon was left behind and made a prisoner one hour later.

Lydon told the court that he felt 'just helpless' when ordered to fight the enemy. Captain Lomer, asked him, 'Were you afraid?' Lydon answered, 'No. Just a sickly feeling in the head. I felt paralysed.' Asked again if he was afraid, Lydon said, 'I must have been.' Lydon said he might have given the impression of being a coward because he was blown into a trench by a shell.

A psychiatrist, Dr T.M. Cuthbert, said that Lydon had been wounded in the head by shrapnel four weeks earlier. He thought that Lydon had been mentally sick since that event. Another psychiatrist, Dr Donald Webster, said that Lydon's mental age was about 12.

Lieutenant Bateman in his evidence stated: 'I said … "Lydon where are you going … where's your rifle?" He said, "I'm hurt, I'm frightened …" He said he had broken his little finger, but it seemed perfectly all right to me. He was lying on the floor under a shelf dug into the side of the trench the whole time … I said several times, "Get up and fight" and Lydon replied, "I can't. I'm hurt. I'm afraid."'

Captain Lomer said Lydon lay in the bottom of the trench shivering, whimpering and muttering 'Tow Shong', while his comrades repulsed the enemy. He added that Lydon was 'a coward who did not, in everyday language, have the guts to go in these horrible circumstances.'

The defence said, 'Whatever Lydon did it was not the result of a criminal mind, but something over which he had no control ... He was mentally ill.' The court was told that two members of his family had had nervous breakdowns and Lydon himself was 'socially inadequate', suffered from 'pathological anxiety' and had a mental age of 12. A psychiatrist testified that Lydon should never have been sent into combat.

In the KOSB archives is an unpublished account written by Corporal A. Laidlaw DCM of A Company who recorded information from C Company survivors:

> But 'C' (Coy) did have a 'cuckoo' in the nest. And Lt A.E. Bateman had a hell of a job getting him interested in the battle whilst manning a Bren. The 'cuckoo', a bag of nerves, lying at his feet wouldn't face the foe no matter how the bold lieutenant kicked and prodded. He wouldn't rise even for his platoon sergeant, Sergeant Burgess, no matter the 'inspiration'. The soldier was a Northumberland Fusilier, who had already been wounded on the battle for Long and returned to the sharp end – too soon some of his mates said. Wounds leave more marks on the mind than on bodies sometimes. Anyway, this 'Fighting Fifth Fusilier' failed to live up to the honourable motto of his regiment – refusing to fight and taking the first opportunity to wave a 'Tow Shong' (Surrender) pass at the first sober looking Chinaman. He was last seen at the bottom of a hole – petrified, he wouldn't stir.

The hearing was adjourned for the day and continued on 21 October. For twenty minutes, the five members of the court, all officers with combat experience, pondered the case. Their verdict was guilty. The sentence was: 'You will be jailed for one year and discharged from the Army with ignominy.'

When the finding was announced, Lydon's counsel, Mr Philip Niman, said, 'This man lost his nerve. He was a volunteer for Korea and a prisoner of war for 18 [sic] months. He has already suffered greatly.'

When the verdict and sentence were announced in open court it was stated that sentence was subject to confirmation. It was clear from the Army Act that the confirming officer might refuse to confirm the conviction, or confirm part only or send the case back to the court martial for reconsideration.

At this stage a media campaign began led by the newly appointed editor of the *Daily Sketch*, Mr Herbert Gunn, who was clearly seizing an opportunity to make a name for himself. The issue was stoked up by the *Daily Sketch* on 22 October, the day after the sentence, with an article headed: 'All Britain is arguing about the case of Fusilier Patrick Lydon … what do people think of this case?' Further articles were published on 23, 24 and 26 October. While the confirming officer was pondering his decision, the *Daily Sketch* published an article on 27 October which said, 'The Army authorities must be made to realise the strength of this feeling. They must realise that cowardice can no longer be treated as a simple crime.' To heap further pressure on the confirming officer, the *Daily Sketch* then took the extraordinary step on 28 October of publishing an article with the heading: 'The general with cowardice on his mind' with a photograph of the confirming officer, his name and postal address. Without doubt, the general would have received a large number of letters from the public pleading leniency for Lydon.

The Army confirmed his sentence but remitted the prison term. On 4 November 1953, on the second anniversary of the battle, Lydon walked free; he had served only two weeks of his one-year sentence. He was released from prison at the Fenham Barracks, Newcastle-Upon-Tyne, the Regimental Depot of the RNF. It is unclear why this occurred: the Army may not have wanted Lydon in its custody or some leniency may have been shown following a public reaction to the sentence. Lydon requested he stayed one more night at the barracks and the request was granted.

On 5 November, Lydon returned to his home town of Middlesbrough. On his arrival, crowds of people welcomed him as 'a hero' and cheered his car. The crowds blocked the street and police reinforcements were needed. When he stepped from the car outside his house he was slapped on the back by well-wishers. He ran inside to embrace his mother who he had not seen for three years.

Corporal Laidlaw concluded in his account:

> The judge reckoned he had been through enough punishment. John (Smokey Joe) Nelson was called to give evidence explaining the circumstances on the Hinge at the time. As well as Lt Bateman and Sergeant Burgess. The 'evidence' as well as the accused were quite happy to see the end of the sad affair, the sentence being trivial.

A few days after his release, the editor of the *Daily Sketch* appeared in court for alleged contempt of court in relation to the Lydon case. The solicitor general submitted that the published articles were calculated or designed to interfere with the free action and decision of the confirming officer, and that they constituted a serious contempt of court. Sir Hartley Shawcross defended Mr Gunn by saying he was ignorant of the contempt law and that he was 'deeply anxious about the problem of how to treat cowardice in the face of the enemy.' Mr Gunn denied his actions were a journalist stunt to increase the newspaper's circulation.

The judge said that he could not escape the conclusion that the object of the *Daily Sketch* campaign was to put pressure on the confirming officer to influence his decision and that such conduct could not be tolerated.

He added that he was disappointed that only the editor was in court rather than the directors of the company which owned the newspaper. The editor was found guilty and ordered to pay £500 for contempt of court.

Bill Speakman does not remember the Lydon case, although CSM 'Busty' Murdoch does. In an interview with the authors in 2009, Murdoch recalled the incident and had every intention of having Lydon marched off the hill under armed guard even though Lydon was not in his company. But in the heat of the battle there was no time for this: Murdoch was wounded and Lydon was made a POW when the battalion withdrew.

When the case came up in the UK, Lieutenant Colonel Tadman received a plea of clemency from Lydon's mother who asked for charges not to be pressed. Murdoch remembers being called into Tadman's office to give his view. Murdoch was adamant that Lydon should be tried because he had let his comrades down at a critical moment. Even after fifty-six years, Murdoch felt very strongly about the issue and said it was right for the court martial to have taken place despite the controversy it caused. Tadman took Murdoch's advice and testified for the prosecution at the court hearing.

It could be argued that it would have been more convenient for the Army to quietly drop the charges and not bring a prosecution. Colonel Tadman reminded the court that in the same action the KOSB were awarded a VC, DSOs, MCs, DCMs and other decorations for gallantry in the face of the enemy.

The case is unusual for three reasons. First, it was the first case of a court martial for cowardice in the British Army for more than 30 years – possibly since the First World War when some similar cases resulted in the death sentence. It appears that during the Second World War not a single case was heard for cowardice.

Secondly, the case caused controversy in the UK resulting in deeply divided views which may explain why Lydon was released early and received such a warm welcome on his return to his home town of Middlesbrough as a sort of anti-hero (2). There was a public view that Lydon had been unfairly treated by the authorities. The media played a role in making the issue prominent, with the *Daily Sketch* campaigning for Lydon's release.

Thirdly, the act of cowardice took place in the same action as Speakman's VC. Although Lydon was in C Company and Speakman was in B Company, the act of valour and act of cowardice occurred in the same place at the same time. So the two extremes are highlighted in how society sees courage: Speakman received the VC – the highest award for valour – and national fame; he was one of only four VCs awarded for Korea. In contrast, Lydon was court-martialled, charged, convicted, jailed and dismissed from the Army for cowardice and the only case in the war in Korea. The contrast was not lost on the public at the time. It brought into question the nature of courage, what is expected of soldiers in combat and what causes some men to rise to the challenges of peril and danger in the face of the enemy while others opt for self-preservation or, in the case of Lydon, demonstrate a complete inability to do anything.

New Zealand-born Hector Bolitho wrote to the *Daily Telegraph* that despite the evidence of Army psychiatrists, 'the swagger stick proved stronger than reason. I am sure there is not a valiant soldier who does not comprehend the dark fears that beset this boy. Only the brave comprehend fear'. To this a retired officer retorted, 'All men comprehend fear. Bravery is the control of fear.'

In September 1983, the counsel for the defence, Philip Niman, wrote to *The Times* recalling the case. He said that one of the psychiatrists, called to give evidence for the defence, stated that 'the distinction between cowardice and bravery is paper thin' and hinged on the individual's reaction to shock. It was suggested that many people had won gallantry awards because they were 'afraid of being afraid'.

Patrick Lydon was born on 1 October 1927, ten days after the birth of Bill Speakman. He died in Middlesbrough in December 1988, aged 61.

NOTES

(1)   Lord Russell of Liverpool served in the First World War and won the MC and two bars. He was later Deputy Judge Advocate General to the British Army of the Rhine and one of the chief legal advisers during the Nazi war crimes trials at Nuremberg.

(2)   Middlesbrough was not a town without heroes: at the time of the court martial three VC recipients were living there: James Smith VC (1914), Tom Dresser VC (1917) and Stanley Hollis VC (1944), the only VC awarded for D-Day.

SOURCES

The Times, London, 14 November 1953

Philip Niman letter to *The Times*, 1 September 1983

Time Magazine, 2 November 1953

The Sydney Morning Herald, 21 and 22 October 1953

The Argus, Melbourne, 5 November 1953

Barrier Miner, Broken Hill, NSW, Australia, 7 November 1953

The Courier-Mail, Brisbane, 5 and 6 November 1953

The Sun-Herald, Sydney, 8 November 1953

Unpublished memoir by A. Laidlaw DCM in KOSB Museum

www.britains-smallwars.com/korea/KOSB.htm

APPENDIX IV

KOSB MUSEUM, BERWICK-UPON-TWEED

The Regimental Museum of the King's Own Scottish Borderers is in Berwick-upon-Tweed.

The details are:

The Barracks, The Parade, Berwick-upon-Tweed TD15 1DG
Tel: 01289 307426 Fax: 01289 331928
email: kosbmus@milnet.uk.net

Opening times: 10.00 to 16.45 (latest admissions by 16.15) from 1 February to 1 November. Outside formal opening hours private access arrangements are possible throughout the year by appointment.

The history of the regiment can be traced from 1689 to the present by displays of uniforms, medals, weapons and artefacts from numerous wars, battles and campaigns. Tableaux and dioramas dramatically bring to life the regiment's history and aspects of the soldier's life at different points of history.

The regiment has an unrivalled collection of documents, pictures and photographs relating to its 324 year history. Access can be arranged by prior appointment. A complete catalogue of the regimental archives (and relevant material held elsewhere) can be found at www.a2a.org.uk.

The Museum does not hold personal files and service records of ex-KOSB soldiers.

BIBLIOGRAPHY

PUBLICATIONS

Adkin, Mark, *The Last Eleven? Winners of the Victoria Cross Since the Second World War*, Leo Cooper, London, 1991

Allen, Charles, *The Savage Wars of Peace: Soldiers' Voices 1945–1989*, Michael Joseph, London, 1990

Arthur, Max, *Symbol of Courage: A Complete History of the Victoria Cross*, Sidgwick & Jackson, London, 2004

Ashcroft, Michael, *Victoria Cross Heroes*, Headline Review, London, 2006

Bancroft, James, *Devotion to Duty: Tribute to a Region's VCs*, Aim High Publications, Manchester, 1990

Bijl, Nick van der, *Confrontation: The War with Indonesia 1962–1966*, Pen and Sword, London, 2008

Carew, Tim, *Korea: The Commonwealth at War*, Cassell, London, 1967

Chapman, Frederick Spencer, *The Jungle is Neutral*, Chatto & Windus, London, 1949

Connor, Ken, *Ghost Force: The Secret History of the SAS*, Weidenfeld & Nicolson, London, 2002

Cooper, Johnny, *One of the Originals: The Story of a Founder Member of the SAS*, Pan Books, London, 1991

Cunningham-Boothe, Ashley, and Farrar, Peter (editors), *British Forces in the Korean War*, British Korean Veterans Association, Leamington Spa, 1988

Cunningham-Boothe, Ashley (editor), *Marks of Courage: The Complete Record of Honours, Decorations and Awards for Gallant and Distinguished Service Presented* to *Members of the British and Commonwealth Forces in the Korean Theatre of War 1950–1953*, Korvet Publishing, Leamington Spa, 1991

De la Billière, General Sir Peter, *Supreme Courage*, Little, Brown, London, 2004

Farrar-Hockley, Anthony, *The British Part in the Korean War* (two volumes), HMSO, London, 1990–1995

Fisher, Peter, and Lohan, Patrick, *Korean War: 25 June 1950 – 27 July 1953*, privately published

Gaston, Peter, *The Thirty-Eighth Parallel: The British in Korea*, A.D. Hamilton, Glasgow, 1976

Hastings, Max, *The Korean War*, Michael Joseph, London, 1987

Headquarters Training Command, Australian Army, *The Battle of Maryang San, 3rd Battalion, the Royal Australian Regiment, Korea, 2–8 October 1951*, Headquarters Training Command, NSW, 1991

Hickey, Michael, *The Korean War: The West Confronts Communism 1950–1953*, John Murray, London, 1999

Hunt, Derek, and Mulholland, John, *A Party Fit for Heroes. His Majesty's Garden Party for recipients of the Victoria Cross, 26th June 1920*, Naval and Military Press, Uckfield, 2007

MacDonald, Major General John, *The Borderers in Korea*, published by KOSB, Berwick-upon-Tweed

Mulholland, John, and Jordan, Alan (editors), *Victoria Cross Bibliography*, Spink, London, 1999

Percival, John, *For Valour The Victoria Cross: Courage in Action*, Methuen, London, 1985

Perrins, Anthony (editor), *A Pretty Rough Do Altogether, the Fifth Fusiliers in Korea 1950–1951*, The Trustees of the Fusiliers Museum of Northumberland, Alnwick Castle, Alnwick, Northumberland, 2004

Royle, Trevor, *The King's Own Scottish Borderers: A Concise History*, Mainstream Publishing, Edinburgh, 2008

Southern, Patricia, *The Story of Altrincham*, Amberley Publishing, Stroud, 2008

Walker, Adrian, *A Barren Place: National Servicemen in Korea 1950–1954*, Leo Cooper, London, 1994

Woollcombe, Robert, *All the Blue Bonnets. The History of The King's Own Scottish Borderers*, Arms and Armour Press, London, 1980

NEWSPAPERS AND PERIODICALS

Altrincham, Hale & Bowdon Guardian
Medal News
The Borderers' Chronicle
The Cadet Journal
The Daily Express
The Daily Mirror
The Evening News
The Sunday Express
The London Gazette
The Times
The Sunday Times
Torquay Herald Express
The Sydney Morning Herald
The Argus

Sotheby's sale catalogue July 1982

UNPUBLISHED SOURCES

War Diaries 1st KOSB October 1951 (National Archives file WO 281/484)
War Diaries 1st KOSB November 1951 (National Archives file WO 281/485)
War Diaries 28th Brigade October 1951 (National Archives file WO 281/139)
War Diaries 28th Brigade November 1951 (National Archives file WO 281/140)
War Diaries 28th Brigade December 1951 (National Archives file WO 281/141)
VC Recommendation for W. Speakman (National Archives file WO 32/14861).Contains public sector information licensed under the Open Government Licence v1.0.

Canon Lummis VC files, held at the National Army Museum
Documents held at the KOSB Museum, Berwick-upon-Tweed

NEWSREEL FOOTAGE

See British Pathé website www.britishpathe.com and enter the following in search box:

Selected originals –VC's mother hears news of award to her son	Footage of Bill's mother, Hannah Houghton, reading about her son's exploits in the newspapers at her home in Moss Lane, Altrincham (December 1951)
Speakman VC comes home	Footage of Speakman's triumphant return to his home town of Altrincham (January 1952)
Queen's First Investiture	Footage of Speakman and his guests outside Buckingham Palace after his VC investiture (February 1952)
Selected Originals – Queen's First Investiture	Footage of Speakman outside the gates of Buckingham Palace after his VC investiture (February 1952)
Lunch at Palace VCs	Footage of Speakman at a lunch for VC and GC recipients at Buckingham Palace in the summer of 1968

INDEX